D0990387

Cuba's Nicolás Guillén
Poetry and Ideology

Nicolás Guillén (1902–) is regarded as Cuba's national poet. His poetry, which has been translated into more than thirty languages, is read, recited, and sung by millions of people in different parts of the world. Guillén's poems, intimately involved with and deeply rooted in the history of his country, are distinguished for their artistic excellence and for their attachment to well-defined spiritual and ideological values.

Professor Ellis begins by establishing the background for an understanding of Guillén's poetry. He examines both the body of literary theory to which Guillén's writings seem most clearly related and the relevance of many writers, from Marx and Engels to Mariátegui and Portuondo. Ellis also considers Spanish-American literary history, especially the predominant tendency to social commitment in this literature from colonial times to the present, and Cuban historical reality, a topic so fundamental to Guillén's work. He thus offers a comprehensive introduction to the historical, ideological, and literary background of Guillén's poetry.

Ellis provides close, original textual analyses of the works themselves, examining the enormous range of poetic modes by which Guillén displays his concern about such important subjects as Cuban identity, racial problems, u.s. imperialism, class struggle, relations between men and women in situations of poverty, the impulse to revolution, and the building of a new society. In the concluding chapter, the author considers such critical issues as the relationship of Guillén's work to Spanish-American and other poets, to the question of *négritude*, to the development of an innovative style, and to the views of literary theorists and the reading public.

Ellis's synthesis of literary and political history and his scrutiny of the artistic elements of Guillén's poetry in the context of the books in which they appear make this volume valuable for everyone interested in Cuba's historical and cultural life.

KEITH ELLIS is Professor in the Department of Spanish and Portuguese at the University of Toronto and author of *Critical Approaches to Rubén Darío*, *El arte narrativo de Francisco Ayala*, and (with Robert Márquez and Alfred Melon) *Tres ensayos sobre Nicolás Guillén*.

Nicolás Guillén

KEITH ELLIS

Cuba's Nicolás Guillén

Poetry and Ideology

UNIVERSITY OF TORONTO PRESS

Toronto Buffalo London

© University of Toronto Press 1983
Toronto Buffalo London
Printed in Canada

ISBN 0-8020-5619-9

University of Toronto Romance Series 47

To Zilpha and Carmen

Canadian Cataloguing in Publication Data

Ellis, Keith, 1935–
   Cuba's Nicolás Guillén

   (University of Toronto romance series, ISSN 0082-5336; 47)
   Bibliography: p.
   Includes index.
   ISBN 0-8020-5619-9

   1. Guillén, Nicolás, 1902– – Criticism and interpretation. 2. Guillén, Nicolás, 1902–
   – Political and social views. I. Title. II. Series.

   PQ7389.G84Z6   861   C83-094160-6

This book has been published with the help of a grant from the Canadian Federation
for the Humanities, using funds provided by the Social Sciences and Humanities
Research Council of Canada, and a grant from the Publications Fund of the University of Toronto Press.

Contents

Introduction

Nicolás Guillén's first published book of poetry appeared more than fifty years ago. He has continued to be steadily productive since that time, creating works that are constant in revealing his preoccupation with raising the quality of life in his native Cuba and changeable in their diversity of expressive forms that reflect the various historical periods with which he deals. His work has been closely followed in Cuba by an abundance of criticism, a perspicacious selection of which has been made by Nancy Morejón in her book, *Recopilación de textos sobre Nicolás Guillén*.[1] Her collection, which includes work by non-Cuban writers, reflects the fact that in the course of his career a rapidly increasing number of critics have intervened to elucidate the various elements of Guillén's contribution. The vast majority of these interventions have been concerned with individual books or subjects treated in his poetry, sometimes linking them to assumed governing concepts. These studies are overwhelmingly sociological in their approach, showing a tendency to relate readily the examined poetry to aspects of the social and political life of Cuba and their international ramifications. This tendency has culminated in the two-volume work by Angel Augier, *Nicolás Guillén: Notas para un estudio biográfico-crítico*.[2]

In his prologue to this book the Cuban writer Samuel Feijoo assessed its importance when he wrote: 'Augier understands his book to be a biographical-critical study, a collection of data that will be fundamentally important for a definitive knowledge of Guillén's work. Augier's position is humble and wise. We understand that a book like this will not be easily surpassed. It will always have to be consulted for a direct and true knowledge of the poet, his times, his works and his numerous tasks.' Augier's early discernment of Guillén's exceptional talent, his long years of close comradeship with him (dating back to the early 1930s), his devotion to the national life of his country and to poetry are the main factors underlying the achievement that Feijoo accurately appraises. For in addition to the biographical knowledge of Guillén that Augier has been uniquely privileged to possess, his book reveals an ability to relate Guillén's poetry to the course of twentieth-century Cuban history. His emphasis is on the circumstances of the composition of the poems rather than on the analysis of the poems themselves, and the fact that the study was written before Guillén's post-revolutionary production had begun to appear makes a third volume highly desirable. Augier has laid the foundation for such a volume by articles referred to in Morejón's bibliography and by his introductions and notes to the two volumes of Guillén's *Obra poética*,[3] the basic text used for this study.

Augier's reading of Guillén's poetry is informed by dialectical thinking and contrasts methodologically with the synoptical tendencies of those of his predecessors, whose views on Guillén have been widely circulated in histories of Spanish-American literature. Nevertheless, Augier's positive assessment coincides with theirs in most instances. Hence, different generations of readers of Spanish-American literary history have been accustomed to favourable glimpses of Guillén, provided by such widely read writers as Arturo Torres-Ríoseco and Enrique Anderson Imbert.[4] Subsequent to Augier's work, aspects of Guillén's poetry were studied by Adriana Tous and Jorge María Ruscalleda[5] in monographs that appeared too early to take advantage of the illuminating constants prevailing among the changes that mark Guillén's responses to historical circumstances. A similar limitation is evident in Ezequiel Martínez Estrada's vigorous and apparently hastily written *La poesía afrocubana de Nicolás Guillén*.[6]

In English, a contribution has been made by Dennis Sardinha, whose monograph *The Poetry of Nicolás Guillén* is the most visible part of a body of significant work done by some of his colleagues at the University of the West Indies; and Neville Dawes of Jamaica has written incisively about Guillén in the context of Caribbean poetry.[7] Sardinha's book widens the area dealt with by Wilfred Cartey and Frederick Stimson in their 1970 studies,[8] Stimson's article having been enriched by his references to Martha Allen's perceptive but much neglected article of 1949, 'Nicolás Guillén, poeta del pueblo.'[9] In recent years, PHD theses have been written on aspects of Guillén's poetry at such universities as Michigan, Princeton, and the University of California at Berkeley; and a significant MA thesis, a detailed study of one of his poems, has been produced at Carleton University.[10] A wide public has been reached by the pages that Cecil Maurice Bowra has devoted to Guillén in his *Poetry and Politics 1900–1960*,[11] a book that deals with world literature and that touches on the literatures of several of the more than thirty languages into which Guillén's poetry has been translated. Like many other readers of Guillén, Bowra finds him to be entertaining, to have skilfully derived light, sprightly, dancing metres from the popular musical form, the *son*, and to have used his own proletarian experiences as a basis to defend poor Cubans. He finds, as well, that all this is 'salted with a small pinch of Marxism, which does not, however, spoil the taste.' The limited helpfulness of these views is in part explainable by the terminal date of Bowra's project, and the readiness (revealed in his culinary image) to regard a clearly Marxist ideological position as unappetizing may well impede the just reading of Guillén's poetry.

In *Self and Society in the Poetry of Nicolás Guillén*,[12] a major study that has appeared within recent months, Lorna Williams has attempted to define Guillén's racial identity and to evaluate his socio-political attitudes in that light, with ample reference to his poetry. Appearing almost simultaneously, and as an indication of the quickening pace with which serious studies of Guillén's work are now appearing, Nancy Morejón's book, *Nación y mestizaje en Nicolás Guillén*,[13] offers among its many virtues a detailed accounting of the circumstances that make self and society inseparable in Guillén's consciousness.

The issue of the relation of Guillén's poetry to politics and society is as important as it is complex. It falls within a category for which a theory of sociological literary criticism has been developed. It is useful as a first step to consider the development of this theory in order to facilitate an understanding of the extent to which it is applicable to Guillén. This procedure is one of the ways of indicating the broad significance of his contribution. This contribution is rooted in a specific Cuban historical and geographical setting, which comes to be progressively widened by Guillén's awareness of similar circumstances throughout the West Indies, in Latin America, and elsewhere. The fundamental preoccupation with Cuban history displayed in his works prompts, also in the first part of this book, the explanation of the appropriate historical background as a clarifying measure.

But the effectiveness of a poetry that conveys a concern for social development rests on other factors, on the poet's selection or discovery of forms of organization and expression, of syntactical and lexical elements, that make the poem itself appear as the matrix from which emerges the substance of concern. The fact that Guillén's poetry has not been studied extensively with regard to the function of its artistic elements makes it necessary to place the central emphasis of this study on an examination of the poems in the context of the books in which they appear. The poems studied in particular detail are those that illustrate crucial representative strategies of Guillén's craft or that have been previously read in disputable ways. An examination of all the major collections of his poetry exposes an enormous range of poetic modes and techniques. It is necessary to probe beyond the centrifugal effect of this diversity and make a part of the task of close reading an apprehension of the unified, firm ideological content of his poetry. This probing is aided by vigilance with regard to the function of such elements as counterpoint, irony, and paradox.

A consideration of the results of the analysis of the poems undertaken in the second part of this book, in the light of the theoretical and historical framework provided in the first part, permits several conclusions about Guillén's work. An attempt is made to assess the principal technical bases of his versatile expression, to situate him among the renowned Cuban poets and among poets in general, to evaluate the relevance of such topics as *négritude* and magical realism to his practice, and to consider the relation in his work of poetry to ideology – ideology being understood as the forms of thinking that promote the aspiring to, struggling for, welcoming and building of the desired structure of national and international life.

Unless otherwise indicated, the translations from other languages into English in this introduction and throughout the book are mine. A glossary of literary terms follows the notes at the end of the volume.

Cuba's Nicolás Guillén:
Poetry and Ideology

1

The Theoretical and Historical Framework

The work of an avowed Marxist poet who writes with a keen sense of the historical conditions that have shaped his social circumstances naturally elicits, in the course of the evaluation of his work, a consideration of the theoretical bases on which the category of literary criticism known as Marxist criticism is built. It is fitting, therefore, that a study of Nicolás Guillén's work should begin with an examination of such a theoretical framework, particularly since certain aspects of the theory viewed in the light of his practice need to be adapted and elaborated on in order to accommodate his unique contribution. While the general purpose of this study is to describe and characterize this contribution, the immediate task is to view the development of Marxist and other relevant sociological literary criticism from a viewpoint that is attentive to the character of Guillén's work.

Marx himself had a lively interest in literature. He wrote poetry, attempted drama and a novel; and in the fields of theory and practical criticism, apart from writing several brief articles and an unpublished manuscript on art and religion, he planned a journal of dramatic criticism, a full-length study of Balzac, and a work on aesthetics.[1] Besides, in his essays on political economy he showed a special alertness to literary style and to the concept of coherence; and just as these literary characteristics are present in his political writings, so also do these writings contain concepts that include the field of imaginative literature in their scope.

Marx expressed the view (in *The German Ideology* and in the preface to *A Contribution to the Critique of Political Economy*) that the production of ideas, concepts, and consciousness is linked inextricably to the way in which people's material life is produced. In *The German Ideology*, the view was stated as follows:

Morality, religion, metaphysics and all the rest of ideology, as well as their corresponding forms of consciousness, thus lose all semblance of autonomy. They have no history, no development; it is rather men who by developing their material production and their material relationships transform, along with their own real existence, their thinking and the products of their thinking. It is not consciousness that determines life but life that determines consciousness.[2]

Literature, as a form of ideology, is for Marx a part of the apparatus of state organization that serves to protect the base or infra-structure, which is essentially the relation of the worker to the system of production. Thus literature, far from being isolated or autonomous, is involved subordinately in a hierarchical pattern of social organization; and it is besides, as the product of labour, subject to examination as a component of infra-structure. The interrelation of these two aspects of literature is influential in diverse and complex ways on the character of the literary product.

The other principal effect on the perception of the possibilities of literature derives from the general nature of Marx's philosophy. Rather than being a systematic philosophy with metaphysical content and a body of static codes and permanent canons, it is a critical philosophy that is dialectical in its procedure of examining the relations between social phenomena at the different stages of their historical development. Hence it is a constantly applicable tool, a form moving in time, as Frederic Jameson has put it;[3] and since such social phenomena include everything that is dependent on the means of material production, it is virtually all-embracing in its scope. It permits analysis of the extrinsic realities bearing on the production of literature as well as those intrinsic to the product. Artists are seen to have changing attitudes to literary activity; and, since changing times carry with them changing content for literature, the writer must keep finding the appropriate form for the proper representation of the changing reality.

It is doubtful that Marx saw the possibility, in any of the European societies in which he was primarily interested, of literature playing a leading role in their transformation. He seemed rather to want, indeed to expect, the industrial workers of those relatively developed societies to take possession of the means of production. With the subsequent end to their condition of alienation and their cultural development, they could read literature from the classics to the present with the enjoyment that comes from expanded powers of discernment. Both he and Engels were far from encouraging to their contemporaries who attempted to produce literature that was clearly tied to political schema. They were not impressed by the examples of literature that aimed, without due regard to the internal demands of these works for literary coherence, at directing the consciousness of the reader to their own high political consciousness. Engels's often-cited letter to Minna Kautsky of November 1885 sums up their position: he states, 'I am by no means an opponent of tendentious, programmatic writing (*Tendenzpoesie*) as such';

and after classifying Aeschylus, Aristophanes, Dante, Cervantes, Schiller as *Tendenzpoeten* and certain Russian and Norwegian dramatists as *Tendenzdichter* he adds: 'But I believe that the thesis must spring forth from the situation and action itself, without being explicitly displayed. I believe that there is no compulsion for the writer to put into the reader's hands the future historical resolution of the social conflicts which he is depicting.' In his letter to Margaret Harkness of April 1888, he further counselled: 'The more the opinions of the author remain hidden, the better for the work of art.' It is important to note the historical conditions in which Engels presented these views. It was at a time when Marx's life work had recently ended (he died in 1883) and when Engels's own major contribution had already been made. They had laid the programmatic basis on which the advanced industrial workers of Europe could organize, propagandize, and participate in non-violent activities leading to the seizure of power by the proletariat – a seizure that would be facilitated by the internal contradictions of capitalism. Engels in fact stated all this in his introduction to the 1895 edition of Marx's *The Class Struggles in France (1848–1850)* in which he discussed the futility of revolutionary warfare, of the conventional urban uprising. He was buoyed in his optimism about the collapse of capitalism by the grave world economic depression that had begun in 1873 and was to last until 1895 and by the new tensions over trade arising among the imperialist countries after the apparent truce provided by their agreement at the Conference of Berlin (1884–85) to share among themselves select parts of Africa. In such circumstances, Balzac's critically realistic presentation in *La Comédie humaine* of the internal conflicts of a society based on money served as an example of good art and of the revolutionary possibilities of artistic endeavour. Essentially, then, European society seemed to Marx and Engels so ready for change that any literary presentation of it showing it in its realistic fullness would reveal this readiness, even to a reader of lower revolutionary consciousness and irrespective of the novelist's intention. Accordingly, Marx, in his negative criticism of Lassalle's verse drama *Franz von Sickingen* and of Eugène Sue's novel *Les Mystères de Paris*, cited the insufficient scope of their realism.

Some years later, Lenin's perception of the conditions facing his party in 1905 yielded his essay of November of that year, *Party Organization and Party Literature*. The work was written at a time when the crisis facing the czarist government over the dismal showing of the Russian army and navy against the Japanese created the opportunity for what Lenin called 'the bourgeois proletariat revolution,' and for the expansion of the Bolshevik party, which won the right to have a legal press. In the circumstances, he sought to mobilize all the talents of his comrades, including those of the writers, to the effort. He wrote in calculated opposition to the Menshevik position, and also to Plekhanov, alluding to their terminology:

Literature must become Party literature ... Down with unpartisan *littérateurs*! Down with the supermen of literature! Literature must become a part of the general cause of the proletariat, 'a small cog and a small screw' in the social-democratic mechanism, one and indivisible – a mechanism set in motion by the entire conscious vanguard of the whole working class. Literature must become an integral part of the organized, methodical and unified labours of the social-democratic Party.

This quotation from Lenin's essay and the earlier ones from the two letters by Engels are taken from the well-known essay by George Steiner, 'Marxism and the Literary Critic.'[4] He calls them 'three celebrated and canonic texts at the origins of the Marxist theory of literature'[5] and proceeds to emphasize the difference between the views of the two writers and to stress Lenin's deviation from a properly open attitude toward literature. The passages quoted are the selections most favourable to Steiner's argument; but his position is made untenable by his failure to take properly into account the historical circumstances in which the passages were written and by the in-adequacy of his representation of Lenin's views. His use of the adjective 'canonic' is also questionable, for the three opinions are not expressed as permanent doctrine. Nor is it useful to refute Steiner by claiming, as Terry Eagleton[6] does, that Lenin had in mind not imaginative literature but party theoretical writing. Lenin clearly had in mind all the forms of literature writ-ten by those who called themselves Bolsheviks. What needs to be done is to place Lenin's statement in the proper perspective of his expressed views on literature: his abiding belief was that the great works of world literature were the heritage of his contemporary socialists. He stated this as early as 1897 in his essay 'What Heritage are we Rejecting?'; and in his addresses to several congresses in 1920, he repeatedly stressed his view that commun-ists were people of highest development who enriched 'their memories by a knowledge of all the riches humanity has created.' His appreciation of Tol-stoy, like Marx's and Engels's appreciation of Balzac, was made possible by the notion that 'the subjective intentions of writers do not always corres-pond to the objective meanings of their writings'[7] and by the related view that partisan adhesion derives not so much from the arbitrary will of the writer but is inherent in reality itself and is revealed by the comprehensive repre-sentation of reality. He employed this theory in his six articles on Tolstoy, written between 1908 and 1911, to show how the great novelist rejected capitalism and failed to join in a proletarian struggle against it but was, nevertheless, 'the mirror of the Russian revolution,' as Lenin called him in the essay of 1908. Thus Lenin's views on literature did not place him at odds with Engels, especially when it is understood that for both men partisan-ship, be it overt or deducible, was always the goal. They both saw art and ideology as closely linked.

One distinguishing feature remains between them, however. While Marx and Engels could assume a relatively developed and sizeable reading public in Europe, Lenin was faced with formulating a real policy on writing for a population that was predominantly peasant and largely illiterate (73 per cent, not including children under nine years old, is Lenin's figure). He wanted the best literature written before the revolution to be a part of the people's heritage; for the present his own cultural preferences were determined by the national situation. His favoured medium was film and in literature he liked traditional non-vanguardist forms to which the population at large could have easy access. But at the time of his death in 1924, following an incapacitating illness that afflicted him in 1922, no lasting answer had been found to the question of what role literature should play in the revolutionary society. Trotsky's combative *Literature and Revolution*, with the Formalists his main target; the appearance in 1917 of *Proletkult*, on which Lenin had frowned, with its aggressive fostering of a proletarian culture to accommodate the class of new importance; the 1920 Congress of Proletarian Writers; the All Russian Association of Proletarian Writers; the Soviet Writers Union; the 1934 Congress of Soviet Writers, which officially endorsed the doctrine of socialist realism and the subsequent decrees were all, in a pioneering, groping, or desperate way, projects for dealing with a major problem in the new society. It was an internal problem affected by other internal problems, some of them as serious as the survival of the revolution itself, and these problems were exacerbated by external developments that culminated in the Nazi invasion of the Soviet Union. In order to deal with the problem of literature, some of the above projects introduced repressive measures; little regard was paid to the fact that artists are sometimes, by vision, temperament, and self-esteem, very special people who are not suited to extensive co-operative projects, no matter how noble or useful these projects might be. Undoubtedly, had there been in the Soviet Union a few writers who could combine exceptional literary skill with an ability to perceive and represent sympathetically the legitimate national goals as they emerged, and who at the same time possessed firmness, stability, and a gift for diplomacy, the problem of literature and the revolution might have been less acute. This combination of attributes is not, as we shall see later, unattainable.

Meanwhile, theories were being developed with the aim of explaining literature in its varying relations to society by writers who were for the most part outside of the turmoil of the Russian experiment. They examined such factors as the effect of historical conditions on the nature of writing, the representation of politics in literature, objective versus subjective realism, questions of form and content, the limits of dialectics and of coherence, among other matters. Most of these writers were European and it is worth examining the relevances and limitations of some of their theories, bearing in mind the broad aspects of Guillén's achievement in his creation of a body of poetry that furthers the possibilities envisaged by these theories.

The Russian writer Georgi Plekhanov provides a good starting point. He was the first major elaborator of Marxist literary theory. His writings on literature, which formed but a small part of his work, covered the field of European, particularly French, literature. He considered the history of art and literature to be the principal proving ground of his theory that the social mentality of an age is conditioned by that age's social relations. He held the view that the idea of art for art's sake was a direct consequence of the aversion felt by the French romantics, Parnassians, and early realists for the bourgeoisie. The romantics, he says, starved themselves to look pallid, greenish, cadaverous in a reaction against bourgeois satiety. They felt that to produce useful art was to serve the detested bourgeoisie, and so they addressed themselves to a limited public. Flaubert wrote for 'les amis inconnus' ('unknown friends'), and Leconte de Lisle believed that the popularity of a writer was a 'signe d'infériorité intellectuelle.' From such observations Plekhanov derives his dictum that, on the one hand, 'the belief in art for art's sake arises when artists and people keenly interested in art are hopelessly at odds with the social environment'[8] and, on the other hand, that 'the so-called utilitarian view of art, that is, the tendency to impart to its productions the significance of judgements on the phenomena of life, and the joyful eagerness, which always accompanies it, to take part in social strife, arises and spreads wherever there is a mutual sympathy between a considerable section of society and people who have a more or less active interest in creative art.'[9] Plekhanov goes on to explore French literature from 1848 to 1852, a period in which Marx had great political interest, and finds further evidence for his argument. During this period, begun by the February revolution of 1848, Baudelaire and his colleagues became very interested in social issues, putting out the journal *Le Salut Public* and denouncing the idea of art for art's sake as puerile. With the success of the counter-revolution they readopted art for art's sake, with Leconte de Lisle writing in the preface to his 1852 *Poèmes antiques* that poetry could no longer stimulate heroic action and could only express small personal emotions. The new role of poetry, he declares, is to 'donner la vie idéale à celui qui n'a pas la vie réelle' ('give an ideal life to those who have no real life'). Guillén's steady writing of a poetry quite removed from expressions of art for art's sake in an environment that was hostile to the point of obliging him to live in exile for several years would seem to cast immediate doubt on Plekhanov's theory. But instead of simply declaring that Guillén's career refutes the theory, it will be more useful later in this chapter, when the social and literary conditions in Spanish America and more specifically in Cuba are examined, to see why a theory that appears to be so convincing when it is demonstrated on the basis of nineteenth-century France should not hold true for Guillén's Cuba. For the moment, let it be said that with an attitude of mind different from Baudelaire's and Leconte de Lisle's, Guillén perceived a historical situation in pre-revolutionary Cuba that, unlike the situation perceived by Baudelaire in nineteenth-century France, led him to feel, even in the face of the hostility of the governing classes, that the general national interest dictated his utilitarian view of art.

How does the artist expose reality so that its proper utilitarian or ideological value can be revealed? An answer that has partial application to Guillén is given by György Lukács. It is partial because Lukács's theories are based primarily on the novel in a European setting – from Tolstoy to Thomas Mann – and as such they cannot be expected to embrace all the elements that we will later observe to be functioning to this effect in Guillén's poetry. Lukács provides, however, two points of general theory that are particularly applicable. They are elaborations of positions taken by Marx, Engels, and Lenin in whose terms (and if we recall Engels's list of *Tendenzpoeten*) the question at the beginning of the paragraph may be rephrased simply: What constitutes great art? Lukács's concepts are presented in answer to this question. The first concept is conveyed in his declaration that

[The aim] of all great art, is to provide an image of reality in which the opposition between phenomenon and essence, between the particular case and the general rule, between immediate experience and concept ... is resolved in such a way that in the impression given by the work of art both poles of the opposition meet in a spontaneous unity, both form for the reader an inseparable unity. The general appears to be a property of the particular and of the singular; the essence is made visible and perceptible in the phenomenon: the rule is revealed as the specific motivating cause of the particular case which is specially exposed.[10]

The concept represented here and on which Lukács insists in various parts of his work resembles the individual-type relation of which Engels wrote and which has been explored as a concept by non-Marxist theorists as well. W.K. Wimsatt, for instance has examined it fruitfully under the designation 'The Concrete Universal.'[11] It is the combination of this and the other prominent concept of Lukács that brings home the force of his theory. This latter concerns the comprehensiveness of the portrayed world. He writes of the use of succession and gradation in the production of a vigorously articulated and ordered world, a world that is not merely a product of mimesis but that is made alive and readily recognizable through the author's partisanship. The greater the artist, Lukács believes, the firmer is the control he assumes over his world, and the more profoundly does he understand the place in history of the world produced in his work.

Lukács uses Balzac and Tolstoy as his chief examples. He sees them, without the ideological reservations Marx, Engels, and Lenin had shown, as exemplary artists who have created full and harmonious bodies of work. He elsewhere criticized Kafka, opposing him to Thomas Mann, for offering without relief or hope the narrow, oppressive world of bureaucratic control. Kafka has been praised by other Marxist critics for showing the need for change by doing just that.[12] The importance for Lukács's aesthetics of dealing with a fullness of reality from which certain practical messages may be drawn thus seems to be primary. At the same time it must be remembered that neither he nor Marx nor Engels had the chance to know an author whose body of writing is comprehensive in its presentation of a national reality (a comprehensiveness that relies largely on the individual-type relation advocated by Lukács), who demonstrates mature ideological adherence to Marxism in his understanding of history, and whose message springs from the appropriateness of the form in which reality is presented. Nicolás Guillén being such a writer, Lukács's comments on him would have provided an excellent basis on which to test the accusation made by Bertolt Brecht, among others, that Lukács aesthetics tended to be reactionary.

The question of the relation of art to its public is one to which a number of theorists have made significant contributions, and the range of their views has been wide. The views in one way or another touch on Guillén, who is generally regarded as a 'popular' poet. The theorists define such words; and Adolfo Sánchez Vázquez may be referred to immediately, since he reminds us in his essay 'El arte verdaderamente popular'[13] that so-called popular art is usually characterized by artistic inauthenticity and the superficial representation of a people. He goes on to state that truly popular art is characterized by 'the profoundness and richness with which [it] expresses the will and the aspirations of a nation in an historical phase of existence.'[14] He agrees substantially with Antonio Gramsci on the indispensability of ideological and moral content as well as tendentiousness in popular art. All this indicates the validity of the opinion popularly held of Guillén. Much of this opinion is based on Guillén's ability to represent political matters in poetry and one would have thought that the criterion given above held room for political content. But Sánchez Vázquez later in his essay agrees with the distinction made by Gramsci between the politician (promoting change for the future) and the artist (representing the present). He further agrees with Gramsci that the political should not be transformed into the artistic. This position coincides with the predicament of Peter Demetz who, upon reading Lukács's theory of the convergence of fullness and particularity, asks: 'How can a work of art as a mirror reflect the present and the future simultaneously?'[15] It will be shown in a later chapter that Guillén in his practice has provided an answer to this, since one of the characteristics of his pre-revolutionary poetry is, by several devices, to project the future while dealing with the present.

Largely irreconcilable with Guillén's poetry is the perspective (and perspectivism) of José Ortega y Gasset. Ortega has contributed to a sociological criticism in such a way as to make his contribution, because of its superficiality in that field, hardly recognizable as sociological. He begins his well known essay *La deshumanización del arte* by pointing to what he views as the inadequacy of the French sociological critic Jean Marie Guyau's principal work, *L'Art du point de vue sociologique* (1890) because it encouraged human content in art, by positing the idea of art as a harmonizing force in society. Ortega instead attempted to establish a veritable dichotomy between art and whatever preoccupation with humanity it may embody. 'That preoccupation with the human aspect of the work is, in principle, incompatible with the strict artistic enjoyment of it,'[16] he writes, and adds: 'The artistic object is artistic only to the extent that it is not real.'[17] He prognosticates a new society to suit a growing purification and 'impopularidad' of art but, with the looseness of the sociological analysis that characterizes the essay, he does not indicate how this new society will come into being or what the general profile of its different strata will be. His society is, in fact, nothing more than the product of a tautological process:

The time is approaching when society, from politics to art, will reorganize itself, as it ought to, in two orders or ranks: one made up of learned men and the other made up of vulgar men ... we will reach a point at which the human content of the work is so diminished that it will be scarcely visible. Then we will have an object that can be perceived only by those who possess the special gift of artistic sensibility. It will be an art for artists and not for the masses; it will be an art of the elite, and not demotic.[18]

Ortega has not predicted rightly, and Guyau, were he to view the literary scene today, would perhaps lament, not any absence of human content, but the formal difficulty with which this human content is sometimes portrayed, particularly in his own country. He would perhaps regret too the relative scarcity of works which have that capacity of great works of every age to interest inexhaustibly different levels of awareness and even to stimulate the raising of those levels in the reader. On the other hand, he would probably be encouraged at the prospect of the greater social role for literature made possible by the easier access to books now enjoyed by so many more people in so many more countries, and who make increasingly discriminating judgments about what literature is worthy of their time.

The Austrian critic Ernst Fischer has taken a position on this general topic that is largely at odds with that of Ortega. Fischer does not see 'the masses' as a permanent, static phenomenon in society. On examining particularly the socialist countries, he finds a constant growth taking place in the capacities of millions of people as readers and a demand created by them for an increasingly higher level of cultural life. He applauds the rescue of many from the 'narcóticos artísticos' – comic books, etc. – of their previous alienated or marginalized existences and expects the development to continue. In these circumstances he declares that 'the decisive task of socialist literature and art – that of presenting the new reality through appropriate expressive means – is intimately bound up with another contemporary problem: the access of millions of people to a cultural life.'[19] Within the context of his view of development, he casts doubt on the existence of 'el hombre sencillo' ('the simple man'), considering the term to be a cliché that had its real application in primitive social conditions where works of art were a mixture of instinct, intuition, and tradition. He speaks of a tension created between generations of revolutionaries by the drive to innovation and modernity that exists in the young, who demand appropriate new styles. Fischer writes: 'The very well-educated sons and daughters of the working class ... smile when their parents shiver at names like Moore, Léger, Picasso; or when they dismiss Rimbaud, Yeats or Rilke as being "obscure"; or when they say that twelve-tone music is the work of the devil.'[20] One may agree with the judgment of the older generation of one or another of the examples given by Fischer. Bertolt Brecht, for instance, believes that a writer like Rilke cannot be popular and that this is not due to formal difficulties. He is not as difficult formally as Maiakovski, but his poems 'ne disent rien au peuple'[21] ('say nothing to the people'). Rather they reveal the poet's hostility in two ways: either by showing an attitude of pity – and pity, Brecht feels, should be directed only at criminals – or by his boring aristocratic pretensions. Fischer, by making the point that new forms do not long remain indecipherable to the people at large, addresses an issue to which Guillén has been discreetly attentive. It is interesting that the Cuban literary theorist and critic José Antonio Portuondo refers extensively to Fischer in his introduction to Guillén's post-revolutionary book of poems *Tengo* (1964) in which he observed the renovating tendency in Guillén's poetic styles. Fischer's thoughts on the question of 'el hombre sencillo' are apparently in conflict with Guillén's frequent use of this concept in his work. It will be noticed later, however, that quite apart from the fact that he deals with a society that has only recently been making significant strides toward development, compared with the 'industrialized and urban civilization' of which Fischer speaks, Guillén's concept of simplicity is one that includes the idea of improvement and that possesses the firm expectation of comprehensive development and equality.

The question of the degree of complexity to which the new styles should attain is one involving several of the aspects of theory that have already been explored. Complexity in literary forms really means the obscuring of coherence, or at least this is the principal way in which it is to be understood by followers of the Hegelian tradition for whom the concept of coherence is indispensable, and who include all the Marxist critics we have dealt with to this point. Fischer, perhaps the most restless of them, implies that the members of the younger generation in socialist societies do resolve the obscurities of some apparently mystifying works. How do they resolve them? As objects that yield to explication or only as the products of certain processes of thinking, processes that are discernible as a result of thinking about thinking? The latter procedure is favoured by Frederic Jameson in his book *Marxism and Form*. The procedure has the attractiveness of being able in theory to deal with any artistic work as part of the history of aesthetics or ideology and it prompts unrestrained experimentation. It nevertheless also has its drawbacks and these can be seen most clearly in cases where the artistic object in question does not accede, assuming reasonable and intelligent effort, to the requirements for coherence or where what is yielded makes the expense of time, which in a useful life is a scarce commodity, seem inordinate. The latter would likely be the case if the minimizing of human content within complex structures advocated by Ortega were to be realized. The gravity of the situation is compounded if we bear in mind the public, not only of the industrialized, urbanized world, but also of the part of the world from which Guillén comes: of those countries parallel to and south of Cuba that are characterized by labour-intensive methods of subsistence and even that only where there is access to employment and to land.

But before we come to look at these matters with regard to historical conditions that affect certain attitudes to literature in Spanish America, brief mention will be made of two or three other European critics who enjoy significant reputations, and who represent positions on our topic that distinguish them from the theorists whose views are to a significant degree readily applicable to Guillén's work. The French theorist Pierre Macherey has suggested[22] that the literary text is never a coherent artistic whole but rather a series of unresolved oppositions and contradictions. Its incompleteness is due to its silences, which reflect ideological prohibitions. The best reading of the text will reveal how its oppositions and contradictions are tied to ideology. It would seem that these views, which Macherey bases mainly on the novel, may have some validity in their application to docile, ambiguous, or what Roland Barthes calls 'blank writing.' Or the theory might be developed to include on a macro-level the gaps in national literatures caused by ideology. This question is addressed by Jean Franco in an admirable essay dealing with Spanish America.[23] One of the points she makes is that centuries of suppression of the cultural offerings of the indigenous and disadvantaged sectors of the Spanish-American population have caused the literature of those countries to be incompletely represented. The long denial of access to the medium of print that these sectors have experienced requires that the written literature of Spanish America be supplemented by probing the still largely unknown oral literatures of the region. This, however, is not the concept of silence with which Macherey deals; and in a case like Guillén's, where a writer produces with a clear political orientation and takes a firm, lucid, ideological initiative, the French theorist hardly applies. The German critic Walter Benjamin[24] paid his main critical attention to Bertolt Brecht and shared Brecht's enthusiasm for the search for new forms. As a theorist, Benjamin accentuated the formal aspect and not Brecht's manifest application of forms in successful, communicative dramatic works. He came to think that the most progressive works of art are the ones that incorporate the most advanced techniques. In the production of these techniques the artist behaves like an innovative, specialist industrial worker. The parallel efforts of function create a bond between artist and worker. Benjamin's theory runs the peril of hypothesizing a condition in which artist and worker may be on parallel courses that never converge, for specialists are prone to be absorbed in their own speciality. Besides, even in an industrial society where specialists abound, a significant part of the reading public falls outside of that category and would become marginal in a program based on the experience of specialists. Convergence between highly skilled artists, highly skilled industrial workers, and the population at large is better assured when it is taken into account that the artist and the worker are producing their techniques to some common end. It is in the area of content, or more precisely in the conveyance of content by appropriate form, that this end is best suggested by the artist. Guillén's evident realization of this is a factor that keeps him distant from Benjamin's theories.

Theodor Adorno, a compatriot of Benjamin's, takes theories of communication to the limits of reason and perhaps beyond them. In his book *Negative Dialectics*,[25] he posits the impossibility of dialectical thinking and therefore is occupied not with the process of renewal that results from the action of latent reality coming into being and displacing older reality through the catalyst of tension, but rather with what he considers to be the contradictory nature of social phenomena that makes it impossible to specify or characterize them. The concept of coherence is shot to pieces here, and randomness advances in status. The prominent part Adorno played, through his writings on the sociology of music, in nurturing twelve-tone music into a certain prominence is an indication of his pessimism regarding the forces of reason.

Having examined the views of some of the well-known critics who function outside of the Spanish-American literary world – bearing in mind their relation to certain broad aspects of Guillén's work and having made reference in doing so to a difference in historical circumstances that informed the perspective of those theorists – I will now refer to some of the main aspects of Spanish-American literary history with the aim of showing the currents that lead to the quality of commitment shown by Guillén.[26]

SPANISH-AMERICAN HISTORICAL REALITY AND LITERARY THEORY

While the European societies analysed by Marx and Engels could show evolution from feudalism to mercantilism to industrial capitalism and imperialism and to some vain attempts to move beyond capitalism, Spanish America spent more than three centuries of this period under unswaying colonial rule, victimized by many of the successful European developments. The control of literature during that period was a key pillar of colonial and ideological control. The efforts to make Christians of the conquered indigenous people made the Bible and associated religious literature the principal instruments of Spain's primitive literacy campaign in America. Royal decrees were pronounced, one in 1531 and the other in 1543, prohibiting the export of novels of fantasy that constituted the major part of the fare of the Spanish reading public. The aim was to protect the reputation for veracity with which the missionaries in the colonies had endowed the religious literature. The rest of the writing approved for export was devoted chiefly to the other main parts of the colonial superstructure – administration and jurisprudence.[27] The controls, although not practically effective, served to communicate to the early colonists the spirit of seriousness with which their mission was to be undertaken and to stimulate the production of literature that aided the program of colonization, while discouraging and depriving of prestige imaginative literature that was uncommitted to the task. The chronicle, describing the new acquisitions, justifying or repudiating actions, was the new form that flourished in these conditions. Some chronicles were written with considerable political perspicacity, such as the *Cartas de relación*, most of which were written by Cortés. He stressed Mexico's (or New Spain's) large population of potential Christians, its wealth, and his own indispensability for the project of bringing the territory under Spain's control. He thereby showed his perfect assessment of the arguments to which his king, Charles I, would be susceptible and which would earn the ambitious Cortés *post factum* legal status as conqueror and ruler of Mexico.[28] The other genre to thrive was epic poetry, which in its substantial narrative aspect is closely related to the chronicle and which provides in Ercilla y Zúñiga's *La araucana* a striking early example in Spanish-American literature of the tension, explicitly referred to in the poem itself, between form and content. Ercilla struggled with the idea of how a form inherited from Homer and Virgil through the Italian Renaissance could be accommodated to the rude environs of sixteenth-century Chile, where a tenacious indigenous tribe was giving lessons in valour and organization to the Spaniards.

By the seventeenth century, the firm establishment of colonial order and its associated silencing of the large masses of indigenous people not co-opted to the colonial cause brought an attempt to dispose of any conflict between form and content by simply removing Spanish-American reality from a position of prominence in literary representations. Imitation of the metropolitan models of poetry became the norm. Complex conceits in the manner of Góngora were reproduced by members of the small privileged class, a number of priests among them, for the exclusive enjoyment of their own class, which was most firmly tied to metropolitan interests. When Spanish-American content was treated, form and content tended to be in an uneasy alliance in flawed poems such as Sigüenza y Góngora's 'La grandeza mexicana.' The *Quijote* and the picaresque novel were read in some clandestinity and not imitated, as the shadow of the official disapproval of prose fiction in general hung over them. The finest Spanish-American dramatist of the period, the Mexican Juan Ruiz de Alarcón, went against the religious current that swept the genre and crossed to Spain to write plays of social morality. Meanwhile, the dispossessed Indian people, with no recognized outlets for their artistic expressions, sang, danced, recited, and narrated only in unrecorded, remote performances, in contrast to the colourful festivals and mammoth contests they had known in pre-Columbian times. Spanish-American literature in the colonial period, then, faithfully served metropolitan ends. At first, by force of law, it helped to instil the spirit of seriousness in the colonizers and later, through imitative tendencies of the dominant sector of the population, it contributed to the firm establishment of colonial society. The choice of forms dictated the near exclusion of a Spanish-American viewpoint even in those cases where an attempt was made to deal with Spanish-American topics. The envisaged audience was metropolitan, no matter whether the writers were Spaniards of short sojourn or creoles born of Spanish stock in Spanish America.

The Enlightenment, associated principally with France and its eighteenth-century 'philosophes,' had authentic manifestations in Spain and in Spanish America. Their names may not be as well known as those of many writers of the Golden Age, but such writers as Gaspar Melchor de Jovellanos and Meléndez Valdés showed the all-round interest in remedying Spain's national condition, an interest that reflected the responsibility felt by many intellectuals and artists of the times for correcting, by means of a pluridisciplinary effort, the ills of their society. Francisco de Goya y Lucientes, for example, whose paintings reveal an ardent interest in his country's political, economic, and social life and include allegories on 'Commerce,' 'Industry,' and 'Agriculture,' played an important role, in co-operation with intellectuals like Moratín, Iriarte, Jovellanos, and Meléndez Valdés, in creating practical projects aimed at stimulating Spain's development. Thus artists and writers whose formation took place in the eighteenth century, the Age of Decadence (as it is widely known), attempted to right the ills of the heritage of the Golden Age, whose debased character Cervantes, Quevedo, and, sometimes, Góngora understood so well.

At a time when enlightened but not as yet predominant sectors of the educated class in Spain were searching for a way to build the country internally and, consequently, to lessen its dependence on the colonies, some intellectuals in Spanish America were also starting to demonstrate a spirit of comprehensive interest in the area's well-being. This spirit is shown most dramatically in its Spanish-American beginnings by Simón Bolívar. As an essayist, he quickly reached the conclusion that Spanish America's principal problem lay in its subjugation and exploitation by Spain. To this intellectual perception he joined the military means, thus becoming in a direct sense the liberator of the northern and central South American countries. While he engaged the Spaniards, the rest of the Spanish-speaking parts of the continent set out to achieve their independence. His example of liberation in the military area was quickly followed in the literary area – and at least once at his personal instigation. He asked the Ecuadorean poet José Joaquín de Olmedo to write a poem celebrating his victory at Junín (August 1824). Olmedo responded with his 'Canto a Bolívar' in which he departed from historical accuracy by giving Bolívar credit for the victory at Ayacucho (December 1824), a battle in which Bolívar did not take part, but which by marking the winning of Peruvian independence achieved the final triumph of his military plan. This alteration was a measure of Olmedo's will to make the occasion of his poem serve as fully as possible the advancement of independent America. He looked beyond Bolívar to the distant past as well as to the future of the Spanish-American countries, demonstrating thereby a quality that would mark much subsequent Spanish-American poetry: its transtemporality, its involvement with history, and its concern about the future. Crucial to the mythological system of his poem (and here, too, making a new departure for Spanish-American poetry) is his use of Huayna Capac, the Inca who ruled the huge pre-Columbian empire of Tavantinsuyu before it was split between his sons Huáscar and Atahualpa, as the voice urging peace and unity for the continent. Spanish-American landscape, primarily the Andes, also plays its role as witness in this poem in which various American elements combine with one of the flexible traditional verse forms – the *silva* – to express a message of celebration and concern regarding America.

A theory of literature was already being elaborated to support this kind of practice. Its founding figure was the man of letters Andrés Bello, Bolívar's compatriot. As if to demonstrate his view of the usefulness of poetry, poetry itself was used to convey the essence of his theory. In Bello's poem 'Alocución a la poesía' (1823) he suggested that Spanish-American poets should now bring to an end the imitation of European models and find their inspiration in America, its history, its landscape, and its vegetation. Bello's views were taken up in forceful, even strident prose by the Argentinian writer Esteban Echeverría. There were two main reasons why Echeverría found himself in bad spirits. First, his romantic notions acquired in France about freedom and liberty were contradicted on his return to his country by the reality of the regime of Manuel Rosas. He used literature as a weapon in his struggle against this regime both by his formation in 1838 of a group of liberal anti-Rosas writers, the Asociación de Mayo, and by his own scathing literary, principally allegorical, attack on Rosas. Secondly, Echeverría was irritated by those in Spanish America who continued to think that Spain had a contribution to make to the continent's cultural development. Answering these, in articles later published in his *Dogma Socialista* (1846) he wrote of the obligation that Spanish-American writers had to represent Spanish-American reality in their writings, to make writing not abstract or vague but, by imbuing it with a sensitivity to history, useful to the national cause. This wedding of literature to Spanish-American reality came to be known as literary Americanism, and by the mid-nineteenth century the concept held sway over Spanish-American literature. The preoccupation with the kind of content advocated by the literary Americanists – liberal politics, the furthering of the cause of independence, nature as witness, the beauty and powerful presence of landscape, the luxuriant vegetation, and the produce of the varied geographical zones – was compatible with the freedom of forms allowed by romanticism. But the history of literature continues dynamically, and out of the tension caused by the relation of prescribed content and increasingly abundant forms, with romanticism having formally supplanted neo-classicism, would grow a new spirit of renovation. The tension (which comes under the purview of Plekhanov's theory about the occurrence of art for art's sake) was rooted in the fact that, despite the years of writings showing an American sentiment, the socio-political situation in several Spanish-American countries had stagnated or regressed; independence itself was observed to be incomplete or illusive. A new imperialism exercised by the United States, Britain, France, and Germany was growing harsher in its effect.

Writing in the last fifth of the century, it was difficult for the contributors to the movement of renovation, which the Nicaraguan poet Rubén Darío came to lead and call modernism, to realize that they were in fact products of the process of literary Americanism. Darío spoke quite harshly of his predecessors for their limited ranges, and the critics who defended them attacked

Darío in turn for forsaking the trend. Of those critics steeped in the trend, only the Uruguayan José Enrique Rodó, who perceived something of the course of the literary development, managed to reconcile himself, and that, uneasily, to the transition from literary Americanisn to modernism. Captivated by the mastery of Darío's art, he went from the position of declaring that 'Rubén Darío is not the poet of America' to the statement 'I am a Modernist too.'[29] Of the writers who took part in the process of renovation, only the Cuban José Martí, to whom we shall return later, possessed a lucid understanding of the controlling socio-political developments and formulated a conscious reaction to them, reflected in his establishment of a hierarchy of literary genres. He placed his essays and newspaper articles, in which he conveyed such fine perceptions as those contained in his essay 'Nuestra América,' ahead of his poetry and prose fiction,[30] where artistic elaboration was more clearly evident. As if the desperation brought about by the contrast between the ideal life and the real life was sometimes overpowering, Darío responded on occasion either in poetry or in prose with an uncharacteristic forcefulness to developments in the socio-political sphere. The blatantly imperialistic actions of Theodore Roosevelt prompted the poem 'A Roosevelt,' in which the ideal/real opposition is in clear relief. Such actions also exerted a sobering influence that, combined with other developments of the period (such as the vulnerability of Hispanic cultural traditions in America following the defeat of Spain in the Cuban–Spanish–American War of 1898), resulted in the prominence of social content in his works that appeared in the first decade of this century.

A new cleavage soon sprang up between writers who emphasized social content on the one hand, and on the other, those young, aggressive poets who, their expectations heightened by the renown Darío had won, were anxious to dominate Western literature with their innovations even as Darío had dominated Hispanic literature. The Chilean Vicente Huidobro made through his creationism a significant contribution to those vanguardist movements that were nurtured by the confusion resulting from World War I. The Argentinian Jorge Luis Borges, too, came to public notice in this period by his interventions in the expressive theories of another of the vanguardist movements, ultraism. He argued that poetry should be purified by the placing of greater emphasis on its primordial element, the metaphor; that content which depended on discursive or anecdotic forms had no place in poetry; and that identifiable settings, regional topics, and local colour should be similarly excluded. Although Borges ignores almost all of the precepts in his subsequent book of poetry, *Fervor de Buenos Aires* (1923), some of them are to be later observed in the books of short stories, such as *El Aleph* and *Ficciones*, in which his years of laboured apprenticeship come to fruition. His early views have their recrudescence in Borges's most significant later statement on literature, his essay entitled 'El escritor argentino y la tradición'[31] where, in opposition to those writers concerned with the literary representation of Argentinian society, he posits a universalist orientation that eschews local colour and national concern. These attitudes have prompted a spectrum of hostile reaction from the considerable range of defenders of an Americanist position. There are those who argue, coinciding in theory with the Mao Tse Tung of the days of the 'Yenan Forum on Art and Literature,' that no writing is simply universal or Western; that rather, all writing is aimed at and is on behalf of certain class interests; and that Borges, at the expense of the real interests of the Argentinian people, uses his talent to pander to groups that are ultimately oppressive. Others cite Borges's expressed disdain for Latin America, his infantile desire to be English, and his undemocratic and even pro-Fascist statements whenever he ventures commentary on politics. Still others see him as simply showing the irresponsibility that comes of immaturity, while others admire how he writes but not what he writes.[32]

As the Russian Formalists had to contend with Trotsky, so did the wave of vanguardist theorists in Spanish America have to contend with the Peruvian José Carlos Mariátegui in the 1920s. He related the views of his compatriot and predecessor Manuel González Prada to developments of his own time and was able to understand Spanish-American socio-economic phenomena in their global context. Mariátegui came to hold the view that the problems of the dispossessed Peruvian people could begin to be solved only by a thoroughgoing Marxist revolution. He founded the journal *Amauta*, which served as an organ for views he regarded as being more scientific than those that were being expressed by his former colleagues in APRA (Alianza Popular Revolucionaria Americana) led by Haya de la Torre. His numerous publications in this journal and elsewhere reveal the great importance he attached to literature in the formidable task of improving the conditions of his people, the millions of Peruvians among whose surest expectations were daily hunger and nightly pain. He regarded it as the normal human response of the writer to concern himself with, in addition to aesthetic matters, ethical, moral, and political issues; he considered it natural that these factors should be taken into account in the assessment of literature. The writer should also be conscious of history and understand that nineteenth-century satisfaction with the mere presentation of local colour was seriously inadequate in the twentieth century, when the real and urgent interests of the people lay in alleviating their misery by overthrowing the oppressive system under which they lived. César Vallejo won his approval for the way in which he sometimes combined the elements of his poetry to expose the ravages of suffering on the psyche of the Peruvian people. On a global scale, however, he was dismayed at the indifference writers were showing to the human condition, at their lack of 'positive capability,' if we may invert the Keatsian phrase, at the ethical, moral, and political void in their works. He cites the case of the Italian writer Massimo Bontempelli (an early exponent of 'magical realism'), who declared that in 1920 he felt almost communist and in 1923, the year of the march on Rome, almost fascist. In this context Mariátegui makes an assertion that reappears frequently in his writings: 'The contemporary artist, in most cases, has an empty soul ... Mankind cannot progress without a faith, because to be without a faith is to be without a goal.'[33] As far as the Hispanic world was concerned, he lay some of the blame for the impotence of art and artists on the shoulders of Ortega y Gasset (for reasons we have already explored), who, Mariátegui finds, by 1926 had become the chief Hispanic promoter of chic vanguardist and surrealist vogues and of 'cosmic' writers who had no feet.

The Cuban theorist José Antonio Portuondo, to whom we shall later refer, has developed theories furthering those of Mariátegui; and extensive work has been done in recent years by Adolfo Sánchez Vázquez, a Spaniard long resident in Mexico, in exploring the relation between literature and society. As is characteristic of the Spanish-American critics of the post-Mariátegui era, Sánchez Vázquez is solidly acquainted with world-wide trends in literary criticism and is thus able to be comprehensive in his analysis. He begins with the basics of the Marxist position, seeing art as a social phenomenon, the artist as a social being, and the work of art as a bond or bridge between creator and the other members of his society. He credits the work of art with the power to affect the aims, ideas, and values of a society. He employs broad historicity in suggesting that in different historical periods the relations between art and society manifest themselves differently. The religious emphasis of the Middle Ages, for instance, gave way to the emphasis on material production in the post-Renaissance period, reflecting man's growing dominance over nature. The worker and the artist subsequently became tools in the service of this production. The artist recognized his alienation in the romantic period and refused to go on being merely a part of the production process. This later gave rise to art becoming destined for the privileged few, the large masses being treated to 'narcóticos artísticos,' to use Fischer's term. Sánchez Vázquez writes: 'We see, then, that in the conditions prevailing in capitalist society, the economic and ideological interests of the dominant class are tied to a mass consumption or aesthetic enjoyment that can only be represented, in general, by a banal art; while true art, to which great masses of human nuclei have no access, tends to become a privileged art. This situation ... has to be felt by the artist to be a limitation on the radius of action of his work.'[34] From this he deduces a common interest between the artist and the social sectors that struggle to achieve change. He agrees with most Marxist critics that the artist should assist in this struggle but sees his power in this regard as limited, since the task is a social rather than an artistic one in which the proletariat, the class most interested in ending its alienation, will play the decisive role. Sánchez Vázquez's broad view, expressed in categories that appear to be precisely European, could be salutarily corrected by greater attention to the Spanish-American experience. As was observed earlier, his agreement with Gramsci's views led him to a questionable distinction between the artist and the politician; and here such a factor as the special, socially constructive character given to romanticism in Spanish America by its links with literary Americanism is not brought to bear on his argument. Nor does he give significance to the fact that in the later history of Spanish-American literature, within capitalist or capitalist-dependent societies, artists in various fields[35] have placed their art and themselves in the vanguard of movements for social change in such a way as to erase any trace of separateness from the members of the proletariat, and – since it is of limited usefulness to speak of a proletariat in sub-capitalist countries – from the peasants and the dispossessed as well. In fact Mariátegui would have been pleased at the number of leading Spanish-American writers who, since his time, have shown the kind of commitment he demanded and who have involved themselves, although not often in a systematic way, in discussions of the theory of commitment. Pablo Neruda illustrated the tendency vividly in his 'arte poética' entitled 'Explico algunas cosas' ('I Explain a Few Things') in which he accounts for his shift from intuition to history as the source of a new poetry of social involvement that would be transmitted in appropriately more open forms than those of his preceding poetry. He would in this phase of his poetic life, in the final line of his poem 'Las alturas de Macchu Picchu' ('The Heights of Macchu Picchu'), entreat the oppressed to 'Speak through my words and my blood!' More recently, other leading writers have been revising the concept of literary Americanism, stirring up polemics and adding new refinements in keeping with the historical stages their societies have reached.

The Colombian writer Gabriel García Márquez, for instance, has viewed the search for excellence in expression as part of the writer's political duty. The other part is to reveal to his readers the social and political realities of his society. He has said: 'I believe that the principal political duty of a writer is to write well. Not only to write well in the sense of writing correct and brilliant prose, but to write well. I do not mean sincerely, but in accordance with his convictions.'[36] Speaking of his novel *Cien años de soledad* (1967), he elaborates:

The whole drama of the banana massacre is established in my novel in accordance with my convictions. The position I take is definitely in favour of the workers. That is clear. And I think that the great political contribution of the writer is not to evade either his convictions or reality, but to help the reader through his work to understand better the political and social reality of his country and of his continent, of his society; and I believe that that is a positive and important political task and that that is the political function of the writer.[37]

García Márquez has subsequently given clear indications of his deepening socio-political activity: he has founded a journal, *Alternativa*, devoted to literature and society; and especially notable among his writings in the journal was his chronicling of the Cuban military and other aid to Angola.[38]

It is evident from Julio Cortázar's works that his primary concern is with personal identity and the relentless search for techniques and expressions suitable for upsetting complacent relationships with everyday reality. Yet, in declaring his ideas on literature, he is sympathetic to the view that the Latin-American novel should address itself to the problems of the area and he has expressed allegiance to the socialist cause in Latin America.[39] He is considered by García Márquez to be 'profoundly Latin American' in contrast to Borges,[40] and his novel, *Libro de Manuel* (1973), is considered to be revolutionary in a political sense, as advocating a socialist revolution.[41] Cortázar has endorsed this view of his novel.[42]

Mario Vargas Llosa's study[43] of García Márquez's *Cien años de soledad* has given rise to a lively series of exchanges between Vargas Llosa and the Uruguayan critic Angel Rama on the question of socio-political involvement. The central views of the role of the writer put forward by Vargas Llosa were that each novel is a deicide, a symbolic assassination of reality. The novelist, however, is not conscious of why he rebels. A demonic madness pushes him to it. He must therefore abandon himself to the irrational, which is a basic element in his work. It follows from this that the novelist is not free. He does not choose his themes; they choose him. Rama, from his Marxist viewpoint, considers this posture to be idealistic, irresponsible, and regressively romantic. He adds: 'Opposing the idea of art as social and human work, as Marxism holds, Vargas Llosa reconstructs the idealist thesis of the irrational (if not divine, at least demonic) origin of the literary work.'[44] Rama asks that the writer be a 'writer-producer,' responsible to a society or to a sector of it as García Márquez becomes after *El coronel no tiene quien le escriba* (1961). In his replies, Vargas Llosa, while curtly rejecting Marxist aesthetic theories as being too conservative, gives prominence to the public usefulness implicit in his theories. He explains that the novelist's demons are obsessions that arise from the clash between individual and world history. The novelist is therefore dealing with what is social, what is real. Despite the fact that Vargas Llosa, unlike Cortázar and García Márquez, has distanced himself from the Cuban Revolution, he proclaims, and with justice, that his exposure of institutions in his native Peru, particularly of the military, is of the kind that may provoke the desire for new social values.[45]

The necessity for writers like García Márquez, Cortázar, and Vargas Llosa to claim social commitment may well be due in part to a reaction by some Spanish-American critics to one result of the concern for technique and expression. Because of the history of this concern in Spanish America – the frequent coincidence between the striving for artistic effects and the disclaiming of specific interest in Spanish America – critics may be reluctant to see Americanism or social commitment in the works of those who are praised universally as consummate artists. On the other hand, they have notoriously overlooked the artistic methods of those who are obviously committed. In this connection Fernando Alegría comments aptly when he states that the contention that García Márquez, Cortázar, and Vargas Llosa are apolitical compared with novelists of an earlier generation like Jorge Icaza, Aguilera Malta, and José Revueltas may be due to a simple optical illusion, since, in fact, the younger writers do not remove themselves from social reality as some have supposed.[46]

All this, then, represents the large theatre in which Guillén as a Spanish-American poet has been operating. It establishes the fact that long before Jean Paul Sartre's divulgation of the idea of *littérature engagée*, before his confusing conundrum of Marxism and existentialism, the concept of commitment was a live, consciously observed one in Spanish America. In the colonial period it had a largely conservative purpose. From the beginning of the independence movement onward, it has had revolutionary purpose. The overt presence of commitment in both periods makes it one of the distinguishing features of Spanish-American literature. The preponderance of the idea of literature as a tool has included the idea that the tool should be kept sharp; and much is owed in this regard to those like Huidobro and Borges who have made their best contribution in the realm of expression. We shall see that Guillén's alertness to matters of expression permits him to represent with impeccable appropriateness any adjustment in the area of content suggested by his attentiveness to history. But more precisely Guillén is a Cuban poet, and in the geographical and especially in the historical sense this fact has considerable significance. To examine the Cuban background, then, is to sharpen the focus on the context in which his contribution has been made.

CUBAN HISTORICAL REALITY AND LITERARY HISTORY

The two salient features of Cuban history up to the late nineteenth century to which literary activity is closely tied are the country's colonial status and the institution within it of slavery. Cuba has its colonial status in common with the other Spanish-American countries; those general features of that status that have already been described apply to Cuba. In comparison with the large and relatively advanced mainland civilizations, however, Cuba's indigenous people lacked the resources for a struggle against the Spaniards.[47] It was soon controlled, settled by 1510, and used as a base for other conquests. The quick establishment of the colony led to a cultural life that showed obeisance to the metropolis and exhibited a less-than-remarkable literary output. The idea of African slavery as the most economical form of manual labour emerged because the indigenous population had been nearly wiped out by the brutal conditions imposed on it by the Spaniards. Spain became a customer in the slave trade carried out principally by the master of the seas and of the trade – England – and Cuba was one of the main destinations. Thus slavery and colonialism came to form the issues that dominated Cuban life for centuries, the two having complex interrelations.

The haughty individualism that drove the illiterate Francisco Pizarro to head the exploration company that destroyed the comprehensively structured Inca civilization was to be found in more temperate manifestations throughout the colonies. We have already seen how Cortés had embarked illegally from Cuba on his successful quest for power and glory in Mexico. The ruthless individualistic ethics of Pizarro and Cortés were reflected and perpetuated in colonial Cuba by the Spanish authorities. There emerged, nevertheless, an ennobling spirit of defiance on the part of the slaves struggling for freedom and from creoles (descendants of Spaniards) who later came to struggle for independence. Creoles wanted control over their economy, their politics, and their culture. Although there were times when the slave and creole struggles merged through personalities or groups, they were not always in reliable partnership. Every stage in the process of enslavement met with some resistance. There were captives who resisted on African soil, on board ship, and as soon as they landed on Cuban soil. During the sixteenth and seventeenth centuries the primary form of resistance was escape. Runaway slaves, or maroons (*cimarrones*), sought out remote, usually hilly, areas (*palenques*) as refuge from their pursuers (*rancheadores*). Records of brutal exemplary killings of captured maroons date from 1533;[48] and the slaves in reprisal for such cruelty helped the enemies of Spain whenever they could, as they helped the French in the sacking of Havana in 1538. There were also significant uprisings against the authorities in 1677 by maroons attempting to protect their freedom and in 1731 by slaves in the copper mines attempting to win theirs, both occurring in the region of Santiago del Prado. All these incidents involved the direct opposition between slave-master and slave and left relatively untroubled other segments of the society. By the late eighteenth century this began to change as national and international developments turned slavery into an absorbing issue confronting the whole population. The first international event to affect the character of uprisings in Cuba was the Haitian revolution that began in 1791. French families from that country and Spaniards from Santo Domingo fled to neighbouring Cuba to bolster the numbers of those who wanted slavery maintained in its rigid form so that a second domino would not fall to blacks of the Caribbean. A further wave of immigrants largely in favour of the Cuban status quo arrived in 1797 from Trinidad, which had been occupied by the English. At the same time, the desire of mulattos and blacks for normal status in Cuba grew strongly and they found some limited support among creoles.

A new kind of conspiracy against the colonial authorities was led by Nicolás Morales, a free mulatto, in 1795. His objectives were to secure for mulattos equal rights with whites, the lifting of certain taxes, and a redistribution of land. The plan, involving Oriente province, was betrayed to the authorities by one of Morales's colleagues. Morales was arrested, brought to trial in Bayamo, and hastily executed.

The second group to show its restlessness under the Spanish regime were some wealthy merchants and landlords. Prohibited from trading with the United States and feeling the adverse effects of other Spanish decrees, they started, in 1809, a protest movement led by Ramón de la Luz, Joaquín Infante, and Luis Francisco Bassave y de Cárdenas. They were joined by several freed blacks and by some slaves who welcomed any anti-colonial agitation. The leaders and many of the participants were arrested and jailed overseas, but one of the participants who was not detained was to lead the third of the new kinds of rebellion.

He was José Antonio Aponte, a freed black, carpenter, artist, and soldier. He took advantage of his military training and his Lucumí heritage to organize, for the purpose of ending slavery in Cuba and toppling the colonial government, the most extensive liberation movement to that date (1812) in Cuban history. Acts of insurrection had no sooner begun than the movement was betrayed by a supposed supporter. Aponte was hanged along with a number of freed blacks and slaves; and, as was done by the authorities with ritual frequency, their heads were cut off and exhibited on stakes. Aponte's effort was exceptional in that his enormous plan and sacrifice were carried out on behalf of others, he himself having already the rights and privileges he attempted to make general in his country.[49] Meanwhile the authorities remained unrelenting, unmoved either by the frequent uprisings on sugar estates (chiefly in Oriente province) or by the sniping attacks carried out by the maroons. While some creoles saw independence and the abolition of slavery as desirable, the authorities kept most of them loyal by warning of the Africanization of Cuba that would result. The situation is well summed up by Sergio Aguirre. He writes:

The Cuban bourgeosie defends itself, in the end, from the danger that any slave uprising represents for it. Its wealth is based on the work of the African slaves and
their descendants; upon the overseer's whip it builds a whole economic, social and
political evolution; but it lives besieged by the fear that what happened in revolutionary Haiti in 1791 might be reproduced in Cuba. For it slavery is at once the source
of economic exaltation and a political yoke. For fear of the black man there is no
uprising against Spain. And in spite of all we have said, we have to agree that this is
probably the principal reason why Cuba suffered a historical set-back of eighty years
on the way to its liberation.[50]

The climate in Spain's colony was different from what it was in Britain's
neighbouring colony, Jamaica, largely because of differences between the
two metropolitan countries at that time. The liberalism and prosperity that
Goya and his encyclopedist friends had planned for Spain did not take root
and the absolute, repressive monarch Fernando VII held sway until 1830.
By contrast, England's industrial expansion, its increase in production, and
demand for labour exposed the harsh conditions of the workers (many of
them children), especially alongside the wealth their labour yielded. A sentiment sprang up in favour of improved labour practices that provided a remote yet helpful analogy for the cause of freedom for slaves. The sentiment
had its real base in industrial growth and could become practically effective
and achieve its goal only when it converged with another aspect of industrial
growth: a market for British machinery that would replace freed slaves. The
slave-holders could foresee ancilliary economic gains, particularly a pool
of cheap labour that would be provided by the freed slaves, who would
become landless peasants. Moreover, this pool could be made desperately
insecure by supplementing it with growing numbers of immigrants from
India who, marginalized by the economic drain being visited on their home-
land, were soon to be encouraged by the authors of the drain to emigrate to
the Caribbean as indentured labourers. It is at this point of convergence of
profit and sentiment that the slaves were freed in Jamaica in 1834. British
economic interests would also be served by abolition in Cuba that would
create industrial markets. The issue, however, was put forward as a moral
one. By agreements in 1817 and 1835, the British terminated slave-trading
compacts with Spain. British representatives in Cuba, Richard R. Madden
and later David Turnbull, gave high priority to seeing to the effectiveness
of the agreements and to matters of slavery in general. The hidden motive
of profit – for Cuba was, after all, Spain's territory – caused the British to
work somewhat clandestinely. This, in turn, contributed to the ambivalence
shown by some of the leading Cuban writers of the time and was to have,
combined with other factors, a disastrous consequence for the anti-slavery

movement, and especially for the leading black figures of the 1840s. These circumstances are conveniently examined by focusing on the career of Domingo del Monte.

The depressing conditions of colonial life drove from Cuba José María Heredia, its greatest poet of the early nineteenth century. Having written stirring patriotic *silvas* about freedom from the colonial condition, he left the country in 1823 at the age of twenty to continue his career in Mexico and other Spanish-American countries and, very briefly, in Canada. He left behind a confused literary situation. Padre Félix Varela, an admirer of the Spanish Enlightenment, had lectured at the Seminario de San Carlos on the Spanish constitution, which the liberals had brought into being in 1820. At this time, he became a deputy representing Cuba at the Spanish Cortes. Because of having voted against the accession to power of Fernando VII, he was condemned to death; to avoid this penalty, he was forced to live outside the Spanish Empire, in the United States. He was an ardent independentist and his ability as a writer and lecturer had attracted wealthy young Cubans with literary aspirations such as José Antonio Saco, José Luis de Luz Caballero, and Domingo del Monte to a liberal outlook. They came to reflect the Spanish Enlightenment view that intellectuals should attempt to come to grips with the ills of their society, and so they felt obliged to adopt positions on the two great issues of their day: colonial status and slavery. When the regime suppressed the Academia Cubana de Literatura (which they and their colleagues had founded) and banished Saco, the focal figure of the group became del Monte. In private *tertulias* in his mansion and in voluminous correspondence with the promising young writers of his time, he impressed upon them the view that the poet 'will consider himself a *man* and then a *poet*, and in that way will use all the strengths he can command to co-operate with the other artists and philosophers of the century, who are worthy of calling themselves men, that is, who have the spirit of men, and have in their breasts whole and manlike hearts, to improve the condition of their fellow men.'[51] At the same time, however, del Monte, though wandering apparently close to the boundaries of his class interests never strayed beyond them. He considered himself and his circle to be in the vanguard of the landed gentry and, knowing he had a great deal to lose in a radical social upheaval, worked with sedulous deviousness for the peaceful transition of power to this group. He was on extremely good terms with Mr Madden and believed in the kind of mechanization of sugar processing that the British were promoting; he encouraged and supported *literary* attacks, in neo-classical rather than romantic temper, on slavery. The novel *Francisco* by Anselmo Suárez y Romero was read and corrected at his *tertulia* as it was being written.[52] He encouraged the slave Juan Francisco Manzano to write his autobiography and contributed to the purchase of his freedom. Furthermore, he urged other writers inside and outside of Cuba to write about slavery.[53]

In the meantime, slave rebellions had continued throughout the country. An illicit slave trade was carried on that was so large it can hardly be called clandestine.[54] Britain's insistence that the agreements of 1817 and 1835 prohibiting the trade be observed became vociferous, with Palmerston in London (1840) threatening Spain, while Turnbull (who succeeded Madden in Havana) angered the slave interests by making several demands, including that all those blacks who had been enslaved since 1820 be freed. In this atmosphere of heightened tension, Domingo del Monte, apparently fearing that the radical social upheaval he had worked hard and surreptitiously to avert was at hand, sent a letter in late 1842 to an American diplomat, Alexander Everett, informing him of a plot by the British, their agents in Cuba, and the blacks for a general uprising that would free the slaves and remove Cuba from Spain's domain. The allegation was passed to the Spanish and it received elaborate embroidery from the slave interests, including a rumour that an invasion was being prepared from Jamaica. Spain dispatched a new captain-general, Leopoldo O'Donnell, to the island. On the further report of a slave-owner that one of his slaves had told him of a plan for a rebellion, he set up a military commission charged to investigate the conspiracy of non-whites against whites. The result of what became known as the Conspiración de la Escalera of 1844 was the killing of some 7000 blacks. Among those selected for slaughter were many of the most prominent of the incipient black bourgeoisie who had distinguished themselves in various fields, including the violinist and conductor José Miguel Román, the Paris-trained dentist Andrés Dodge, and one of Cuba's best-known poets of the nineteenth century, Gabriel de la Concepción Valdés, known as Plácido. Another leading black poet of the time, Juan Francisco Manzano, was sent to prison. Following his letter, del Monte and his wife had gone to the United States and thence to France. He learned there that, being easily identifiable as one of the British agents, he himself had been denounced and was wanted in Cuba for trial as a conspirator. He never returned to the island. His close friend Luz Caballero, also wanted for trial, returned from Paris to deny having had any part in what he called the horrible conspiracy by blacks; he was freed.

The case, and perhaps with Guillén as our ever-present subject we might say the lesson, of Plácido deserves close attention. A humble typographer, he was a gifted, self-taught poet who, producing at a time when Spanish romanticism was at its height, adopted as his models such writers as José Zorrilla, José de Espronceda, and Francisco Martínez de la Rosa. The pathos inherent in the contradiction between his choice of models who exercised freedom of form and exuberance of tone to reflect the environment created by the death of the tyrannical Fernando VII and Plácido's own reality of a slave society was one that marked his whole career. He was troubled by the insincerity that led him to dedicate panegyrics to government officials and the landed gentry. Betrayed by the latter and condemned to death by the former, in the isolation of the eve of his execution, he wrote to his wife: 'I do not send regards to any friends because I know I have none. I send regards only to don Francisco Martínez de la Rosa, don Juan Nicasio Gallego, and don José Zorrilla.'[55]

A search for a more authentic romanticism in which Plácido also participated found expression in those poems fixing on selected aspects of life in the Cuban countryside. The poems based on the small tobacco producers, the *vegueros*, and were written in *décimas*, the form most closely associated with country folk, the *guajiros*, were one such manifestation. Another form, which revealed a desire to escape from the tensions of contemporary times, was an imagined indigenism, *el siboneísmo*, by which readers were transported to idyllic scenes of supposed pre-Columbian bliss.

The harsh colonial slave-master (*negrero*) hold on Cuba gave rise to diverse reactions. The regime had firm support from those whose economic interests were directly tied to slavery and from those, including some blacks, who were susceptible to propaganda in various forms, including shows of military power, that was aimed at bolstering the system. There were annexationists who schemed at perpetuating conservative Cuban politics by making that country a part of the United States. Their visible activity was centred largely in the United States: their man of military action was the Venezuelan adventurer Narciso López. The autonomists, matching the political profile of del Monte, had built their wealth on the colonial structure but were not averse to certain changes in methods of production or to a degree of agitation that did not go further than being unsettling. They expected to have the reins of power fall to them. There were the heroic slaves, maroons, freed blacks, and the mulattos who, despite the repeated exhibitions of heads on stakes and tortures from previous crushed attempts, continued in more or less spontaneous uprisings to show their revulsion at the inhuman institution they considered slavery to be and their determination to bring it to an end. To complete the spectrum, a group that had been growing in significance came to be recognizable as revolutionary in the last third of the century. It grew out of elements of some of the above groups in a changing economic climate. A crisis in the world economy during the 1850s, particularly in 1857, had a serious effect on relations between the classes. It affected the tobacco industry and spurred a new consciousness among the workers in that industry. Their newspaper *La Aurora* joined the reformists' organ *El Siglo* in opposition to the establishment's slavery-supporting newspaper, the *Diario de la Marina*. Also, since the Spaniards wanted to take every advantage possible in the difficult economic situation, a real rift developed

between them and the creoles resulting in a new will among the latter for
independence and in a new invulnerability on their part to the regime's
warning against the Africanization of Cuba. In Oriente yet another plan was
drawn up by a freed black, this time Augustín Da, for a rebellion to end
both slavery and the colonial system. The attempt failed with the customary
fatal consequences; but in the same year, 1866, the creole[56] Sociedad
Republicana de Cuba y Puerto Rico, headed in New York by Juan Manuel
Macías and with links to some large landholders in Cuba headed by Carlos
Manuel de Céspedes in Manzanillo, declared that 'the firm and only purpose
of the society is the independence of the Antilles and the absolute freedom
of all its inhabitants, without regard to race or colour.' The basis for a popular
movement was being laid and two years later, with rebellions in Oriente
and Camagüey, the Ten Years' War began.

   In the difficult times leading up to 1868 the writers did not distinguish
themselves, either by their perception of the historical situation or by their
literary achievements. Several of them had behaved ignominiously in the
affair of the Conspiración de la Escalera, scurrying to vindicate the regime's
brutality. They persisted for a long time in the path of the early Spanish
romantics and chose, without fine discernment, contemporary European writers for imitation and translation. The verses devoted to patriotic questions
fell in the large shadow cast by Heredia. Gertrudis Gómez de Avellaneda,
one of the most polished of these writers, participated in the tendencies
that were in vogue during her stay in Cuba: indigenism and romanticism.
The exotic, sentimental aspects of these movements were displayed in her
novel dealing with slavery, Sab. Only in the last two decades of the century
did two poets, Julián del Casal and José Martí, in their quite different ways
lift the level of writing to a position of prominence in the Spanish-American
field. Casal, known as one of the accomplished modernists, channelled
those distantly inspired experiments of poets like Juan Clemente Zenea and
Francisco and Manuel Sellén as well as direct French Parnassian models
into elaborately decorative and at the same time precise expressions of despair
and escapist urges. If one were to relate the few poems he wrote that deal
with Cuba's political and social scene to the general tone of his poetry, one
would ascribe Casal's despair and pessimism partly to his sense of an
apparent endlessness of the quest for independence. The enthusiasm with
which the war against the Spanish had been launched faltered on the dis-
agreements that arose among landholders on the grounds of their degree of
commitment to a revolutionary position. A measure of the revolutionary
character of the struggle was the leadership role that black Cuban patriot and
staunch anti-colonialist General Antonio Maceo had come to play in it. An
indication of its shortcomings from this standpoint was the exasperation shown
by Maceo and his brother José when the inconclusive Paz de Zanjón was

reached in 1878. Antonio Maceo, determined to fight until independence was won, to wage the Thirty Years War instead of the Ten Years War, co-operated with other firm revolutionaries, notably Máximo Gómez and José Martí, meeting with them in Costa Rica and in Jamaica where he spent much time and where all three leaders made fruitful plans. The Maceo–Martí partnership signifies the fruition of the Cuban revolutionary spirit. The descendant of slaves (let the slave-master be ashamed, as Guillén would say) and the son of a Spanish soldier posted in Cuba joined in leading the un-compromising struggle for independence from Spain and for the equality of all Cubans under the law. Martí, imprisoned and then banished from Cuba to Spain at the age of fifteen for independentist activities, had spent years of his exile in Spanish America and the United States. He employed his time being actively patriotic – in all his writings, teaching, planning of constitu-tions – and showed great concern about the situation of all Latin America. He had observed that in independent Spanish America the spirit of the colonies had continued into the republics, undermining them and making them vulner-able to a new imperialism. He was, therefore, determined that the bases of the independence of Cuba should be so constructed as to make the country impervious to any intrusion that would sap its vital energies. Something of Martí's conviction and of his ability to communicate it, in short, something of the essential personality of Martí is conveyed in the eloquent words ad-dressed to General Serafín Sánchez by José Maceo shortly before he was to fall in the field of battle. He talked of the frustration he had felt after years in the struggle, of the irritations caused by bad faith and intrigues, and stated that despite his love for Cuba and his dedication to the revolution he had planned not to return to the war. But he did, because of Martí. 'Only Martí could lure me from my love nest, only he. He compelled me with his patriot-ism and seduced me with his words.'[57] The combination of patriotism and words well characterizes Martí. His words, used to convey his sentiments and his well-reasoned perceptions, were managed with a level of art that put him in the front rank of Spanish-American writers. His patriotism had mani-fold expression in his lifetime, which ended finally in fruitful martyrdom to the cause.

By February 1895, the war had become intense again, and the poets were numerously inspired by this new phase of it. They devoted themselves as much to the writing of verses in support of its aims as to seeking material aid for the effort within Cuba and on the American continents. Some of them joined in the combat and died in it. The years between the two active phases of the war had witnessed a new spirit developing in Cuba's literary circle. By 1895 the neo-classical restraint under which del Monte and Luz Caballero had held intellectual opinion as well as the escapist modernism of Casal had given way to the positivist attitudes of Enrique José Varona. As editor of the *Revista Cubana* (1885–95), Varona advocated persuasively a scientific, sociological approach to literary activity, stressing the necessity for writers to be abreast of the governing events of their times and to make literature work for the improvement of their societies. He thus helped to open the way to a meeting of minds between writers on the one hand and Martí and Antonio Maceo on the other, the latter himself encouraging literary support of the war by his sponsorship of the journal of the revolutionary fighters, *El Cubano Libre*.

The military action ended in 1898 with the comprehensive defeat of the Spaniards as a result of the United States' intervention and declaration of war on Spain. This circumstance would make the Cuban fight for independence inconclusive and prolong the militancy of some writers. It became clear once more that the persistence of José María Heredia in the Cuban literary imagination is due not so much to the excellence of his art as to the continuing appropriateness of his declamatory patriotic tone during the more than 100 years in which hopes to achieve the goal of independence were repeatedly frustrated. Again the Heredian model of patriotic verse came into service as poets like Enrique Hernández Miyares and Bonifacio Byrne, men who had worked and written vigorously on behalf of the independence struggle, now expressed their alarm at the flying of both the United States and the Cuban flags over Cuba. They coupled alarm with the determination that annexationism should not triumph after all. However, disillusionment soon set in, brought by the awkward reality of an empty republican status. Instead of the anticipated implementation of Martí's *Bases y estatutos secretos del Partido Revolucionario Cubano* and of the *Resoluciones adoptadas por la emigración cubana de Tampa*, names of difficult pronunciation for most Cubans, such as General Leonard Wood, Howard Taft, and Colonel Enoch Crowder had their way in debates on the Cuban constitution. The Republic of Cuba was established on 20 May 1902. Through the Platt amendment to the constitution, the U.S. 'legalized' its subsequent interventions to protect its interests in Cuba. The amendment also allowed for U.S. supervision of Cuban foreign and finance policies. Corruption and inequality that were antithetical to the ideals expressed by Martí soon became rife; and the festering recrudescence of racism led to an ugly explosion in 1912 in which the losses among the black population were severe. In such a climate the encouraging gesture of Pedro Henríquez Ureña visiting from the Dominican Republic and urging a Spanish-American cultural identity could be communicated only to a few young writers. The methodology of Fernando Ortiz's pioneering exploration of the roots of Cuban society was hardly noticed. In these circumstances, the founding in 1910 of the officially sponsored Academia Nacional de Artes y Letras seemed like a parody.

Parody was in fact a primary literary style of the period. It reflected the

bitterness of the writers of the first republican generation. It is true that the founding, in 1913, of the journal *Cuba Contemporánea* represented an attempt to analyse in its pages the principal socio-political problems of the country; but in the world of fiction, parody ruled in novels such as Carlos Loveira's *Generales y doctores* (1920), *La última lección* (1924), and *Juan Criollo* (1927), and in Miguel de Carrión's *Las honradas* (1917) and Jesús Castellanos's *La conjura* (1909). In the theatre, pathos and pessimism dominate in the work of José Antonio Ramos (see *Tembladera*, 1916), the most significant dramatist of the period. The search carried out during this decade in Spanish America and elsewhere for new expression beyond those points reached by the masters of modernism is joined in Cuba, too. The principal participants are Regino E. Boti with his *Arabescos mentales* (1913) and José Manuel Poveda, who showed a wide range of initiatives in his *Versos precursores* (1917), while Felipe Pichardo Moya modernized the expression of national sentiment found in earlier poets like Bonifacio Byrne. The novelties introduced by Boti, Poveda, and Pichardo Moya would be useful in the following decade when the level of anti-establishment political activity was raised and sought various, including literary, expression.

The year 1923 saw the stirrings of political activity among a select group of the already small number of students privileged to attend the University of Havana. Led by Julio Antonio Mella, their first action reflected their embarrassment at their exclusivity; they pressed for university reform. An outcome of this was the establishment by Mella of the Universidad Popular José Martí. He was helped in this endeavour by other young intellectuals of the time (who would later constitute the Grupo Minorista), one of whom, Rubén Martínez Villena, headed what came to be known as the *protesta de los trece*, the protest of thirteen intellectuals, who in a manifesto criticized the government of Alfredo Zayas for its numerous shortcomings. Its aims included attempts to right some of the wrongs felt since 1901. Members of the group tended to engage in literary pursuits. Jorge Mañach, for instance, condemned in eloquent writings the republican constitution, which he would later call 'that mockery of a republic, that illusion of nationality in a colonized, humiliated people.'[58] Emilio Roig de Leuchsenring and José Antonio Fernández de Castro reassessed aspects of Cuban history, the latter joining with Félix Lizaso to include the history of modern Cuban poetry. In addition to his manifestos, Rubén Martínez Villena wrote cultivated verse in which he conveyed his national conerns. So did Juan Marinello who contributed sober, deeply contemplative poems. The founding of the first Cuban Communist Party in 1925 owed a great deal to the new militancy of this group and to the need to combat the dictatorship that Gerardo Machado had begun to establish in that same year. However, the rampant vogue of art for art's sake and for vanguardist emphasis on expression in the main centres of Western literature and the rapid communication of the new Parisian literary fashions to Cuba through the pages of the *Diario de la Marina* affected many of the writers of the group with the Gramscian notion of the distinction between art and politics. Several of them began to opt for one or the other. Martínez Villena, for instance, gave up poetry for praxis when he became active in the party in 1927.[59] On the other hand, the political activity of the Grupo Minorista waned in 1927 and *Cuba Contemporánea* gave way to the *Revista de Avance*. Directed by stalwarts of the Grupo Minorista such as Juan Marinello, Jorge Mañach, Francisco Ichaso, and Félix Lizaso, the *Revista de Avance* shunned political involvement and fostered those aspects of trendy expressionism that would have pleased Ortega. In two articles[60] published in the journal, Marinello showed his inclination to view poetry and politics as incompatible, a view now upheld by Mañach. The way was therefore clear for the *jitanjáforas*[61] and other experiments by which Mariano Brull hoped to arrive at 'pure poetry,' for the *calligrammes* of Manuel Navarro Luna, and for the *negrista* poetry of Ramón Guirao and a host of other practitioners. Apollinaire, Valéry, Proust, Gide, Breton, Cocteau, Giraudoux, and Marinetti were names of influence. Eugenio Florit is among those Cuban poets attracted to the ideal of purity, but his scholarly turn of mind and his spiritual serenity lend an exceptional maturity to the poetry of this tendency, while Emilio Ballagas restlessly goes from playful exercises to *negrista* musicality to religious piety.

It is possible that the attractiveness of the idea of art for art's sake during the lifetime of the *Revista de Avance* (1927–30) confirms Plekhanov's theory about the phenomenon. It could be that Cuban writers felt 'hopelessly at odds' with their society under the Machado dictatorship. Nevertheless, the eventual convergence of an important sector of the Grupo Minorista and the searchers after 'pure poetry' serves to bring into clear relief the fact that throughout the whole period following the war of independence, throughout the post-Martí period, the economic, political, and cultural interests of the large masses of Cubans were being substantially ignored. They were inadequately represented even by the most progressive elements of Cuban society and their abandonment was almost complete when art for art's sake reigned supreme. The black population of Cuba lay almost entirely within that ignored quantity. It was precisely during this period that Guillén began to establish the foundation for his contribution and, incidentally, to disobey Plekhanov's law. The groundwork of his edifice was his presentation of real aspects of the life of the black sector in Cuban life. This edifice grew to include all the main elements that constitute Cuba's cultural identity and the links of that identity with humanity in general.

The factor in Spanish America and the Caribbean that makes the area resist the umbrella of a law like Plekhanov's is that the writer there who is deeply sensitive and is ambitious for the scope of his art can hardly but be aware of the fact that, beyond the small public that he can envisage as readers, there is an immense body of people whose aspirations include being able to purchase and read books of literature. It is readily apparent to such a writer that the reader as a concept is in fact an integral part of the process of development. The desire for cultural and other forms of social development being shared by writer and reader, the achievement that the formation of new readers represents, and the possibility that new readers are being reached make it difficult for writers to adopt for long a form of art that creates a distance between the writer and his potential public. The sort of sustained contempt and disdain for the bourgeoisie noted by Plekhanov in the French writers of the nineteenth century would be out of place in Spanish America where such a defined, stable class of readers does not exist. And rare is the writer who is capable of contempt for people in general.

Guillén was not, of course, the only significant writer of this period to go against the 'pure' tide. As a minor current, there began to appear in the *Revista de Avance* a kind of poetry that recognized, with seriousness of tone, the presence and struggles of working people. Lino Novás Calvo and Ramón Guirao essayed such poems, but its most accomplished early manifestation was Regino Pedroso's poem of 1927, 'Salutación fraterna al taller mecánico.' Pedroso continued in this direction in poems collected in his *Nosotros* (1933). Concern for the worker was shown also in the poetry of Angel Augier and Mirta Aguirre during the 1930s; Navarro Luna had by then also been turning away from 'pure' poetry, as had several writers associated with the *Revista de Avance*. The life of the peasants was depicted with evident interest in their well-being and with ever-increasing deftness in matters of technique by Onelio Jorge Cardoso and Novás Calvo in the short story genre. A novel of the period dealing with prison life, Carlos Montenegro's *Hombres sin mujer*, brought cynical punishment from the regime to some writers, including Guillén, who was jailed for allowing part of it to be published in the journal *Mediodía*, which he edited. The *negrista* movement was extended to the novel and the short story. With shipment of African slaves to Cuba continuing, as we have seen, until 1880, cultural links between Cuba and Africa were kept alive in the twentieth century to a degree not approached in the rest of the Caribbean. This fact was taken advantage of by writers such as Alejo Carpentier, Rómulo Lachatañeré, Lidia Cabrera, and Ramón Guirao, who either based fiction on the African ethnic background or published collections of stories and legends told among the black population. Slavery is also examined by a writer in the movement in Novás Calvo's novel about a slave-master's life, *Pedro Blanco, el negrero*.

The essayists who in the years 1927–30 had taken an excursion into the field of 'pure' literature returned in the 1930s with renewed resolve and vigour

to the struggle against Machado; and after he fell in 1933, their target became the continued u.s. control. Viewing his society, Jorge Mañach was
not convinced that it was harmful and in fact impossible to separate the
cultural from the political – 'la zona de la cultura y la zona de la devasta-
ción'[62] as he called them. Juan Marinello wrote and worked tirelessly and
with declared communist commitment, serving with Guillén on the editorial
board of *Mediodía* and, like Guillén, daring to run for public office.[63]
Mediodía had been founded in 1936 to fill the need for a journal that would
represent with maturity the links between literature and society in Cuba.
Among other members of its editorial board were Carlos Rafael Rodríguez
(who had come to literary notice as an elegant and combative essayist),
Mirta Aguirre,[64] Angel Augier, and José Antonio Portuondo. Raúl Roa analyses the pre-*Mediodía* period from a firmly nationalist viewpoint in his *Bufa
subversiva*.[65]

Portuondo was later to be active in developing theories of literature based
on his Cuban experience but which have a broad relevance. In his early work,
El concepto de la poesía,[66] he shows an interest in poetry as an art of discovery, expressing and revealing the hidden essence of things, including
social phenomena. The intertwined nature of these capacities, the merging
of form and content, is the basis of the power of poetry. When this power is
fully realized, what is communicated evokes a collective response because
a dynamic essence, a vital rhythm has been revealed. This creative fulfilment
is beneficial to both writer and reader, and, being the result of a creative
process, it is constantly refreshing. By contrasting the vitality of the poet with
the rigidity of the philosopher, Portuondo seems to have seized on an
opposition that possessed far greater validity than Gramsci's opposition between poetry and politics. In fact, the aspects of vitality and collectivity in
Portuondo's characterization of poetry indicate a potential similarity between poetry and certain forms of politics. This relation is made clear in his *El
heroísmo intelectual*,[67] where he urges the writer to undertake, in conjunc-
tion with other intellectuals, the task of identifying the roots of the real problems affecting the lives of so many suffering people in Spanish America
and to present their work in such a way that the need for change is made
compelling to the reader. He decries writing that glorifies the irrational, that
attempts to make heroes of psychopaths, and that occupies itself with problems that have little or no significance for most people and no conceivable
solutions. As the writer should work for change in the pre-revolutionary
society, so should he in the post-revolutionary society play his part in the
task of reconstruction. The writer, Portuondo has frequently insisted, should
always strive for formal excellence. A sharp attentiveness to history and an
ability to assess his times are qualities that are always present in the writer of
consequence. From this view Portuondo has derived his generational ap-

proach to the study of literary history. Like Pedro Henríquez Ureña before him, he finds that writers are assessable with respect to their generational duty and he attempts to define the generational task of each of the periods he examines. This procedure is evident in his indispensable work on Cuban literary history, *Bosquejo histórico de las letras cubanas*, as well as in his books *Estética y revolución* and *Crítica de la época*.[68] Portuondo's clearest precursor is José Carlos Mariátegui. The emphasis by both of them on what is rational, moral, and ethical, and the breadth of their social concern together with their belief in artistic excellence make Spanish America well represented in matters of literary theory. And whereas Mariátegui often referred to César Vallejo's work to demonstrate his views, the poetry of Nicolás Guillén illustrates in many ways, as we shall see, Portuondo's theories.

It was seen in the examination of the relation of literature to society in Spanish America that cases of emphasis on formal matters tend to lead both to an ensuing emphasis on social involvement and to an enrichment of the formal means of presenting social content in literature. The abundance of Cuban poets who, between 1940 and 1958, turned to the example of Mariano Brull and Eugenio Florit and beyond Cuba to other exquisite poets of the period who preferred not to deal with immediate social questions (like the American T.S. Eliot and the West Indian Saint-John Perse) could be taken as one indication of the event of enormous historical importance with which this period in Cuba would end. The writers of this period, the second republican generation, founded a number of journals of small circulation and intended their work for a fit few. The best known of the journals was *Orígenes* (1944–56) and Lezama Lima, with an outlook that made him enamoured of the unusual and the difficult – 'Sólo lo difícil es estimulante'[69] ('Only what is difficult is stimulating'), he wrote – was the luminary of the group. From it have come poets of the considerable stature of Cintio Vitier, Eliseo Diego, and Roberto Fernández Retamar. This was also the period in which Alejo Carpentier blended art and history to make his mark internationally as a novelist, when short story writers like Félix Pita Rodríguez and Onelio Jorge Cardoso developed their art, and Virgilio Piñera carried out influential popular adaptations of classical theatre. The formalist attitudes in writing did not go unchallenged among the writers who were coming to the fore. The tendency toward creolization of the theatre shown by Piñera was finding parallels in other forms of writing, too, and soon the journal *Ciclón* (1955–58) edited by José Rodríguez Feo presented an alternative outlet. Guillén meanwhile spent many of these years, some of the 1940s and most of the '50s, in exile.

The very large number of poets who may be listed as constituting the second republican generation may give the misleading impression of a healthy, dynamic literary climate in Cuba. That the situation of the writer was

indeed desperate can be gathered from two sad accounts. One was written
during the pre-revolutionary period and appeared as an editorial in an early
number of *Ciclón*. Its editor, José Rodríguez Feo, reflects the concern of
his group for the moral condition of his country and the prevailing disregard
for culture as he writes:

In our country where culture has always been somewhat improvised and superficial,
the artist has lived on the fringes of society. Unappreciated and without the slightest
encouragement from the State and its official institutions, he is the true outcast of
the nation. To publish a book, sell a painting or a sculpture in these adverse circumstances is almost impossible. One reason for this is that in Cuba almost no one reads
and least of all native works; it is sad to admit it. Whenever the Cuban State has
tried to make itself Protector of the Arts, its cultural policy has been vitiated by
demagoguery and false concepts. Thus recently they established a new and spark-
ling National Institute of Culture (the very name gives it away) where the old 'hierarchs'
of national culture immediately gathered.[70]

The other account is the retrospective view of Roberto Fernández Retamar
of the real economic hardship facing writers in the years preceding the
revolution. The account is given in the context of an essay where he expounds
his adoption of a theory of literature in which the economic bases of the
production of literature have significance. He writes:

With us it has been normal for the writer to be in economic difficulties. During the
twentieth century, until the coming of the Revolution, Cuban society, deformed by
imperialist penetration, seemed to have no remedy for this persistent problem, unless
the painter changed to doing billboards, the novelist to a writer of serials, the
essayist to a newspaper reporter, the composer to an arranger, the poet to anything
whatever. I mentioned Luis Felipe Rodríguez, dead from hunger, as I could have
mentioned, with reference to other arts, the painter Fidelio Ponce de León. The great
painter Víctor Manuel, a master to several generations and not only of painters, is
still going from café to café in Havana drinking beer ... He has taught fidelity to art,
sincerity, courage as well as disdain for a stupid society. I focus on him because his
case is characteristic, but the condition of our writers in general, if not so extreme, has
been at least clearly precarious. Small bureaucratic activities have permitted Lezama
Lima and Labrador Ruiz to survive: magazine articles and I do not know what random
duties, Samuel Feijoo. I am not certain but I believe that Carlos Felipe worked on
the railways and Navarro Luna in the insurance business, while Pita Rodríguez and
Cardoso were wearing themselves out writing for the radio, which has sucked in and
deformed many, as has writing for the newspapers. A few, worn out, gave in to what
passed for politics here, and degraded themselves; but if it was an honest and revolutionary politics, as was the case with Guillén or Marinello, it means persecution
and exile. In any case they were in a precarious personal situation. And of course there

were those who had to sleep out of doors, like Rolando Escardó who I know slept often in the Plaza de Vapor, and one night, they assure me, at the foot of the statue of Máximo Gómez.[71]

The two views reflect a vexing situation that prevails in many Spanish-American and Caribbean countries.

Such, then, was the state of affairs with regard to Cuban writing and writers when the revolution came. Many writers had helped to bring it about: some in mountainous guerrilla warfare, some in the cities and towns in clandestine activity, and still others through years of writing, lecturing, and other forms of militancy. Many of the latter, easily spotted and apprehendable within Cuba, were forced to choose exile. Among them were Guillén, Marinello, and Mirta Aguirre. Something of the enormous landmark that the revolution represented for them may be transmitted even in the literal, unrhymed translation given below of Mirta Aguirre's sonnet, written on the occasion of Marinello's death.

RECUERDO JUAN ...

Recuerdo Juan, cuando estrechamos manos.
Era el exilio. Era una tierra ajena.
Distancia y pena, Juan, distancia y pena:
lazos de acero para unir hermanos.

Recuerdos de pesares muy lejanos.
Y en ellos, tú. Tu plenitud serena
sirviendo de sostén a la cadena
de nuestro breve grupo de cubanos.

Recuerdo, Juan, Pepilla y tú, nosotros,
diciendo: 'Aunque ninguno vaya a verlo
lo que se debe hacer, vamos a hacerlo.'

Y se hacía, Juan, pensando en ojos de otros.
Mas hoy, si algo consuela es que te fuiste
después de verlo, Juan. ¡Después que viste!

I REMEMBER, JUAN ...

I remember, Juan, when we shook hands.
It was exile. It was a foreign land.
Distance and pain, Juan, distance and pain:
bonds of steel joining brothers and sisters.

Memories of distant sorrows.
And in them, you. Your serene fullness
serving as sustenance to the chain
of our little group of Cubans.

I remember, Juan, Pepilla and you, us,
saying: 'Even though none of us may see it,
what is to be done, we are going to do it.'

And it was done, Juan, thinking of the eyes of others.
And today, if something consoles, it is that you left
after seeing it, Juan. After you had seen it![72]

Guillén returned to Cuba from exile some three weeks after the overthrow of the dictatorship of Fulgencio Batista on 1 January 1959. His contribution to the revolution was acknowledged almost immediately: he was invited by Ernesto Che Guevara to read his poetry to a large gathering of the Revolutionary Army. The revolution meanwhile moved speedily to create appropriate cultural institutions. The Biblioteca Nacional 'José Martí' became one of its focal centres; with an emphasis on film reminiscent of Lenin's liking for the medium in a revolutionary society, the Instituto Cubano del Arte e Industria Cinematográfica was founded. So was Casa de las Américas, the institute and the journal, which was intended to strengthen cultural links with Spanish America, a role which it has come to fulfil with dynamic efficiency, expanding its sphere of interest to include the English and French-speaking Caribbean. All these institutions were functioning by July 1959. In 1961, the Consejo Nacional de Cultura was founded, replacing the old Instituto Nacional de Cultura. It assumed responsibility for diffusing culture throughout the country. One of its first achievements was the massive literacy campaign of 1961. In the meantime Guillén, in addition to writing poetry and essays, was at work preparing the First National Congress of Cuban Writers and Artists amid the revelry, experimentation, and uncertainty of his young colleagues.

To complete the survey of writers and their attitudes to the revolution, it must be added that there were those who felt regret and even guilt at not having taken up arms for the revolution, those who felt outside of it and simply wanted to be writers, and those few who were hostile to it. And writers entertained a variety of expectations with regard to the revolution. This, of course, also applied to other groups. There were peasants, for example, who thought that once the revolution had gained control of the government they would be able to move to the cities and enjoy immediately a more advanced life-style. It was necessary to explain to them that since the basis of Cuba's economy was agriculture, a productive rural population was indispensable and that the aim of the Revolution was to bring to the rural population, to the extent affordable in an underdeveloped country, the amenities and best advances of the cities, to do away with the treadmill of monotonous chores and habits, and to eradicate what Marx had called 'the idiocy of rural life.'

Some writers had concerns that were infinitely more complex than those of the peasants. There was the question of artistic freedom, for instance. Artists generally insist on the freedom to choose and present their subjects as they see fit. In a society in which the goal of co-operative effort in building a new society where the level of development and the history of the recent past make what is to be done blatantly obvious, it is not difficult for the artist to be troubled by the suspicion that his inclination to express 'true inner individual feelings,' unrelated to the tasks at hand, is a symptom of immaturity and ir-responsibility. Moreover his disquietude may be even more pronounced if the 'true inner individual feelings' are really the product of distant (in time and / or space) environmental forces, of a lagging superstructure, the true function of which is to foster a system that in its individualism or class allegiances runs counter to the co-operative ethos. On the other hand, the revolution, particularly in light of the hostility to it of the United States and other great powers (a hostility that grew to fierce dimensions when it became clear that Cuba's economic base was changing), had to do what it could to protect itself and its resources, among which it counted and valued highly its artists and writers. The chief organ of the young writers who blossomed in the exhilara-ting first days of the revolution was *Lunes de Revolución* the weekly literary supplement of the newspaper *Revolución*. It was edited by Guillermo Cabrera Infante; Pablo Armando Fernández served as deputy editor and Antón Arru-fat, Heberto Padilla, and Manuel Díaz Martínez collaborated closely. The works published in the supplement during the nearly three years of its exis-tence display exciting formal devices and an almost anarchistic mood. Every kind of freedom was manifested as writers searched for forms and content to suit their different conceptions of writing.[73] Some of them alarmed them-selves and others into wondering if they were overstepping the limits of what the new governmental permissiveness would allow. All this while the u.s. media encouraged defection and welcomed defectors. Cuba, it was suggest-ed, was a disaster from which its citizens, especially its distinguished ones, should flee, for a race was on there between the total collapse of the economy and a general uprising to overthrow the revolution. In April 1961, a u.s.-backed invasion of Cuba took place at Playa Girón in the expectation of the general uprising. In an organized and disciplined effort, the revolution de-stroyed the invasion force. No small part of the discipline involved keeping Cubans from all parts of the country from converging on the invaders. The seriousness of the task of defending and building the revolution was demonstrated to all sectors of the population. One of the ways in which the writers and artists were affected was that their National Congress, being prepared by a team headed by Guillén, had to be postponed until August 1961. A preparatory series of discussions for the congress took place in the Biblioteca Nacional 'José Martí' in June 1961, dealing with the relations between writers and artists and the revolution. The leader of the revolution and prime minister of the country, Dr Fidel Castro attended all three sessions and gave the closing address to the gathering. I quote at some length from his address, which has come to be known as 'Palabras a los intelectuales' ('Address to the Intellectuals') because, in addition to being directed at the immediate Cuban situation, they represent a way of approaching a problem that, as was shown earlier with regard to the Russian Revolution, has dogged revolutionary societies for many years.

Allow me to tell you first of all that the Revolution defends freedom; that the Revolution has brought to the country a very large number of freedoms; that the Revolution cannot be essentially an enemy of freedom, that if some of you are worried that the Revolution is going to stifle your creative spirit, that that worry is unnecessary, and there is no justification for it ...

What are the rights of the writers and artists whether they be revolutionary or not? Within the Revolution, everything, against the Revolution, no rights.

And this is not any kind of special law for artists and writers. This is a general principle for all citizens. It is a fundamental principle of the Revolution. The counter-revolutionaries, the enemies of the Revolution, have no rights against the Revolution, because the Revolution has a right: the right to exist, the right to develop itself and the right to succeed, and who could jeopardize that right of a people who have said FATHERLAND OR DEATH, that is to say, the Revolution or death?

The Revolution cannot attempt to stifle art or culture when one of the goals and one of the fundamental principles or purposes of the Revolution is to develop art and culture, precisely so that art and culture may become a real patrimony of the people. And just as we have wanted a better life for the people in the material realm, we also want for the people a better life in the cultural realm. And in the same way that the Revolution is concerned about developing the conditions and strengths that will allow the people to satisfy all their material needs, we also want to develop the conditions that will allow the people to satisfy their cultural needs.

So too we ought to provide the conditions necessary for all those cultural benefits to reach the people. That does not mean that the artist will have to sacrifice the value of his creations, and that he will necessarily have to sacrifice their quality. It means that we have to try in every way to make the artist produce for the people and to make the people raise their cultural level so that they may get closer to the artists. It is not possible to make any general rule, all artistic manifestations are not exactly of the same nature, and at times we have discussed things here as if all artistic manifestations were exactly of the same nature. There are expressions of the creative spirit which by their very nature can be much more accessible to the people than other manifestations of the creative spirit.

Because of that it isn't possible to make a general rule, because, in which artistic expression should the artist try to reach the people, and in which should the people get closer to the artist? Can a general affirmation be made in this regard? No. It would be too simple a rule. It is necessary to strive in all manifestations to reach the people, but in turn it is necessary to do everything possible so that the people may understand more and more profoundly. I believe that that principle does not run contrary to the aspirations of the artist, and least of all if he bears in mind the fact that people ought to create for their contemporaries.[74]

This was not Fidel Castro's last address on the subject of the role of writers and artists. He was to return to it from time to time, personally or by his contributions to official documents and declarations – and always to clarify or elaborate on the basic attitude of the revolution, enunciated here, to writers, artists, and culture in general.[75] The attitude, particularly in relation to those special temperamental characteristics artists enjoy, has had remarkable success in satisfying and even inspiring many of those writers who were earlier indifferent to or misunderstood the possibilities of their relations to the revolution. True, some defections have occurred in subsequent years. There was the Heberto Padilla affair which, during the period of Padilla's conflict with the revolution and until he left for the United States, generated great reaction, particularly outside Cuba, from a range of interests. There were those who were genuinely concerned about the problems of a talented poet, those who welcomed and attempted to exacerbate anything that might be represented as a crisis for the revolution,[76] and those who were susceptible to the confusions of Jean Paul Sartre.

Shortly after the First National Congress of Writers and Artists, the Union of Writers and Artists of Cuba (UNEAC) was established with Guillén as its president. *Lunes de Revolución* ceased publication in November 1961 and in early 1962, UNEAC founded two journals, *La Gaceta de Cuba* and *Unión*. The first publishes works produced locally for the most part, on a monthly basis; the second appears quarterly and is devoted predominantly to contemporary international currents in literature, literary theory, and criticism. The Cuban poets who frequently serve as translators of poetry and prose from a large number of languages for *Unión* display an outstanding level of skill and dedication to their tasks. Ediciones Unión is one of the several publishing outlets in different parts of the country, functioning as units of the Instituto Cubano del Libro, through which they and their colleagues have their books published. The Instituto in turn is under the aegis of the Consejo Nacional de Cultura, founded in 1961. As a result of early drives, such as publishing

100,000 copies of *Don Quijote* and selling them at twenty-five cents each, and publishing Cuban, Spanish-American, and other works in an attempt to satisfy the demand that was rising in keeping with the revolution's cultural policy, the number of books published was raised from fewer than one million in 1958 to 8.7 million by 1967, to 18 million by 1972, and to 49.5 million (representing 1499 titles) by 1981. Including imports, an average of six books per year have been sold to each Cuban since 1959 at an average price of sixty centavos (less than the price of a bottle of beer or a packet of cigarettes), and sixty per cent of the total number of books have been distributed free of charge. Cuban writers and artists are enjoying an ever-expanding public, thanks to the country's broadening international relations. (Cuba had, in 1979, technicians in twenty-eight countries, and twice as many doctors serving overseas in underdeveloped countries as the World Health Organization of the United Nations; while in the cultural field, *Casa de las Américas* is by far the most widely circulated journal published in Spanish.) The general growth of cultural activity envisaged by Fidel Castro in his 1961 address may thus be seen as an illustration of the views of Sánchez Vázquez (discussed earlier) about the artist's real interest in social progress.

The fact that the members of UNEAC share in general Guillén's enthusiasm for the revolution does not mean that they show uniformity in their approach to their work. The pages of *La Gaceta de Cuba* have carried lively controversies between them dealing with literary theory and film.[77] The spirit of accommodation of different aesthetic approaches manifested in Fidel Castro's address is clearly evident in the recognition given to poets of different tendencies. I earlier mentioned three poets, Eliseo Diego, Cintio Vitier, and Roberto Fernández Retamar, who were affiliated with the pre-revolutionary formalist journal, *Orígenes*. They have differed from each other in their poetic manifestations since the revolution. Diego has carved elegant images in remote settings to construct delicate poems that reveal a metaphysical inclination and claims to have no talent for social poetry; Vitier, while striving for more directly communicative poetry than he wrote earlier, has not abandoned his Catholic orientation; and Fernández Retamar has come to write social poetry, producing some of the most notable poems about the revolution itself. At the same time, they all hold important positions in Cuba's cultural institutions. Diego is in charge of public relations for the literary section of UNEAC and is a tireless searcher for new reading material for Cuba's children; Vitier leads Martí studies in the Sala Martí of the Biblioteca Nacional 'José Martí'; and Fernández Retamar is the editor of *Casa de las Américas*.

The writers and artists led by Guillén span three generations, the first and second republican generations and the one whose formation took place almost entirely under the revolution. In the first generation are writers like

Angel Augier, Raúl Roa, Regino Pedroso, José Zacarías Tallet, Félix Pita Rodríguez, José Antonio Portuondo, and Dora Alonso all of whom, along with the recently deceased Mirta Aguirre, worked alongside Guillén in the thirties. The much more numerous second generation has at the top, chronologically, such writers as Eliseo Diego, Cintio Vitier, Onelio Jorge Cardoso, and extends to younger ones such as the poets Manuel Díaz Martínez, Nancy Morejón, Pedro and Francisco de Oraa, Otto Fernández, Miguel Barnet, and Georgina Herrera, the novelists Manuel Cofiño, José Soler Puig, and Lisandro Otero, the short story writer Sergio Chaple, all of whom, fully or partly formed before the revolution, have come under its sway. A host of young writers compose the generation of the revolution. Born in the late forties and fifties, many of them have two or three books to their credit. Among them are poets like Waldo González López, Osvaldo Navarro, Nelson Herrera Ysla, Cos Causse, and Eliseo Alberto, the novelist Manuel Pereira and the short story writer Omar González Jiménez. The remarkable poem by Nelson Herrera Ysla, 'Defensa del coloquialismo,'[78] in which the poet shows an acute awareness of his historical and literary times, could serve as an 'Arte Poética' for many of the poets of his generation. A conversational poem about uplifting conversation, its links to Guillén lie in the uncompromising manner in which form and content are made to merge and in the convincing way in which thoughtfully positive images of the revolutionary experience are made to spring from the poem itself. All these writers, named and not named, are finding, as are other artists, the following principal ways of fulfilling themselves: by their production of aesthetically pleasing works; by taking advantage of the outlets of publishing, publicity, and distribution through which their work reaches an ever-growing public; and by their participation in the progressive and creative undertaking that they find the revolution to be.[79] There is a spirit of renovation in most of them that blurs the distinction between generations.

CONCERNING FORM AND CONTENT

In the examination I have carried out so far of literary theories and of Spanish-American and Cuban literary history, one of the questions that has been frequently mentioned is the relation of form and content. To a reader who regards literature as art for art's sake and who spurns the idea of social commitment in literature, even a provisional separate consideration of these two topics will seem hardly to the point; for if literature is conceived of as being ahistorical, then a focus on content can scarcely be made valid. A poem in which the subject is landscape, a tree, some daffodils, a falling leaf, the song of a bird, a cat, a distant star, a loved one, a religious or magical experience, a birth, or a death, for example, may be judged from that perspective to be a preferred piece of literature if it has no demanding historical dimension. Historical content may be seen to act distractingly during the synchronic examination of how the poem is constructed. Something memorable or persuasive about the emotion evoked by the landscape or the falling leaf may be conveyed by the way in which the elements of the poem – imagery, rhythm, tone, etc. – cohere to represent the recollected or imagined experience. In such cases, disregarding the historical aspect of the relation of form and content makes of little value the discussion of them as separate topics.

When a historical perspective is used, however, the poem may be seen from a distance that allows it to be evaluated along with its circumstances or in the light of its broad social content. New areas of inquiry are then discovered, such as: Of what social significance is the choice of the daffodils as subject? Does the poem confront or conceal crucial issues of its time? To what sector of the public is it primarily addressed? Does historically significant content arise from the treatment of the subject? Are the formal elements adequate to the historical content? Where the reading public has been prepared by the preponderance of theoretical opinion to be conscious of social commitment in literature, as is the case in Spanish America and certainly now in Cuba, the historical approach is even more encompassing. In such a society the poet tends to be seen as existing among the people. The provenance of his poetic gift is not mysterious, since it is related in part to his social provenance and to the consequent social awareness that he shares with his fellow conscientious citizens. He is a part of a pluridisciplinary national project. His special talent lies in his repeatedly demonstrated ability to express in lastingly attractive and resounding ways what was on the tips of the tongues of his progressive compatriots. Hence there is a special alertness to and recognition of what he says, as well as a keen appreciation of his individual way of expressing sentiments that those compatriots might hold. Thus content and form are evident and prone to consideration as entities, at least provisionally, until the final overall evaluation is given of the work in which they function. What finally emerges, then, is an evaluation that is more comprehensive than that achieved by an ahistorical habitude, because appraisals of social and historical relevance and correctness do not substitute for others but are added as criteria in determining the achievement of coherence.

There are certain general formal concomitants of literature produced in such conditions of historical and social consciousness. The principal one concerns formal accessibility. Because of the topicality of content, the concern that it should reach a broad and growing public, and the importance in this literature of didacticism and dialogue, communicability is one of its principal characteristics. Sophisticated reading publics have for more than a century now prided themselves on their taste for metaphor.

Despite the special promotion of metaphor by Aristotle, it was regarded as one among several favoured rhetorical figures from the time of classical writers to that of the neo-classicists. It came into its own as the dominant figure in the nineteenth century, promoted by those French poets who have been described by Plekhanov as being completely at odds with their society.[80] Metaphor's position of dominance has been reaffirmed by other proponents of art for art's sake. Borges, as we have seen, wanted it to occupy a place of highest importance; André Breton declared that compared to metaphor and simile 'the other "figures" which rhetoric persists in enumerating are absolutely devoid of interest. Only the analogical process excites us';[81] and Ortega's *Revista de Occidente* revelled in it.

In fact, metaphor has achieved so much prestige among certain groups in our century as to prompt a tendency among those groups to regard as 'anti-poetry' manifestations of poetry in which its suzerainty is not apparent. This implies a relegation to secondary status of the production of poets, especially of those who use fewer figures and a smaller repertoire of verse forms than Guillén (Ernesto Cardenal, for example) and who in their quest for the communicability that is a feature of social poetry do not give special emphasis to metaphor. The attitude also marks a significant gain for those who are not disturbed at the idea of poetry being removed from, or in conflict with, a broad public. But this conception of poetry involves a myopic and restrictive view. Myopic because it takes into account only a limited part of the history of poetry; for when Borges stated in the second decade of this century that poetry should return to its primordial element, the metaphor, his characterization of poetry could have seemed valid only to those who limited their view to the previous fifty or sixty years of, particularly, French poetry. Also, by focusing on expression, this view falls into the error of regarding as 'anti-poetry' a poetry dedicated to uplifting the lives of a large section of humanity.

The 'now you don't see it, now you do' trait of metaphor and its capacity to permit movement from analogy to analogy while an abstract quality is maintained make a concentrated use of it conducive to the representation of the indefinable, of mystery, of magic, and of play. The prominence of these kinds of content has corresponded to the championing of metaphor as a form. It is possible, of course, to employ metaphor in such a way that its more restrained aspects have primary functions and in structures where it occurs along with other rhetorical figures that lend concreteness to poetic expression. Metonymy is one of these other figures, and while it may be regarded as a type of metaphor, it possesses significant intrinsic qualities. Its greater capacity for concreteness derives from the fact that it exploits the relationship between a phenomenon and its function instead of suggesting the aspect of resemblance between dissimilar objects as metaphor does. The concreteness in turn permits a general intimacy with what is being presented. It is the latter combination of metonymy and unobscure metaphor that in a variety of associations with other figures has been employed principally in poetry that deals with social matters. The great modernist poet Rubén Darío, for example, who in his predominant mode wrote the adorned, playful prose of 'El rubí' and the dualistic poetry of his metaphorical sonnet 'Venus,' later wrote his famous poem 'A Roosevelt' in which he turned to the representation of a socio-political subject.[82] The relative concreteness and accessibility of this poem is indebted to the easy interplay of metonymy and metaphor with which allusions to historical personages and events harmonize. In fact, the historical allusions also have a metonymical character, since through them certain qualities or functions of the named objects are made active in the poem. Roosevelt (Theodore) is the readily identifiable historical personage who has engaged in and may further engage in actions harmful to the Spanish-American people. He is the spearhead and embodiment of certain traits of aggressiveness characteristic of the society he leads. In contrast to these, and existing on a more elevated plane, are those manifestations of different stages of Spanish-American history that point to superior spiritual qualities. The readily perceived interrelations that stem from this metonymical process in the poem is the key to its broad social communicability. Darío was aware of his achievement in 'A Roosevelt' and was satisfied that, despite its differences from his previous work, the poem met securely his stringent standards as far as its artistic quality was concerned. He passed judgment on it by declaring, in his metaphorical modernist mode, that 'my protest [against Roosevelt] is written on the wings of the immaculate swans' and thus is ultimately bound up with his quest for the ideal.

Socio-historical content in literature is best conveyed by a formal system that allows metaphor to approximate the directness of metonymy. This means that metaphor can hardly occur in prolonged paradigms, but is better used with the restraint that is characteristic of metonymy and with a degree of precision that makes it compatible with history. Darío's poem is one particular illustration of how these basic elements are successfully elaborated with others. Spanish-American literature contains, as might be expected, many examples of this usage. It should be realized, however, that this is not simply a Spanish-American idiosyncrasy. It has a rich universal heritage. Several of the classical and neo-classical writers, Dante, Cervantes, and those other writers whom Engels has called *Tendenzpoeten* have represented mankind's social concerns, aspirations, and achievements and have found language unburdened by obscurity to be the fitting vehicle. In a very general sense, Aeschylus' view of Prometheus as undertaking a noble, daring task on behalf of mankind's advancement can serve to characterize the attitude of these writers. None of these authors participated by their writing in the revolutionary transformation of their societies, as Guillén has done. But by their attitudes – revealed in the moral content of their works and in the further attractiveness lent by their formal means – they gave stimulus to later writers to continue to find new expression appropriate to the concerns of their times. The more scientific political thinking available to later writers has led in some cases to a heightening of their desire to produce committed writing and to an awareness of its complexities. The producers of this literature care intensely about their work reaching the public and several complications arise in this regard. First, a reader may be unreceptive to the work only because he or she is unsympathetic to the viewpoint advanced. Also, writings about socio-political problems can easily be uninteresting to readers who are either too little or too greatly distanced from the problems. The former may tend, because of their familiarity with the problems to find their literary representation to be trite and superfluous. The latter, conversely, may find it to be remote and trivial. The need in such writings, then, is for mature perception invested with art. But then there are other difficulties, principally the subtle distracting powers of art with which Bertolt Brecht in his quest for committed theatre constantly wrestled.[83] Aggravating this difficulty is a tendency for poetry to be seen as containing essentially pseudo-statement, (as I.A. Richards[84] would have it), as stating only provisionally and not containing concepts in which there can be a real basis for belief. Having exposed these questions and shown the broad theoretical framework and the historical tradition to which Guillén's work is related, I will examine his achievement in the rest of this study.

2

The Poetry

Nicolás Guillén was born in Camagüey on 10 July 1902, some seven weeks
after the Republic of Cuba was established. He was the first of six children
born to Nicolás Guillén y Urra and Argelia Batista y Arrieta.[1] His parents,
both of them descendants of Africans and Spaniards, were well established
in Camagüey. His father served as editor of the local newspaper, *Las dos
Repúblicas*, and was a leader there of the Partido Liberal Nacional which
vied, mainly on the basis of personality clashes, with the Partido Republicano
Conservador for what local control existed of the nation's political life.
From 1909 to 1912, with the Liberals in power, he represented Camagüey as a
senator and when his term of office ended in 1912 he became editor of its
newspaper, *La Libertad*. In the meantime Nicolás and his brother Francisco
had learned typography in their father's printing shop, which was housed
in their residence.[2] What had begun as a voluntary apprenticeship, the product
of their fascination with the marvel of printing, soon became a dire familial
necessity. Their father had joined in an armed protest against the machinations
of Mario García Menocal to hold on to the presidency after his term of office
had ended in 1916. As a result, Nicolás's father was one of the few to be
assassinated in 1917, leaving Nicolás, then fourteen years old, as the main
support for his family. The young Guillén had written his first poems in
1916 and, while he continued his education mainly through night classes with
the aim of pursuing a career in law, he became increasingly attracted to
poetry. He completed his secondary schooling in just two years, while gaining
prominence among the young poets of Camagüey, where his poems began
to appear in the journal *Camagüey Gráfico* in 1919. In the following year he
left for the Cuban capital to enrol in the School of Law of the University of
Havana. Pressing financial needs forced his early return to Camagüey; but he
went back to Havana in 1921 and managed to remain interested enough in
his studies to complete his first year. Guillén has provided evidence of the

conflict that led him to abandon his legal studies in a series of three sonnets entitled 'Al margen de mis libros de estudio' ('In the Margin of My Textbooks'). He begins the first sonnet with the quartet:

> Yo, que pensaba en una blanca senda florida,
> donde esconder mi vida bajo el azul de un sueño,
> hoy, pese a la inocencia de aquel dorado empeño,
> muero estudiando leyes para vivir la vida.

> *I, who thought of a white flowery path,*
> *there to hide my life under the azure of a dream,*
> *today, despite the innocence of that golden endeavour,*
> *I die studying law to make my way through life.*

and ends the last sonnet with the tercet:

> tendré que ahogar, señores, mi lírica demencia
> en los considerandos de una vulgar sentencia
> o en un estrecho artículo del Código Penal ...

> *I shall have to stifle, gentlemen, my lyrical madness*
> *in the considerations of a vulgar judgment*
> *or in a narrow article of the Penal Code ...*

During his year in Havana, Guillén had made the acquaintance of the group of bright and outgoing young men who frequented the Café 'Martí,' many of whom were later to become prominent in the fields of literature and politics. His first relations with them were not fruitful. When, therefore, he gave up his studies in Havana, he decided to live in Camagüey. There he founded, with the strong support of his brother Francisco, the literary journal *Lis*, the first number of which was published in January 1923. The journal reflected the prolongation of the modernist mode in Cuba, both in the original works, mainly by writers from Camagüey, and in the reproductions of Spanish-American and other writers that appeared in *Lis* during the six months of its existence. This publishing venture also revealed Guillén's capacity for initiating and organizing a serious literary project. One of the senior contributors to the journal, José Armando Pla, significantly characterized the Guilléns as talented and simple, quite the opposite of those who ' "simulate talent in the quest for personality and a living." Let them be known by their work: They have brought into existence an interesting journal, well written and with an appearance that is enchanting for its beautiful simplicity.'[3] This characterization, coming at this early stage in Guillén's career, emphasizes and entails an understanding of simplicity that approximates the use Guillén will make of it in his poetry. Pla here uses the adjective to describe a person who shows an honest devotion to work and the expectation of consequent positive results. Indeed, when the journal ceased publication because of lack of funds, Guillén was severe in his denunciation of the philistine attitudes exhibited by Camagüey readers. But this situation, as we have seen earlier, was symptomatic of a national condition. The exigent aspect of this simplicity was displayed, too, in the criticism Guillén pubished in *Lis* of contemporary Cuban poetry. He complains of the host of poets, most of them quite without talent, who were writing in Cuba without the corrective benefit of effective literary criticism.

CEREBRO Y CORAZÓN AND OTHER EARLY POEMS

In 1922 Guillén put together for publication a selection of his early poems, several of which had appeared in *Lis*. The collection, which he entitled *Cerebro y corazón*, remained unpublished, perhaps because of the unavailability of prompt financing, perhaps because of the poet's later re-evaluation of it. It was abandoned by Guillén and rescued from oblivion by Augier who reproduced a copy of it as an appendix to his study[4] from its first edition of 1962. If Guillén finally suppressed the manuscript for aesthetic reasons, as is most probable,[5] he might have done so because, true to its title (*Brain and Heart*), the inclusive nature of the collection makes its unity elusive. The *varia* represented by its fifty-four poems suggests the exercise of budding poetic talent that still had to find amenable channels for its aptitudes. Guillén demonstrates here a firm mastery of the musical elements of poetry. He easily overcomes the formal rigours of the sonnet and shows, by selecting twenty-two of them, his liking for the form. Seventeen of them are in eleven-syllable verses, two in fourteen-syllable (Alexandrine) verses,[6] two in eight-syllable and one in twelve-syllable verses. They display a variety of rhyme schemes including those established in the Renaissance, those introduced by the modernists, and an innovative one employed in the poem 'Madrigal trirrimo' ('Three-rhyme Madrigal'), where monorhyme is used for the two quartets and a different monorhyme for each of the tercets. The example of Rubén Darío is evident here, from the subtle intrusion of the cadence and some syntactical patterns of his 'Lo Fatal' into Guillén's Alexandrine sonnet 'Soledad' ('Solitude'), to the ubiquitous employment of Darío's favourite symbol, the swan, to the clear reflection of the Parnassian aspect of his modernism in such poems as 'Nácar' ('Nacre'), 'Jardín I' ('Garden I'), 'Hoja de álbum' ('Page from an Album'), 'Pétalo' ('Petal'), 'Mariposa de cristal' ('Glass Butterfly'), 'Tú' ('You'), and 'Capricho' ('Caprice').

The last four of these poems express an attitude of happiness in love; but this is exceptional in *Cerebro y corazón*, where the overwhelming majority of the poems reflect a brooding disillusionment. Love destroyed is the most often-treated topic; it is dealt with in the four sonnets 'Rosas de elegía' ('Elegy Roses'), in 'Corazón adentro' ('Inside the Heart'), 'Jardín I' and 'Jardín II,' 'Rima ingenua' ('Ingenuous Rhyme'), 'Gota de hiel' ('Drop of Gall'), and 'Siempre' ('Always'), while the longing for love is treated in 'Granate' ('Garnet'), 'Mariposa' ('Butterfly') and 'Madrigal trirrimo.' Unrelieved sadness is represented in the two sonnets on 'El piano,' in 'Tras la dicha' ('After Happiness'), 'Sólo la flauta' ('Only the Flute') and 'Canción de invierno' ('Winter Song'). All this, combined with the bitterness expressed in 'La amarga ironía' ('The Bitter Irony') and the paradoxes resolved by the idea of suffering in the poem 'Mujer' ('Woman'), in addition to the anguish of 'Madrigal,' make the attractiveness of death and insinuations of suicide represented in other poems seem like a natural development. This development is represented by 'Rima triste' ('Sad Rhyme') (with its echoes of the Colombian modernist poet, José Asunción Silva), 'Rima amarga' ('Bitter Rhyme'), 'Sonata crepuscular' ('Twilight Sonata'), 'De profundis' ('From the Depths'), 'El espejo' ('The Mirror') and 'La balada azul' ('The Blue Ballad'). This exquisitely delicate poem, in its Christian allusions and the attraction the cemetery holds for its speaker, carries echoes of the Cuban modernist poet, Julián del Casal.

There are several poems in which an even stronger Christian outlook is exhibited. In the order in which they appear in the collection, they are 'A Jesu-Cristo,' 'Señor' ('Lord'), 'Nocturno' ('Nocturne'), and 'Salmo lírico' ('Lyrical Psalm'). Devoutness characterizes the sonnet 'A Jesu-Cristo'; 'Señor' is a prayer of contrition, while 'Nocturno' is an exercise in mysticism. In 'Salmo lírico,' belief has apparently ebbed. Christ seems no longer to have any redeeming power and evil holds sway in society:

> Cristo, Cristo, Cristo, ya no nos ayudas;
> ya no enjugas llantos, ni disipas dudas;
> está vivo Judas,
> está vivo Judas y estás muerto tú.

> *Jesus, Jesus, Jesus, you no longer help us;*
> *you no longer wipe away tears or dispel doubts;*
> *Judas lives,*
> *Judas lives and you are dead.*

Two poems seem to bear directly on the title of the collection. They are 'Blasón' ('Coat of Arms'), the first of the Alexandrine sonnets, in which the preference is expressed for heart over brain, and 'El mal del siglo' ('Le mal du siècle'). In the latter poem he finds both brain and soul absent from the century in which he happens to live and he declares:

> Yo no puedo vivir en este siglo
> sin cerebro y sin alma.

> *I cannot live in this century*
> *that has neither brain nor soul.*

Since the enumerated characteristics of the century lack precise historicity and could apply to other centuries, the poem seems to follow a formula known to the French romantics and to those other nineteenth-century French poets who suffered the *mal du siècle* and spoke of the *poète maudit*. It also resembles Darío's statement in the 'Palabras liminares' to his *Prosas profanas*: 'I detest the life and the times into which I was born.' This aspect of the poem 'El mal del siglo' is manifested in the collection in general and accounts for the absence from it of the strength that is derived from a poetic voice that achieves authenticity by its links with history. Here the voice is at times anxious for retreat from society as in the sonnet 'Silenter,' the last tercet of which is:

> ¡Déjame, vida, indiferente o loco,
> misantrópicamente, poco a poco
> dormirme en el silencio de mí mismo!

> *Let me, life, indifferent or crazy*
> *misanthropically, little by little*
> *go to sleep in the silence of my own being.*

This turning inward is an attitude to life and poetry that here results in poetry as neurosis – revealed in expressions of self-pitying lovelessness, desperate religious dependence, and preoccupation with suicide and death. All this is in contrast to the constructive social poetry that will result later from an involvement with broad national concerns.

Nevertheless, *Cerebro y corazón*, both in some of its details and in some of its broader aspects, has recognizable links to Guillén's more accomplished poetry. In general terms, his demonstrated mastery of traditional forms and his tendency to explore new ones reveal a confidence in this regard that facilitates his adopting more unusual forms suitable to the new content of his later poetry. One detail of form that is to reappear in Guillén's pre-revolutionary poetry is his method of presenting alternatives that have equal negative effective value, as in the last verses of 'Sólo la flauta':

> si canto, parece que lloro;
> si lloro, parece que canto ...

> *if I sing, I seem to be crying;*
> *if I cry, I seem to be singing ...*

Although it is used figuratively in the poem 'Gota' ('Drop'), the image:

> *the slave that misses his master,*
> *a master who beats him ...*
> *What an incomprehensible slave!*

is infused with the kind of impatience about an intolerable situation that functions in many of Guillén's poems. He will also continue the production of love poetry as well as poetry in the elegiac mood begun here. It is this latter genre to which the important poem 'Ansia' ('Anguish') belongs. The poem may be considered the first 'Arte poética' written by Guillén. The guitar used in it symbolically as the vehicle of his art is to reappear in the same role in all the important stages of his poetry:

> La palabra es la cárcel de la idea.
> Yo, en vez de la palabra,
> quisiera, para concretar mi duelo,
> la queja musical de una guitarra.
> Una de esas guitarras cuya música
> dulce, sencilla, casta,
> encuentra siempre para hacer su nido
> algún rincón del alma ...

> *The word is the prison of the idea.*
> *I, instead of the word,*
> *want, to represent my mourning,*
> *the musical moan of a guitar.*
> *One of those guitars whose*
> *sweet, simple, chaste music,*
> *always finds for its haven*
> *a corner of the soul ...*

Apart from 'duelo' and 'queja musical' symbolizing the elegiac tendency, the other lasting aspect of the poem, considered as an 'arte poética,' is the modification of the desired guitar music by the adjective 'sencilla.' As I have already indicated, this will be shown to be a concept of special importance in Guillén's work.

In a poem in which he sets out a code of conduct, 'Palabras fundamentales' ('Fundamental Words'), Guillén proposes a resolutely combative attitude that contrasts with that exhibited in most of the poems of the collection:

> Alza tu voz sobre la voz sin nombre
> de todos los demás, y haz que se vea
> junto al poeta, el hombre.
> ...
> ¡Sacude el ala del atrevimiento
> ante el atrevimiento del obstáculo!

> *Raise your voice above the nameless voice*
> *of all others, and cause to be seen*
> *next to the poet, the man.*
> ...
> *Flap the wings of boldness*
> *in the face of the boldness of the obstacle!*

Here, however, the lack of concreteness, of a suggested context within the poem or elsewhere in the collection to which this should be applied or from which it arises serves to expose the largely rhetorical character of the verses and the resemblance they bear to the earlier quoted words of Domingo del Monte. The last poem in the collection, 'Ritmo' ('Rhythm'), contains four tercets of disparate content, each followed by an antithetical two-syllable command. The final antithesis is of real significance:

> Alma mía, que mueres
> de pena y angustia;
> alma mía, que mueres:
> ¡Lucha!

> *O my soul, that dies*
> *from pain and anguish;*
> *oh my soul, that dies:*
> *Struggle!*

By confronting thus the predominant attitude shown in the overwhelming majority of the poems with the combative attitude shown in 'Palabras fundamentales' and 'Ritmo,' promise is suggested of the ascendancy of the latter attitude in his subsequent poetry.[7]

This promise took some time to be fulfilled, primarily because Guillén wrote no poetry between 1922 and 1927. He had worked as editor of the newspaper, *El Camagüeyano*, and tiring of the limited scope of activity in his native city, he returned to Havana in 1926, a year after Gerardo Machado came to power. A friend of his late father secured him a position in the Secretaría de Gobernación, the equivalent of the Ministry of the Interior, where he worked as a typist. By 1927, when he began to write poetry again, the political and literary movements earlier described were having their chief impact on Havana. But still feeling the unease he had felt in 1922 with some of the gentlemen of Havana, he forsook the *Revista de Avance* and *Social*, a literary supplement of the *Diario de la Marina*, edited by José Antonio Fernández de Castro, and published instead in the Manzanillo journal *Orto*.[8] These poems and others written before the appearance of *Sóngoro cósongo* in 1931, are published in Guillén's *Obra poética* in the section 'Poemas de transición.' The section is aptly titled, for in regard both to form and content, the works, while paying some homage to vanguardism, may be seen as constituting a bridge between Guillén's beginning poetry and the mainstream of his poetic career.

The formal aspect is characterized by a growing confidence. Instead of wanting to retreat into silence – 'dormirme en el silencio de mí mismo,' as we have seen it expressed in *Cerebro y corazón* – the poet shows a more forthright attitude in the last verses of the poem 'La nueva musa:'

> Ahora, el poeta se mete dentro de sí mismo
> y allá dentro, dirige su orquesta.
>
> *Now, the poet turns inward*
> *and there within conducts his orchestra.*

In the poem 'Romance del insomnio,' he plays upon some of the vanguardist proclivities by employing pervasive hyperbole. A normally static object is endowed with striking mobility, the abstract is abruptly represented as concrete, and there are unusual metonymic associations and noisy alliterations. The same mischievous spirit is evident in the poem 'Elegía moderna del motivo cursi'; but here, in a more constructive mood, he proposes for his own poetry the substitution of everyday reality for the reigning ecstasy over things that have to do with the moon.

The playfulness is observable in other of his compositions of the period. In the vanguardists' eagerness for novelty they showed a fascination with contemporary inventions – the telegraph, the cinema, airplanes, etc. The frivolous Italian futurist Filippo Marinetti had declared that a racing car was more beautiful than Leonardo's 'Mona Lisa' and had advocated burning down the museums. Vicente Huidobro had in turn called futurism old-fashioned. Guillén here in the poem 'El aeroplano' plays a game wth time and projects the airplane into a future so distant that absolute ignorance would exist concerning our epoch. The newly formed consciousness, beginning from *tabula rasa*, would then classify the airplane as extinct fauna. Thus by an elegant conceit Guillén 'outfutures' the futurists. The poem also has significance as a prefiguration of those post-revolutionary poems in which Guillén will develop an important variation of the bestiary, particularly in his book *El Gran Zoo*.

Another kind of poem appearing here that will be prominent in Guillén's later poetry is the elegy, represented by the poem 'Canción filial' ('Filial Song'), the subject of which is the loss of his father during the poet's early adolescence. Guillén's ability to find the apt, unabstruse metaphor is well displayed here:

Quizás no sepas, padre, que cuando tu partiste
yo empezaba a ser triste.
Yo estaba frente al vasto pizarrón de las cosas,
con su sistema de ecuaciones odiosas,
la tiza que me diste, en la mano,
y la frente fruncida,
tratando de arrancarle, en vano,
su incógnita a la Vida.

Perhaps you do not know, father, that when you left
sadness began to take hold of me.
I was already before the vast blackboard of things,
with their system of odious equations,
the chalk you gave me, in my hand,
and my brow wrinkled,
trying in vain to wrest
from life its unknown essence.

Two poems touch on what will become two of the main preoccupations of Guillén's life and poetry. The poem 'Futuro,' first published in October 1927 under the title 'Apunte' ('Note'), contains speculations not only about the future of the airplane but also about the possibility of a future people who would be capable of putting in a subordinate position the Americans 'que nos humillan con su fuerza' ('who humiliate us with their strength'). This is the first reference made by Guillén in his poetry to U.S. imperialism as it affected Cuba. In the poem entitled 'Gustavo E.,' published first in May 1929, a profile of Gustavo E. Urrutia is provided in which two characteristics stand out: his concern about racial problems and his love for and promotion of literature. This down-to-earth Quijote is admiringly presented in simple, narrative, perfect *romance* verse.

> Quijote sin Dulcinea,
> ni Sancho ni Rocinante,
> jinete en palo de escoba
> igual que un muchacho grande,
> va por el mundo Gustavo
> siempre adelante, adelante,
> diciéndonos lo que siente,
> lo que piensa y lo que sabe
> sobre esas viejas cuestiones
> de los problemas raciales.

> *Quijote without Dulcinea,*
> *or Sancho or Rocinante,*
> *horseman on a broomstick*
> *like a big boy,*
> *Gustavo goes through the world*
> *always forward, forward,*
> *telling us what he feels,*
> *what he thinks and what he knows*
> *about those old questions*
> *concerning racial problems.*

It will be noticed that 'problemas raciales' is a climax that is reached after careful preparation. The Quijote metaphor is here divested of its usual perquisites (including the 'Don'), so that this deprived idealist proceeds sedulously, in humility and with simplicity. The simplicity does not mean that he is easily assuaged; rather, it seems to contribute to the completeness of his involvement in a quest for the exposure and correction of an evil. The three verbs 'siente,' 'piensa,' 'sabe' in anaphorical relationship convey the intensity of the involvement, while the adjective 'viejas' indicates the persistence of the evil. The poem goes on to show, with usage that establishes a metonymical relation between Gustavo and pencils and paper, the subject's fostering of literature as an agent in his efforts. In the opening lines of the poem, then, Guillén introduces to his 'world' a personage who is preoccupied with a significant socio-historical Cuban problem. The very ease and familiarity of the form in which it is presented – the *romance* is the oldest and one of the most widely used of Spanish verse forms, usually consisting of eight-syllable lines with assonance in alternate lines – although appropriate for conveying the venerable Quijote metaphor, disguises the importance and unusualness of the topic for the vanguardist times in which the poem was written.[9] While he was demonstrating his mastery of the traditional forms, Guillén came to refer to the two great subjects of his poetry.

As we have seen, the first of these, U.S. imperialism, attracted the attention of Cuban poets, at least intermittently, from the turn of the century onward. The second one, however, racial problems, is missing from the topics treated and elicits hardly a single poem from the numerous poets examined earlier. The allusions made to it by José Manuel Poveda in a few of the poems in his *Versos precursores* (1917) were made to seem furtive by the poet's focus on black art as a way of enlivening his post-modernist expression rather than on the possibility of making the real life of blacks a source of his art. It is in this sense that Poveda may be regarded as a precursor in Cuba of what has been called the *negrista* movement. This exotic aspect of Cuban vanguardism adopted the wave of international artistic curiosity about the picturesque aspects of black life. Africa as a place of novelty had attracted European attention in the nineteenth century when René Caillé's *Récit d'un voyage à Timbouctou et à Djenné* (1830) inspired many subsequent travelogues. The work in this tradition that excited artistic imagination at the time when the vanguardist movements were about to be launched was Leon Frobenius's *Der Schwarze Dekameron* of 1910. He had travelled to Africa in 1905 and his accounts from which the book was later derived soon began to evoke interest. In 1907 Pablo Picasso displayed an Africanized European art in his painting *Les Demoiselles d'Avignon* and in the following year in his *Tête de nègre*. In the meantime jazz was being promoted at the Café Schiller in Chicago, and Stravinski was to show its influence in his *Piano Rag Music* and *Ragtime* in 1919. Blaise Cendrars, the editor of *Anthologie noire*, and Federico García Lorca both dedicated important poems to New York, viewing Harlem with particular favour. André Gide travelled to and wrote about the Congo, and Paul Morand produced his *Magie noire*. A part of this work was published in the *Revista de Avance*, just as the *Revista de Occidente* published Frobenius in translation. Many Cuban poets fell under the spell of this activity. It was not the first time that Spanish-American writers reacted in this way to European currents. In the late eighteenth century and early nineteenth centuries, French writers such as Rousseau, Voltaire, Chateaubriand, and Bernardin de Saint-Pierre extolled, without knowing them, the American Indians for their noble simplicity (simplicity used here definitely in the sense in which Fischer attacks it). For such writers, in their ignorance and lack of real imagination, the Indians were exotic beings who lived in idyllic surroundings. And even in the Andean countries, where writers had every opportunity to see Indians in the reality of their day-to-day lives, in novels predating Clorinda Matto de Turner's *Aves sin nido* (1888), the French fashion was followed, and the Indians were used as an element of local colour.

Apart from a few 'proletarian' poems of Regino Pedroso in which he included blacks among the exploited class, the Cuban poets of the late 1920s,
when Guillén was beginning his major work, continued the exotic trend.
Ramón Guirao's 'Bailadora de rumba,' José Z. Tallet's 'Rumba,' and Alejo
Carpentier's 'Liturgia ñáñiga,' all of 1928, sparked the fashion; and numerous
contributors to it may be counted in Emilio Ballagas's *Antología de poesía
negra hispano-americana* (1935) and Ramón Guirao's *Orbita de la poesía
afrocubana*. Guirao wrote in the introduction to his *Orbita* that 'Our Afro-
cuban poetry is an echo of the European black fashion: a consequence rather
than a true initiative.'[10]

What is the meaning of this absence of the treatment of the real life of
blacks? It would be almost idle to suggest that the writers by and large believed that racial problems did not exist because racial discrimination had
been declared illegal by the Cuban constitution of 1902. No less a critic
than José Juan Arrom has written that 'the white Cuban did not see in the
black an African with necklaces of crocodile teeth, but as another Cuban,
as Cuban as he, a citizen of the same Republic that they had forged together
with machete blows.'[11] My earlier historical account, however, has revealed a long, difficult struggle for the black population, a late end to slavery,
with devastating explosions, such as that of 1912, occurring during the
republican period. Blacks who shared actively the aspirations of Martí and
Maceo for national liberation and unity – Lino D'ou, Juan Gualberto Gómez,
Gustavo E. Urrutia – had gone on during this period to decry the continuing
discrimination. They not only wrote on behalf of racial equality but also
toiled for the creation and survival of organizations and publications that
furthered their aims. At the same time, the protest movements, such as that
of Los Trece and the Grupo Minorista, did not make of the racial situation in
Cuba a matter of high priority. They were chiefly concerned, as we have
seen, with reforms in education, public administration, and above all with full
Cuban independence. In fact, in the nine points that summarize the manifesto (1927) of the Grupo Minorista, there is no specific mention of the racial
situation. In withdrawing from the reunions at the Café 'Martí' during the
days as a student in Havana and in opting for *Orto* over the *Revista de Avance*
for the publication of his poetry when he later returned to Havana, Guillén
was no doubt reacting, in part at least, to the insensitivity he perceived on the
part of some members of those groups to what he considered to be a crucial
issue.[12] From his later writings it is clear that he had an early admiration
for two members of those groups, Rubén Martínez Villena and Juan Marinello, and especially in the case of the latter, he appreciates the contribution
made to the struggle against racism.[13] In general, however, the neglect of
the racial topic must be regarded as an indication of the perception of the
overwhelming majority of poets that it was neither urgent nor of essential
national significance.

Guillén's main sources of encouragement, guidance, and opportunity in the late 1920s and early 1930s appear to have been Lino D'ou and Gustavo Urrutia. Guillén has stated that

my real poetic resurrection was due to Gustavo E. Urrutia, who, following the advice of Lino D'ou asked for my collaboration for the page entitled 'Ideales de una Raza' ['Ideals of a Race'], of which he was the principal editor, and which appeared every Sunday in the *Diario de la Marina*. I declined in a thousand ways, telling him – I was twenty-five years old then – that I was a 'retired' poet. At his insistence I gave him some poems which I myself entitled *Versos de ayer y de hoy* [*Verses of Yesterday and Today*]. There were the vanguardist ones (which were those of today), together with others (those of yesterday) among which were a sonnet to a lily, some stanzas to death, and some others which I do not remember.[14]

If the verses of today were vanguardist at the time of the invitation (December 1928), by May of the following year Guillén had written the poem 'Gustavo E.' and in December the 'Pequeña oda a Kid Chocolate,' two poems dealing with race in a non-vanguardist manner. Indeed, the characteristics of thinking and knowing attributed to Gustavo and the directive to speak 'en negro de verdad' ('as a true black'), especially since in the latter poem imperialism and race converge as issues, are a reflection of the rational approach that was to be a feature of Guillén's whole work as opposed to the irrational tendencies shown by several of the *negrista* poets. True, Guillén was also to produce a 'Rumba' in 1931, but by the time he had done so the rational trend in his poetry was already well established; and this poem is tied to the collection in which it was published by its allusions to real social practices. By joining the quest for national unity, he acted as a poet incited by Prometheus (or by 'Gustavo E.') rather than as one who had abandoned himself to Dionysus (or to Ortega). He had set out on a course much more likely to lead to Marx than to Nietzsche. The compatibility of literature and social action, of which Urrutia came to be for Guillén a powerful symbol, no doubt helped Guillén to overcome the influential contemporary Gramscian notion of the need to opt for the one or the other, and was to be a lasting indicator of the possibilities inherent in employing literature in the realization of social action.

MOTIVOS DE SON

Motivos de son (*Son Motifs*) was first published on the page entitled 'Ideales de una Raza' of the *Diario de la Marina* on 20 April 1930. Angel Augier has documented his own reaction and that of many of his compatriots and others, like Langston Hughes, to the event. Augier writes of his 'pleasurable sensation of discovery of the national lyrical essence' and adds: 'In the following

days – in the course of weeks, months – I would find out that I was only sharing a general opinion, because it is possible that neither before nor after has
a collection of poems provoked a greater journalistic stir in Cuba.'[15] The
reaction, however, was not uniformly enthusiastic (see the quotation from
Guillén's tribute to Marinello, note 13). There was in some quarters the feeling that the *son*, the popular musical form on which Guillén had based the
poems, constituted too extreme an aesthetic initiative and too disturbing a
social manifestation.

If one were to undertake a psychological approach to Guillén's first collections of poetry, *Cerebro y corazón* and *Motivos de son*, without, of course,
high expectations of penetrating results, one would advisedly apply a Freud-
ian approach to the first one, entertaining oneself with the apparent neur-
oses exposed by the focusing of poetic attention on a very restricted world of
inner, personal conflict. On the other hand, a Jungian approach is suggested
by *Motivos de son*. The favourable reaction to it by fellow poets like Augier
was matched by a similar favourable reaction by the Cuban population in
general. It is as if Guillén had touched on something active in the consciousness of a few but which was submerged in the unconscious of most Cubans, something said in a way that the people collectively could recognize as
having been on the tips of their tongues and that awaited the articulation
Guillén gave to it. He himself has written of the circumstances of the origin
of the poems in terms that may prompt this recourse to Jung:

The birth of these poems is linked to a dreamlike experience of which I have never
spoken in public and which produced a vivid impression on me. One night – in
April, 1930 – I had gone to bed and was in that indecisive borderline between sleep
and wakefulness ... when a voice that came from I don't know where pronounced
with precise clarity next to my ear these two words: *negro-bembón* ... The phrase,
accompanied by a special rhythm new to me, swirled about me for the rest of the
night, more and more profoundly and commandingly ... I got up early and began to
write. As if I remembered something I had once known, I wrote at one stroke a poem
in which those words served as a subsidy and support for the rest of the verses. I
wrote and wrote all day, conscious of my discovery. By evening I had a handful of
poems – eight or ten – which I entitled in a general way *Motivos de son*.[16]

On a less mysterious and more verifiable level, the historical contexts – that
of the whole history of Cuba including its literary history and that of the
history of Guillén's poetry – provide an explanation for the appearance of
Motivos de son and indicate that Guillén's achievement here is based on his
acute sensitivity to his times and his confidence in his poetic skill. These
factors combined to make him the medium through which profound latent
content began to make its way to the surface, expressed in a form that chal-

lenged the relevance of the preceding forms. A social condition marked by racial discrimination had followed the abolition of slavery. This condition, while serving the ends of the primitive economic base, had deleterious effects on the whole national life. The predominant artistic approaches before 1930 constituted one of the means by which this condition was hidden. Guillén came to expose this suppressed phenomenon by employing a form adopted from a genre of music, the *son*, that, symptomatically, had also experienced suppression.

The *son*, a musical form of contagious and provocative rhythm, is divided into two parts: the *motivo* or *letra* sung by the *sonero*, the principal voice, sometimes in harmony with a second voice; and the *coro* (which may also be called the *estribillo*, the *sonsonete*, or the *bordón*) in which voices of the players of other instruments reply to or second the *motivo*. The subject matter embraces the vast and colourful material of Cuban popular culture, from *pregones*, or vendors' street cries, such as 'El tomatero,' to flamboyant personalities, such as 'Elena la cumbanchera,' to the musicians and their instruments, such as 'Las maracas de Nery,' which are all in the repertoire of the Septeto Habanero. The *son* is comparable to the calypso and the mento in rhythm and spirit, but the risqué aspect of a calypsonian like Sparrow is unusual in the *son*, as is his developed narrative line. The basic instruments are the guitar, its relative the *tres*, with three pairs of strings, which initiates the rhythm, the bongo drums, the bass, the *claves*, and the maracas. The trumpet and other wind instruments were later added. It has been claimed and disputed that a *son* entitled 'Ma Teodora' dates as far back as 1580. Its known continuing history begins at the turn of this century in Oriente province. From there the Cuarteto Oriental went to Havana where it transformed itself into the Sexteto Habanero in 1920 and into the Septeto Habanero, as it is still known, in 1927. Only after 1930 did harassment against it (typifying the attitude to the *son* in general and particularly to the bongo drum which in some quarters was regarded as an immoral instrument) subside. This change in attitude was due in part to the fact that the Septeto had been contracted by a Hollywood studio to participate in the making of a film in Florida and to make several recordings. This improvement in status allowed its escape from clandestinity within Cuba as the country's bourgeoisie[17] began to show acceptance of it. The doors of the 'Vedado Tennis Club' (now the Círculo Social Obrero José A. Hechevarría) opened to the Septeto Habanero.[18] No doubt the prestige of the *son* was also enhanced by Guillén's artistic use of it.

The eight poems published in the *Diario* soon appeared as a booklet. Later in 1930, Guillén published three more *Motivos* and subsequently substituted one of these, 'Hay que tené boluntá' ('One Must Have Willpower'), for 'Ayé me dijeron negro' ('Yesterday they called me black') of the eight originally published to comprise a definitive collection. A tendency has existed in Guillén criticism to treat his poetry in separate categories: as folklore, or as lyrical, love, social, or political poetry and to consider poems as representative of these different categories. One of the most significant features of *Motivos de son* is that it is precisely in this book that such a procedure becomes inappropriate. Through their simple, inviting form, the poems offer a rich concentration of images and devices that work to open a window on the life of the humble black sector of the Cuban population. In the course of the fifty years since they were published, this richness has led to many impressive studies, emphasizing in particular the folkloric and social aspects of the poems. The use of the *son* rhythm and of a level of popular speech characterized by apocope (the omission of a word's final sounds), aphaeresis (the omission of a word's initial sounds), metathesis (or transposition), and assimilation of consonants, supplemented by *jitanjáfora* and onomatopoeia, supports the folkloric findings, while the characters and their circumstances have suggested the social categories. What to my knowledge has not been observed is that the poems are at the same time and in a central unifying sense, love poems. In a recent interview, Guillén corrected the assumption that 'the universal theme of love does not appear in [his] work until *El son entero*' (1947). He referred to 'La balada azul' and other of his early compositions and added that 'there are many more, not only of that time, but of the period immediately following.'[19] If Guillén had meant by his statement that the *Motivos* ... are to be included among his love poems he might not have been readily understood; for only in a minority of these poems is there a lyrical 'I' expressing internal feelings concerning a love relationship; and in them the emotion itself and its symptoms are not isolated and analysed as in those love poems of the earlier Guillén or in those of other poets of the period such as the Neruda of the *Veinte poemas de amor y una canción desesperada*. What is manifested here, rather, is love as it is clearly determined by the historical conditions in which it attempts to exist. The would-be lovers are defenceless in the face of unrelentingly hostile social forces, principally racial discrimination and poverty, which invade their most basic existence and cause 'the universal theme of love' to be shrouded in misery. The musical elements, the lively rhythm of the *son*, and the innocence of the language function as a counterpoint that heightens the pathos and the tension, so that a poignant bittersweetness results, a sprightly and sensuous dance with a powerful undercurrent of sadness. In fact, although it does not operate semantically here, the oxymoron characteristic of so much love poetry comes to be the controlling figure in the collection. It is this fine tension of contrast between musicality and the harsh experience portrayed that underlies the evocative, disturbing, revolutionary nature of *Motivos de son*. The new form introduced in the collection plays a crucial role in suggesting the contrast between how things are and how they ought to be.

In establishing the definitive eight *Motivos* ..., Guillén excluded from the original eight the one that did not entail a man-woman relationship and substituted for it one of the three he later wrote that did. Within this basic unity he presents a focal dramatic situation in each poem involving a variety of distances between the voice of the poem and its audience. Only in the poem 'Mi chiquita' ('My Little Woman') does the poetic voice speak entirely in the third person and therefore directly, descriptively, to a listener outside the world of the poem. In all the others, there is an implied interlocutor, an imagined presence in a dramatic monologue, as in 'Si tú supiera ...' ('If You Knew ...'), or a silent presence in an implied dialogue, as in 'Hay que tené boluntá.' Through the resulting drama, rendered in authentic popular speech, the causes of the state of relations between the characters are exposed.

In 'Negro bembón' ('Thick-lipped Negro'), racial features regarded as being beneath the somatic norms are given as a taunt which, although no direct causality is given, may have incited the protagonist to warp his relationship with his woman by living illicitly, easily, and well attired off her contributions. In 'Mulata,' the possibility of a liaison between a mulatto woman and a black man is dashed by the colour prejudice that, in its perverse way, has affected everyone.

'Si tú supiera ...' provides an image of the damaging effects of poverty on a relationship. The poem has structural features too important to be overlooked. In it, Guillén uses for the first time *jitanjáfora*, the extra-semantic phenomenon that has eluded the semanticists' theories.[20] Its peculiarity is that it belongs to *parole* but not to *langue* and it may connote but cannot denote. A poem consisting entirely of *jitanjáfora* is therefore a nonsense poem. Its best use as a device reflects the awareness that it depends heavily for meaning on the context in which it is used and therefore demands the environment of appropriately structured compositions. 'Si tú supiera ...,' of all the poems of *Motivos de son*, contains the most intense dramatic monologue. The woman is clearly absent and the speaker's lyrical apostrophe to her is spurred by jealousy as he blames his poverty for the loss of this good-time girl:

A é tú le hará como a mí,
que cuando no tube plata
te corrite de bachata
sin acoddate de mí.

You'll do to him what you did to me,
for when my money ran out
you went off partying,
without remembering me.

After this *motivo* has been well established, he breaks into the *jitanjáforas* that form the *estribillo*:

> Sóngoro cosongo,
> songo be;
> sóngoro cosongo
> de mamey;
> sóngoro, la negra
> baila bien;
> sóngoro de uno
> sóngoro de tre.

The *estribillo* suggests revelry, and recognizable words in it describe a dancing woman. As such, it serves the voice of the poem as a compensatory projection, a frenetic fantasy party that would assuage the man's sense of loss and his dejection. The fantasy cannot last, and in the knowledge of this there is pathos. The music here, then, has the contrapuntal function described above, and *jitanjáfora* is made to contribute meaningfully to the poem.

In 'Sigue ...' ('Go on') the woman is also presented by a spurned, presumably penniless, suitor as bad. Poverty dominates and bedevils the life of the pair in 'Hay que tené boluntá' ('One Must Have Willpower'). One of the techniques used in this poem to convey the misery from which there is no apparent escape is the employment of a construction that normally promises a contrasting alternative but reveals no alternative at all:

> Cuando pongo un ojo así,
> e que no hay na;
> pero si lo pongo así,
> tampoco no hay na.

> *When I move my eye this way,*
> *it means I don't have anything;*
> *but if I move it that way,*
> *I still don't have anything.*

This is a technique that Guillén had employed in his earlier poetry, as we have seen, in a less daring form. The poem 'Mi chiquita' is exceptional for its expression of contentment with however basic a life style, but even here the sad disparagement of blackness, learned in a society affected by racism, is present in the speaker's consciousness. The last poem introduces a new cause of frustration – the unequal status Vito Manué has with the American woman as evidenced by his extreme embarrassment at not being able to speak English in Cuba.

The sixth poem, 'Búcate plata' ('Go Get Money') deserves a more detailed and clarifying commentary because of its importance and because it has been subjected to different interpretations. The text of this poem is:

Búcate plata,
búcate plata,
poqque no doy un paso má:
etoy a arró con galleta,
na má.
Yo bien sé cómo etá to,
pero biejo, hay que comé:
búcate plata,
búcate plata,
poqque me boy a corré.
Depué dirán que soy mala,
y no me quedrán tratá,
pero amó con hambre, biejo.
¡qué ba!
Con tanto sapato nuevo,
¡qué ba!
Con tanto reló, compadre,
¡qué ba!
Con tanto lujo, mi negro,
¡qué ba!

Go get money,
go get money,
for I can't go a step further:
I'm down to rice and crackers,
that's all.
I know very well how things are,
but goodness man, one's got to eat:
go get money,
go get money,
cause I'm going to run away.
Then they'll say I'm bad
and won't want to have anything to do with me,
but love with hunger, man
hell!

With so many new shoes,
hell!
With so many watches, my friend,
hell!
With so many luxuries, my brother,
hell!

Urgent financial need is established at the outset by the repetition of the command 'Búcate plata / búcate plata' given by the woman to her lover. The image 'arró con galleta' conveys the spareness of the basis of her existence. The verse 'Yo bien sé cómo etá to' suggests a willingness to be understanding in the light of prevailing general conditions, but hunger looms, inclining her to accept a descent to lower social standing. The anaphora of the *estribillo* introduces different kinds of desirable material goods on show in the society with the refrain '¡qué ba!' indicating restless deprivation. Augier has understood the poem to mean that the man possesses these things, leaving the woman destitute. However, several aspects of the poem are bases for disputing this view. The speaker's anger does not appear to be directed at her lover. The verse 'Yo bien sé cómo etá to' is certainly conciliatory, and the friendly terms used to address him, 'biejo,' 'compadre,' 'mi negro,' when she is otherwise at the point of fury would suggest that we are here faced with the type encountered in the first poem, 'Negro bembón.' Besides, the reiterated directive 'búcate plata' indicates that the problem is not her lover's misuse of money but his lack of it. The directive would certainly have been different had the man been the owner of so many shoes, watches, and luxuries.

In the final stanza, in which the *motivo* gives way to the *estribillo*, the image 'amó con hambre' initiates the pattern of antithesis that moves from the intimately personal experience – love opposed by hunger – to the broadly social. The antithesis developed later between hunger and luxuries underlines the intolerableness of a general situation that provokes the '¡qué ba!' reaction. The trend from the particular to the general is emphasized by the order 'sapato,' 'reló,' 'lujo.'[21] It should be noted, too, that the possessive form 'mi negro' implies a unity, albeit an impotent solidarity between the man and the woman in the face of this general situation. All this, then, further elaborates on the verse 'Yo bien sé cómo etá to,' and by doing so adds pathos to the poem. The woman's understanding of the general situation and her love are factors favouring the continuation of their relationship. Hunger, on the other hand, threatens to tilt the balance negatively. The implied dialogue used in the presentation of the poem is another of the elements contributing to its pathos by lending significance to the lover's silence. In the face of all she says, his silence suggests helplessness, degradation, and shame whose natural course will lead to anger. The effect of pathos is completed by the *son* form, since what I have said earlier about the contrapuntal role of music in the *Motivos* ... is particularly relevant to 'Búcate plata.' The images of the poem, then, evoke hunger, unemployment, the menace of prostitution, the contrast between affluence and destitution, class stratification – all of these in a little poem that employs a popular traditional form and a popular level of speech in order to show the inimical effects of poverty on what is potentially the warmest of human relations.

In conclusion, it may be useful to enumerate some of the principal accomplishments resulting from Guillén's use of the *son*. He exposes the inadequacy of the *negrista* movement in its playful mode by bringing authentically and forcefully to our attention a neglected sector of Cuban society, without whose inclusion the national spectrum is incomplete. By using a truly Cuban form originating in the confluence of African and Spanish cultural patterns, he challenges the idea, from within a neo-colonial setting, that the source of new forms is necessarily foreign and metropolitan. He makes truly artistic an oral tradition that had been disparaged by much of the privileged sector and elevates it to confront the existing forms of printed poetry.[22] Within *Motivos* ... itself, the *son* is made to contribute to the production of a bittersweetness characterized by pathos. It thereby assists in capturing a profound psycho-social reality, that of a people determined to be joyous in a sad situation. Guillén employs an appealing rhythm, inviting his public not so much to dance as to witness love among the destitute, to see an eternal and universal human right, not 'star-crossed' in the manner of Shakespeare's famous lovers, but violated by poverty and racism. In *Motivos* ..., he thus firmly establishes a complexity of mood that will reappear in various manifestations throughout his poetry.

SÓNGORO COSONGO

In responding to the reaction to *Motivos de son*, Guillén addressed himself mainly to the negative attitudes. It is clear from his comment (quoted in note 13) concerning Marinello's appreciation of the book that Guillén sustained the belief that much of the muted or roundly hostile reaction to it was inspired by a cowardly reluctance to come to terms with a marginalized sector of society. Guillén has recently pointed out, too, that some blacks were among the detractors.[23] At the same time it must be recognized that *Motivos de son* represented an uncontainable challenge to the status quo because the simple and just desire that the underprivileged be noticed carried with it profoundly rebellious potential. On the other hand, to be heard would be the beginning of a dialectical process through which successive goals could be identified and pursued; in fact, the troubling confrontation achieved by this book would lead in a logical sequence to other confrontations.

Guillén seemed to be conscious of this potential when he wrote the combative prologue to his second book, *Sóngoro cosongo* (1931):

I will say finally that these are mulatto verses. They partake perhaps of the same elements that enter into the ethnic composition of Cuba where we are all a little bit naseberry. Does that hurt? I don't believe so. In any case it is important to say it lest we forget it. The African input into this country is ... profound and ... many capillary currents criss-cross in our well-irrigated waterways.

I think therefore that a creole poetry among us will not be realized completely with the omission of blacks. The blacks – in my view – contribute very decisive essences to our cocktail ... The spirit of Cuba is *mestizo*. And from the spirit to the skin the definitive colour will come to us. Some day they will say: 'Cuban colour.'

These poems wish to hasten that day.[24]

Thus having extended recognition to the humble blacks and their cultural expression as part of the nation in *Motivos de son*, in *Sóngoro cosongo* he proposes a unified Cuban nationality based on the integration of the society's Spanish and African components. These aims have certain ramifications with regard to the unifying principles of the two books. Whereas in the first book unity emerged from the steady focus on the blacks' beleaguered man-woman relationships, harmony in a broader sense, embracing the wider society, is the elusive ideal shaped by the poems of *Sóngoro cosongo*. The continuity from one book to the other inherent in this design may be observed in several other aspects of their interrelations. The title of the second book is taken from the *estribillo* of the poem 'Si tú supiera ...' of the first book. The emphasis on music is continued in the second book. Further, notwithstanding the discontinuation of the popular level of speech used in *Motivos de son* in favour of the standard speech befitting the greater inclusiveness of the poetic vision, the central interest continues to be on what Guillén calls 'the affairs of the blacks and of the people.'[25] One of the principal differences between the books is that whereas *Motivos de son* possesses the tightness of a book, the poems of which were envisaged at the time of their composition as its constituents, *Sóngoro cosongo* is made up of poems that were composed during a period of almost two years, some of them predating the former collection. We have already observed that the 'Pequeña oda a un negro boxeador cubano' ('Little Ode to a Black Cuban Boxer') was first published in late 1929. The poems 'Caña' ('Sugar-cane') and 'Organillo' ('Barrel Organ') appeared along with other 'Odas mínimas' in June 1930 on the page of the *Diario de la Marina* edited by Gustavo E. Urrutia. *Sóngoro cosongo* was published in October 1931. The fifteen poems that compose the collection, reflecting absent and elusive harmony, offer three main topics: race, imperialism, and poverty. Various perspectives on the first topic are presented. Some of the poems show pictures of black life – the futile pursuit of happiness in bacchanalian

activity in 'Quirino'; the seductiveness of the dance countered by the circum-
stantial evidence that the dancer is wayward in 'Rumba'; music and dance
as frenzied quest for open expression in 'Canto negro.' Other poems celebrate
the elemental beauty of the black woman, as in 'Mujer nueva' ('New
Woman') and the two madrigals. In 'Chévere' violence dominates, as the
slasher's indiscriminate anger finally makes his woman his victim. The
beauty of music with the fatal undercurrent of violence is elegantly developed
in 'Velorio de Papá Montero' ('Funeral Wake for Papá Montero') and in
'Secuestro de la mujer de Antonio' ('Abduction of Antonio's Wife'). The new
departures regarding race that are of special significance, apart from the
earlier-discussed aspect of 'Pequeña oda a un negro boxeador cubano,' are to
be found in the poems 'Llegada' ('Arrival') and 'Canción del bongó' ('The
Song of the Bongo Drum'). At least one prominent Cuban critic has been
alarmed by 'Llegada' and by those other poems by Guillén like 'El apellido' ('The Family Name') in which images of blacks suggest their undefiled
African roots, that is, their Africanness without slavery. The blacks of
'Llegada' are described by Cintio Vitier as arriving with an 'invasionary,
vengeful, auroral mission' and he adds, 'those men are not really Cubans,
but pure Africans.'[26] The poem does indeed convey the image of blacks
initiating an existence in Cuba. Their presentation is ahistorical in that they
appear to be purged of the experience of slavery. This, calmly read, has the
effect of removing the emotion of either contempt or guilt with which they
may otherwise be contemplated by many of their fellow Cubans who are of
Spanish ancestry. On the other hand, for those of African ancestry, it has
the effect of putting to rest the question of how they got to Cuba so that they
may concentrate on the task of establishing their presence alongside that of
others, and so participate in the building of a Cuban nationality. The refrain in
the poem is

¡Eh, compañeros, aquí estamos!

Well, comrades, here we are!

The blacks are men of quiet strength and of simple and firm aspirations,
which include that of being respected for their contribution:

Nuestro canto
es como un músculo bajo la piel del alma,
nuestro sencillo canto.

Our song
is like a muscle under the skin of the soul,
our simple song.

These, then, rather than ex-slaves, are men who, with 'el espíritu limpio' ('clean spirit'), promise a vigorous participation and who look to the future with confidence. Recognized as such they need not be feared, except by the oppressors whom they promise to conquer. This poem marks the beginning of a long series of attempts by Guillén to deal in his poetry with the pernicious matter of slavery in such a way that it permits the subsequent possibility of a real national spirit in Cuba – with the confident participation of all Cubans in their national life. We will see later, for example, another approach to the question in one of his most recent books, *El diario que a diario* (1972).

The other important departure that entails national consequences regarding race is represented by the poem 'La canción del bongó.' There, as in 'Llegada,' the speaker (in this case the personified *bongó*) is in direct contact with the reader, contributing thereby to the intensity of the impact of what is said. The only line presented from a third person perspective is the first, introductory one:

Esta es la canción del bongó

This is the song of the bongo drum

From what was said earlier about the bongo drum as a persecuted instrument, it can be readily understood that the choice of it as a spokesman is a combative act. At the same time, its choice for speaking of covert matters bears a special aptness since it was known to be in some quarters clandestinely enjoyed while publicly spurned. Its presence is commanding throughout the poem; in round and clear tones, amplified by the use of *romance* verse with assonance in accented 'ó,' it speaks to the people, including unwilling listeners, about hidden secrets concerning race:

Pero mi repique bronco,
pero mi profunda voz,
convoca al negro y al blanco,
que bailan el mismo son.

But my hoarse peel,
but my profound voice,
calls together black and white,
who dance to the same son.

The emphasis of the discourse, coinciding with the subtitle of the book, 'Poemas mulatos,' is on the mixed nature of the population, the reluctance to acknowledge the African content, and the resultant absurdities:

En esta tierra mulata
de africano y español
(Santa Bárbara de un lado,
del otro lado, Changó),
siempre falta algún abuelo,
cuando no sobra algún Don
y hay títulos de Castilla
con parientes en Bondó.

In this land, made mulatto
by African and Spaniard
(Santa Bárbara on one side,
on the other, Changó)
a grandfather is always missing,
when there isn't a Don too many
and there are titles from Castile
with relatives in Bondó.

The last stanza of the poem, with extended anaphora serving to augment
the already established intensity of the poem, reveals the bongó's confidence
that its view of the mulatto character of Cuban society will come to prevail.

It will have been noticed in the passage quoted earlier from the prologue to
Sóngoro cosongo that Guillén used the adjectives 'mulatto,' 'creole,' and
mestizo to describe his poetry and the spirit of Cuba. These and several other
related words – *negra, negrista, negroide, afrocubana,* and *afroespañola*
– have been used to describe the poetry that I have been examining. *Mulato*
describes people of mixed black-white heritage; it is fittingly used by Guillén
to mean the synthesis of the Cuban population and the resulting cultural
manifestations. *Mestizo,* used in a more general sense to mean the mixture
of the Spanish and any other racial group is also employed by Guillén to
describe this national synthesis. The term *criollo* (creole) is more complex.
I stated in the first part of this study (chapter 1, note 56) that its original
meaning of 'someone born in Cuba or elsewhere in Spanish America of
Spanish parents' gave way to a more political meaning in the nineteenth
century. The term came to be reserved for those who, having been descended
from Spaniards, opted for Cuba as opposed to Spain when the idea of independence became popular. When Guillén stated (in 1931) that 'a creole
poetry among us will not be realized with the omission of blacks' he alluded
to the time, now come, when the definition would mean, in a political
sense, the whole Cuban population. The adjectives *negra, negrista, negroide*
(all of them meaning, with different nuances, 'black') do not serve to describe correctly a poetry of fusion and synthesis. For the same reason *afro-*

cubana is inappropriate since it carries the idea that what is Cuban and has African origin is not to be regarded as fully Cuban (especially when no such compound word as *hispanocubano* exists to describe what is Cuban and has Spanish origin). Thus Guillén has favoured the term *afroespañol* and has written: 'The Afro-Cuban, as urgent and hasty critics have said and continue to say? No, the Afro-Spanish, which is our stamp and seal.' In the same essay, on and entitled 'Bola de Nieve,' he uses approvingly the series of adjectives: 'national, creole, *mestizo*, mulatto, ours.'[27] All this is a reflection of the inclusive, national scope of his vision.

In the two poems of *Sóngoro cosongo* that deal prominently with poverty, 'Organillo' ('Barrel Organ') and 'Pregón' ('Street Cry'), Guillén again demonstrates his ability to condense more than one topic into a single short poem. 'Organillo' presents a man who attempts to make a living by selling music. The poem captures the moment of the failure of his enterprise:

> El sol a plomo. Un hombre
> va al pie del organillo.
> Manigueta: 'Epabílate, mi conga,
> mi conga ...'
>
> Ni un quilo en los bolsillos,
> y la conga
> muerta en el organillo.
>
> *The sun beating down. A man*
> *at the foot of his barrel organ.*
> *He mutters: 'Wake up, my conga,*
> *my conga ...'*
>
> *Not a cent in his pockets,*
> *and the conga*
> *dead in the barrel organ.*

Since it occupies the rest of the first line after the caesura, there is an expectant stress on 'un hombre.' But immediately the subsequent and the metonymical 'pie' underlines the subservience, in harsh climatic conditions, of the man to the instrument. The dependency is furthered by his importuning the conga music to wake up. The urgent reason for the dependency, his poverty, is coupled in the final stanza with the realization that the music is dead. On another level the poem suggests, through the silence that exists in place of music, the unrelieved, stark nature of the absence of harmony that economic distress represents.

The impact of poverty is driven home by means of contrast in 'Pregón.' Instead of the third-person presentation used in 'Organillo,' the street vendor exists here with apparent independence, publicizing his fruits with his evocative, picturesque, external song, confessing quietly his own misery and by doing all this functions as the speaker of the poem. In his lively opening exclamation:

> ¡Ah
> qué pedazo de sol,
> carne de mango!

> *Oh*
> *what a piece of sun,*
> *mango flesh!*

the vehicle of the metaphor is linked clearly through colour to the tenor, the flesh of the mango, and thus subtly highlights the colour of the objects presented in the rest of the poem. The stanza of crucial contrast is the one preceding the *estribillo*:

> Sangre de mamey sin venas,
> y yo que sin sangre estoy;
> mamey p'al que quiera sangre,
> que me voy.

> *Juice of veinless mamey,*
> *and I who have no blood;*
> *mamey for whoever wants blood*
> *for I am going.*

As is often the case in Guillén's poetry, what at first seems to be playful local colour comes later to have a dimension of utmost seriousness. In the first line of the stanza the metaphorical 'sangre' enables the paradox created by 'sin venas' to result in the enhancement of the succulence of the fruit. It is natural for an image so brilliantly favourable to his merchandise to be conveyed in a loud voice; and the modulation of volume becomes important in the stanza when it is realized that the following line describing the vendor's own distressing state is certainly not meant for his immediate audience of potential customers and is therefore said *sotto voce*. 'Sangre' in this second line loses its metaphorical meaning and becomes part of a hyperbolic image that emphasizes the vendor's feeble condition. In the third line both the metaphorical and literal meanings of 'sangre' are realized in the representation of the juice of the fruit and its nutritive qualities. A sharp irony thus develops: The distributor vitally needs, but by economic dictate cannot partake of, what he distributes. The contradiction is made more fateful by the final four-syllable line of the stanza because, in this context, in addition to indicating the itinerant nature of his trade, it also suggests his imminent death.

The richness of poetic means that Guillén has shown so far in representing a variety of topics is evident as well in those poems of *Sóngoro cosongo* in which imperialism is a significant subject. Guillén mentions the topic for the second time in the 'Pequeña oda al negro boxeador cubano' of this collection in an image in which metonymy and personification are prominent:

> ese mismo Broadway,
> es el que estira su hocico con una enorma lengua húmeda,
> para lamer glotonamente
> toda la sangre de nuestro cañaveral.[28]

> *that same Broadway,*
> *is the one that stretches its snout with an enormous*
> *   humid tongue,*
> *to gluttonously lick up*
> *all the blood of our canefield.*

The other poem treating the subject was, like the 'Pequeña oda ... ,' first published more than a year before *Sóngoro cosongo* appeared. Also focusing on sugar, as will several later Guillén poems, it is entitled 'Caña.' It is one of Guillén's best known poems and because its apparent simplicity disguises its real intricacy, I will attempt to offer a brief analysis of it. The text is:

> El negro
> junto al cañaveral.

> El yanqui
> sobre el cañaveral.

> La tierra
> bajo el cañaveral.

> ¡Sangre
> que se nos va!

> *The black man*
> *next to the canefield.*
>
> *The Yankee*
> *over the canefield.*
>
> *The land*
> *under the canefield.*
>
> *Blood*
> *that goes out from us!*

The first three of its four short stanzas are of parallel construction, with article, noun, preposition, article, noun. The last noun of the series, 'caña-veral,' forms the constant base in the structure of all three stanzas. The two personal subjects have precise antithetical relations to the base, their designations 'El negro' and 'El yanqui' aiding this antithesis; and the concentration of meaning begins to be clear when it is noticed that the syntactical base is also the economic base. The preposition 'junto a' suggests no distance or intermediary between the man and the cane field. Hard labour is relieved by no mechanization, as the closeness leaves room only for hands or for an extension of them, like a machete. Particularly in view of the perpendicular relation of the two other prepositions to the cane field, the additional connotation in 'junto a' of 'on the same level as' becomes functional here, bearing the implication that the physical proximity also means closeness in kind. In this sense the man and the cane field are liable to being treated as things. That they are exploited as such is clear from the prepositional relation of the 'yanqui' to the cane field. He is in a position of superiority to and control over the cane field, the worker, and the land. For the land, in giving sustenance to the cane field, is at the base of the exploited structure, completing the generalized picture of victimization of Cuban capital and Cuban labour. The final stanza breaks with the earlier established pattern. The exclamatory tone is heightened by the stress that now, in the absence of an article, falls immediately on the word 'sangre.' At the same time the absence of an article makes enjambment obvious between the two lines of the last stanza, quickening its pace to reflect the urgent condition that is described. Also introduced here is the use of the first person plural after the series of third-person stanzas. These changes, which convey the effect of the content of the preceding stanzas on the poet and the nation of which he forms a part, also in themselves carry affective weight. They represent a breakdown of the parallel, apparently distanced presentation of the rest of the poem under the burden of intense feeling. This relation of altered form to feeling is similar in technique to the collapse of the sonnet form in Rubén Darío's poem 'Lo fatal,' where the effect was created of a feeling that was too overwhelming for order to be maintained. But whereas Darío dealt in that poem with a metaphysical question that provokes anguish that is not circumscribed by foreseeable time, Guillén's 'Caña' presents a social problem, and time is precisely the element that is evoked by the urgency conveyed by the last stanza. The stanza is commandingly influential because it contains the only verb in the poem, which in the present tense describes the flowing of collective lifeblood. In the face of this, the reader is prompted to review the poem from the perspective of time.

Such a review allows the perception of another aspect of the prepositions in the poem: the temporal relation they establish between the different subjects and the cane field. In the light of this, the most durable relation is that of the land to the cane field. It is the base on which the cane field rests and this relation will last as long as there is a cane field. This continuity is sustained by a metonymical relation between the land and Cuba. Because of his closeness to the cane field and his destiny to be under the earth when he dies, 'el negro' enjoys temporality that, though threatened as far as his life expectancy is concerned by the exploitative conditions in which he works, is still naturally lasting. On the other hand, 'el yanqui,' who at first reading seemed to be superiorly commanding, now comes to reveal a crucial flaw. Precisely by being 'sobre el cañaveral,' he is viewable as having no true contact with the land, no foot on the ground. This makes his position precarious and temporally unstable. In time he may come plunging to the ground or find it prudent to fly away, leaving the cane field, the land, and those who work on it, so that the flow of lifeblood can be stopped. The urgency and intense feeling expressed in the last stanza reflect the earnest desire for that time to be hastened.

The primary topics dealt with in *Sóngoro cosongo* (not with mutual exclusivity) – the racial situation, poverty, and imperialism – are all treated in such a way that they are subsumed under a broader general topic: the absence of harmony. Although in only one poem, 'Canción del bongó,' is there an explicit future projection of a solution, in all of them the need for change and the resolving of problems so that a full potential may be realized is present. The three topics combined, the three problems to be rectified, show obstacles in the way of national harmony; and since those obstacles are not confined to Cuba, the book has wide applicability. The capacity of the poems to disturb their readers lies in no small measure in the fact that in one sense they present thesis and antithesis, leaving the readers to recognize the way to synthesis and its implications.

Guillén's use of music plays a crucial role in achieving this effect. He continues here the at-once overt and subtle employment of music that had been displayed in *Motivos de son*, so that it is used here not just in the masterful rhythmic design of the individual poems that Augier has described so well. Music is also an explicit part of the subject matter of twelve of the fifteen poems ('Llegada,' 'Pequeña oda ... ,' and 'Caña' are the exceptions). In all of these twelve poems – except 'Organillo,' where music functions negatively through the futile effort to create it and thus forms a ready coherence with the player's deprived condition – it behaves contrapuntally. Its magnificence stands in suggestive contrast to the absent harmony revealed in the text. This contrast, demanding resolution, points to a future of change and synthesis. This technique, discovered for *Motivos de son*, is employed with greater scope in *Sóngoro cosongo*. It is not surprising, therefore, that in the best early responses to the book, the critics dwell on the opening to the future and to the world beyond Cuba provided by it. Two such representative critics are Juan Marinello within Cuba, in a spirited, uncompromising and cogent essay, and Miguel de Unamuno, outside it, in a letter in which his religious-existentialist passion is kept in check.[29] Guillén's achievement in *Motivos de son* and *Sóngoro cosongo* is so distinctive that it ought to discourage the secondary critical activity of discovering influences. Nevertheless, Langston Hughes and Federico García Lorca have often been mentioned in this regard. The influence worth mentioning is not strictly literary. It derives from Guillén's obvious admiration throughout those years for the journalistic struggle waged by certain of his contemporary Cubans who were affected by the ideal of harmony that Martí had proposed and who refused to yield to disillusionment or despair. Among these writers, the stellar figure was Gustavo E. Urrutia who, with pencil, paper, and persistence, fought inspiringly against the old divisive issues. He also had a discerning eye for literary talent. Guillén gave enduring expression to, and brought inescapably to national and international notice, the effort in which, in another mode of expression, Urrutia had engaged himself.

WEST INDIES, LTD.

The broadening scope, as far as subject matter is concerned, that was observed in *Sóngoro cosongo* is carried further and presented by an expanded variety of forms in *West Indies, Ltd.* of 1934. The natural progression from *Motivos de son* is continued here: Guillén seems to follow a path of logical consequences premised on the concept of human dignity and advancement. Thus, while poverty is variously represented in this collection – with an emphasis on the destruction it causes in the poem 'Canción de los hombres perdidos' ('Song of the Lost Men'); as an infuriating trap in 'Caminando' ('Walking'); and as victimization and oppression in 'Balada de Simón Caraballo' –

poverty is also presented as a motive for reasoned rebellion in 'Sabás' and 'Nocturno en los muelles' ('Nocturn on the Wharves'). If racial preoccupations are shown in the exposure of a vain and misguided obsession with physical features in the poem 'El abuelo' ('The Grandfather') and in the terror of the loss of black male offspring in the parable contained in the 'Balada del güije,' they are also shown in clear images of projected harmony in 'Balada de los dos abuelos' ('Ballad of the Two Grandfathers') and in concern manifested about class loyalties in a future class struggle. If imperialism is exploitative and for this purpose establishes seemingly permanent strata in a national population in 'Guadalupe W.I.,' it meets with defiance in 'Maracas;' and 'Sensemayá' carries a lesson in how to exterminate it. There are, besides, two poems, 'Palabras en el trópico' ('Words in the Tropics') and 'Calor' ('Heat'), that indicate the newly broadened geographical setting. The title poem combines within it most of the elements of both form and content that are to be found in the other poems, while the poem 'Adivinanzas' ('Riddles') performs in a subtle way the role of summarizing Guillén's chief poetic attitudes.

The geography depicted in the first poem, 'Palabras en el trópico,' is not a simple reflection of the tropics as seen from the vantage point of the speaker who is 'retozando en las aguas con mis antillas desnudas' ('frolicking in the waters with my naked West Indies'). The picture given is produced at minimal, at times confoundingly close, distance, and is conveyed by a speaker whose acquaintance with the tropics is a matter of intimate, lived experience. This intimacy is reflected in the familiar 'tú' used throughout the poem to address the personalized tropics and to describe a wide range of observations and experiences. These are the harsh, hostile tropics as seen by those, represented by the speaker, who labour humbly in it; the pleasures they know within it are those that derive from the natural environment. They are also the tropics with surreal elements that indicate not magical qualities but, on the part of the speaker, long habitation, familiarity, and a degree of adaptation that reaches the point of domination;

> Te debo los días altos,
> en cuya tela azul están pegados
> soles redondos y risueños;
> te debo los labios húmedos,
> la cola de jáguar y la saliva de las culebras;
> te debo el charco donde beben las fieras sedientas;
> te debo, Trópico,
> este entusiasmo niño
> de correr en la pista
> de tu profundo cinturón lleno de rosas amarillas,

riendo sobre las montañas y las nubes
mientras un cielo marítimo
se destroza en interminables olas de estrellas a mis pies.

I owe you the high days,
on whose blue canvas are stuck
round, smiling suns;
I owe you my humid lips,
the jaguar's tail and the snake's spit;
I owe you the puddle where thirsty wild beasts drink;
I owe you, Tropics,
this boyish enthusiasm
for running along the track
of your profound belt full of yellow roses,
laughing atop mountains and clouds,
while a maritime sky
destroys itself in interminable waves of stars at my feet.

In a social sense 'Palabras en el trópico' presents a virgin setting, an open
field for the establishment of whatever community is desired. This beginning
from *tabula rasa* causes the social situations brought to light in the poems
that follow to possess a conspicuous aspect of imposition and corrigibility.
And the dominance of the poetic presence in the first poem makes the
judgments of subsequent voices that are identifiable with this voice appear
to be authoritative.

One of the distinctive traits in this book is the continuation in folkloric
guise of the use of apparent surreal elements, such as those found in the first
poems, 'Balada del güije' and 'Sensemayá.' The latter poem in fact has been
viewed heretofore as being strictly folkloric. Interesting information about
traditional local practices that seem to bear on the poem has been provided by
Angel Augier, who has linked these practices to Guillén's own account of
the circumstances of its composition on the day of the Epiphany, 6 January
1932.[30] But Guillén's statement consists of facts and conjectures about how
he came to write the poem, rather than an interpretation or an indication
of how it should be interpreted. It would appear that beneath its folkloric
veneer is an essential level of meaning that is consonant with other aspects
of Guillén's practice. On a literal plane, and in keeping with its subtitle
'Canto para matar una culebra' ('Chant for Killing a Snake'), the poem explains, with suggestions of ritual, how to kill a snake. But the poem's atmosphere is so charged with emotion, contributed principally by the refrains
of rhythmic *jitanjáfora* used here as they were used in the poem 'Si tu
supiera' to convey heightened feeling, that the poem becomes too imposing,

and the effort excessively serious, for the mere killing of a snake. This excess suggests that the act has a function of greater significance. It seems to be representative of something, the identity of which has to be sought in the images of the poem. In the first place, the very insistence on the snake, with 'la culebra' being used anaphorically with marked regularity throughout the poem, provokes the idea that it comes to mean something else. A technique is being applied here that is similar to the one involved in the production of allegory, a technique that will later reappear in the form of the inordinate attention paid to the malfunctioning of a defective gear wheel in the poem that forms the prologue to Guillén's later book *La rueda dentada*. The technique relies on the fact that an insistently developed image acquires the status of a symbol. The first lines of the stanza following the opening refrain of 'Sensemayá' are:

> La culebra tiene los ojos de vidrio;
> la culebra viene y se enreda en un palo ...

> *The snake has glass eyes;*
> *the snake comes and wraps itself around a stick ...*

The 'ojos de vidrio' emphasized in this stanza recall the 'pupilas de vidrio' that in the 'Balada de los dos abuelos' were used to represent the white grandfather, and suggest here, particularly in view of the following line, a foreign identity that encroaches on and would affix itself to the people's territory. The characteristics of deceptiveness and deviousness are supplied by the images with which the next stanza begins:

> La culebra camina sin patas;
> La culebra se esconde en la yerba ...

> *The snake walks without feet;*
> *the snake hides in the grass ...*

In the following stanza, the danger represented by the snake, its surviveability, and the need to do away with it definitively complete its profile. The anticipation of the snake's death and the attendant celebration occupy the final three stanzas of the poem. The joy of having gained control over it, which the *jitanjáforas* help to convey, reaches its height in the stanza:

> ¡Mayombe-bombe-mayombé!
> Sensemayá, la culebra ...
> ¡Mayombe-bombe-mayombé!

> Sensemayá, no se mueve ...
> ¡Mayombe-bombe-mayombé!
> Sensemayá, la culebra ...
> ¡Mayombe-bombe-mayombé!
> Sensemayá, se murió.[31]

What, then, is this thing that is guilty of spatial intrusion, that is dangerous in its aggressiveness, that is deceptive and stubborn and that evokes hostile emotion?

It seems that the snake in 'Sensemayá' is a symbol of imperialism, and the poem an allegory of the need for, and means of, definitive liberation. The power of music here provides another example of the subtle relation that exists between music and meaning in Guillén's poetry. The novelty and strength of the rhythm seduces the reader to a poem that appears to be attractively folkloric and thence invites him to ponder a serious proposition. In this sense, 'Sensemayá' represents a furthering of the attitude of the maraca 'con un cierto pudor que casi es antimperialista' ('with a certain shyness that is almost anti-imperialist') which was encountered in 'Maracas,' the poem that precedes 'Sensemayá' in *West Indies, Ltd.*

The increased attention paid to imperialism in this book is, given Guillén's earlier manifestations of interest in the subject, a concomitant of the geographical expanse covered in the collection; for the crucial common denominator of the territories that formed the enterprise conveyed by the 'Ltd.' of the title was imperialism. Besides, West Indians from several islands, Haiti and Jamaica in particular, constituted a part of the work force on Cuban sugar estates, so that the worker depicted in the poem 'Caña' of *Sóngoro cosongo* might have evoked comparisons with the situation of workers in those islands. Guillén added to later editions of *West Indies, Ltd.* the poem 'Guadalupe w.i. – Pointe-à-Pitre' which, as Augier informs us, was written in 1938 on that island. This poem bears some superficial resemblance to 'Caña,' particularly in its representative categorizing of a population, but it is in effect the antithesis of that poem in temper. The elements of its structure combine to yield a controlling image of inappropriate conformity and passitivity.

> Los negros, trabajando
> junto al vapor. Los árabes, vendiendo,
> los franceses, paseando y descansando,
> y el sol, ardiendo.
>
> En el puerto se acuesta
> el mar. El aire tuesta
> las palmeras ... Yo grito: ¡Guadalupe!, pero nadie contesta.

Parte el vapor, arando
las aguas impasibles con espumoso estruendo.
Allá quedan los negros trabajando,

los árabes vendiendo,
los franceses paseando y descansando,
y el sol ardiendo ...

The blacks, working
next to the ship. The Arabs, selling,
the French, strolling and resting,
and the sun blazing.

The sea goes to sleep
in the port. The air toasts
the palm trees ... I shout: Guadalupe!, but no one answers.

The ship leaves, plowing
the impassive waters with foamy noise.
There, the blacks go on working,

the Arabs selling,
the French strolling and resting,
and the sun blazing ...

Class and race are aligned and designated in relation to work in the first
stanza, the first preposition 'junto a' recalling its function in 'Caña.' In the
second, nature (which is portrayed as somnolent and stilled) appears to have
the focus of attention. In effect, its central function here is to serve as an
image of social inertia, as a model to which the people conform. This kind
of conformity, it will be remembered, is a type of behaviour alien to that
shown by the speaker in 'Palabras en el trópico,' who displayed nerve and
daring in his dealings with nature. The speaker in this poem evinces an
identity with that speaker. He is an interested, knowing, dismayed outsider
and his intrusive cry, '¡Guadalupe!,' seeking a response informed by at least
a concern for national identity and harmony, goes unanswered. The cry,
'¡Guadalupe!,' is the metonymical representation of a future nation – aware
and unified – that is the present conception and expectation of the speaker.
The word thus exposes two distinct and conflictive stages of time: one lived
by the separate strata of Guadelupian society and another reached by the

progressive consciousness of the speaker. In contrast to what occurs in 'Caña,' the speaker's overt intervention is in the singular and it comes precisely in the middle of the poem. It is in the seventh verse of the thirteen-verse poem and is preceded and followed by seven syllables in that verse. The image of the ship 'arando / las aguas impasibles con espumoso estruendo' is pregnant with suggestions of abuse. The antithetical relation of the vigour contained in the verb 'arando' to the impassiveness of nature, associated, as we have seen, with the local population, points to the ostentatious metropolitan exploitation that determines the internal one. The ship, which had absorbed the labour of the blacks, revelling in its advantageous position in a system of unequal exchange, leaves Guadeloupe, whose inhabitants continue in their divided state. The poem winds down to close with substantial repetition of the first stanza, reflecting the absence of prospects for change. Yet the repeated phrases do not mean at the end of the poem simply what they meant at the beginning. The intervening cry, '¡Guadalupe!,' with its insinuation of conflict in the course of time, now serves to infuse with tense impatience the orderly enumeration of the constituents of a discriminatory, exploitative situation. The conveyance of impatience owes something to the quicker pace at the end than at the beginning of the poem allowed by the use of fewer commas.

A poem of the collection which, like 'Sensemayá,' has a stong folkloric atmosphere, provided this time by its *romance* verse and by its hyperbolic diction, is 'Balada del güije.' The interpretation of it has also been restricted to the folkloric level. The poem, though, contains features that appear to invalidate such a limitation and to suggest an interpretation that goes beyond the literal level. Its images evoke horror – accentuated by the fact that the speaker of the poem is a mother, and the victim of whom she speaks is her little son. It must be of some significance that the archetype of tenderness that this relation normally connotes should be so radically violated here. Further, within the context of *West Indies, Ltd.*, the poem evokes a separateness of the black world that suggests an epoch when harmony could not yet be conceived of as a goal. Also, while the mother tells of the loss of her son to the river, her experience is part of a collective one, since the muddy and deep waters of the river contain black children's heads. And the *güije*,[32] or evil spirit of the river, divides, defaces, dehumanizes, and binds.

> Le abrió en dos tapas el cráneo,
> le apagó los grandes ojos,
> le arrancó los dientes blancos,
> e hizo un nudo con las piernas
> y otro nudo con los brazos.

He opened his head in two,
he extinguished his large eyes,
he pulled out his white teeth,
and made a knot with his legs
and another knot with his arms.

The *güije* thus carried out acts suggestive of some of the effects and practices of slavery.[33] Besides, the mother ends her story by affirming the real
occurrence of what she had narrated. All this opens the way to the poem
being viewed as consisting of oneiric symbolic images that tap the collective
memories of the horrible institution, slavery, through which the forebears
of a large part of the Cuban population passed.

If 'Balada del güije' deals with past time, 'Balada de los dos abuelos,'
which also has its symbolic ghosts, deals with exemplary present time and,
therefore, with desired future time. Metonymy and rhyme are skilfully
employed here to achieve parallel paradigms and linking effects:

Lanza con punta de hueso,
tambor de cuero y madera;
mi abuelo negro.
Gorguera en el cuello ancho,
gris armadura guerrera:
mi abuelo blanco.

Lance with bone point,
drum of leather and wood:
my black grandfather.
Gorget on his broad neck,
gray warring armour:
my white grandfather.

Apart from assonance in *eo* and *ao* functioning in the parallel parts of the
stanza that apply respectively to the black and white grandfather, the firmer
consonantal rhyme *era* is common to and binds the two parts. This feature
of rhyme anticipates the embrace of the two grandfathers that marks the
beginning of the joyful final stanza of the poem and is one of the fine procedures – the larger variety of verse forms that serve an integrative purpose
in the final stanza is another – by which unity and harmony emerge in the
figure of the speaker from the divergent experience and background contributed by the prominent metonymy.

A different quality of future time is suggested in the poem 'Dos niños'
in which poverty, class, and race converge. As in 'Sabás,' which Guillén

dedicated to Langston Hughes and which bears some resemblances to Claude McKay's famous poem 'If We Must Die,' there is an urging here of an end to abject attitudes. Future time in these poems, therefore, embodies the rebellious means by which social change will come; and the underlying hope is that the bonds formed by shared class experiences will endure.

In 'El abuelo' Guillén uses the Alexandrine sonnet for the first time in a published edition. It is used in a way that continues the modernist diversion from the traditional (Juan Boscán and Garcilaso de la Vega) ABBA, ABBA quartets with the tercets venturing only as far as E. Guillén produces here the scheme ABBA, CDDC, EFE, GFG. The text of the poem is:

EL ABUELO

Esta mujer angélica de ojos septentrionales,
que vive atenta al ritmo de su sangre europea,
ignora que en lo hondo de ese ritmo golpea
un negro el parche duro de roncos atabales.

Bajo la línea escueta de su nariz aguda,
la boca, en fino trazo, traza una raya breve,
y no hay cuervo que manche la solitaria nieve
de su carne, que fulge temblorosa y desnuda.

¡Ah, mi señora! Mírate las venas misteriosas;
boga en el agua viva que allá dentro te fluye,
y ve pasando lirios, nelumbios, lotos, rosas;

que ya verás, inquieta, junto a la fresca orilla
la dulce sombra oscura del abuelo que huye,
el que rizó por siempre tu cabeza amarilla.

THE GRANDFATHER

This angelic woman with Northern eyes,
who lives attentive to the rhythm of her European blood,
knows not that in the depths of that rhythm a black man
beats the hard heads of deep drums.

Under the severe line of her sharp nose
her mouth, in a fine stroke, traces a short line,
and no raven besmirches the untrammeled snow
of her flesh, that shines tremulous and bare.

Oh, my lady! Look at your mysterious veins;
go rowing in the live waters that flow inside you,
and see the parade of lilies, nelumbiums, lotuses, roses;

and troubled you will glimpse, next to the fresh bank
the sweet dark shadow of the fleeing grandfather,
the one who curled forever your yellow hair.

In addition to the skilfully exploited opportunity for the effective use of stress afforded by the polyrhythmic mixture of dactylic and trochaic metres, the well-placed caesuras and enjambments, the harmonies emerging from the vocalic patterns and the graceful precision of the end rhyme round out the rich music of this sonnet. This elaborate form is used with the kind of complex effect with which the *son* is used in poems that reveal situations detrimental to human progress. The difference is that whereas the *son* contributes to the creation of pathos by giving contrapuntally cheerful accompaniment to sad happenings, the Alexandrine is so used here that pathos arises from its measured, sober exposure of a ridiculous fixation on racial stock. The dignity of the rhythm mocks so superbly the absurd pride, the foolish pretention, that the use of this mocking form brings to mind other poets, some from other ages, who have used similar procedures: John Dryden and Alexander Pope, for instance, used the heroic couplet in their mock epics and Pablo Neruda used pathos to sobering effect in his 'La United Fruit Co. Inc.' But it would be difficult to find another poet using the procedure with such skill in a form as concentrated as the sonnet form that Guillén uses here.

The intensity of the sonnet is established in the first quartet where pathos is evoked by the revelation that the woman's obsession is founded on ignorance. The distance between speaker and subject is minimal, enabling observation of the subject's external features and the penetration of her thought process, and, further, permitting the description of the subject. The adjective 'angélica,' with its suggestion of unreal purity, is followed by the complementary adjective 'septentrionales,' both of them describing features that are highly prized in the subject's system of values. These values are arrived at through narrow experience, since the subject's preoccupation is with her European ancestry. The last two verses of the quartet contain knowledge, provided by the omniscient speaker, that is outside of and antithetical to her interests. A tenacious form of irony enriches these verses: they indicate that what she determinedly does not want to know is embodied in her being. 'Septentrionales' finds its antonym in 'hondo,' which also indicates the inner as opposed to the superficial, and insinuates the speaker's countervailing system of values. And when cognizance is taken of the auditive aspect of the imagery, it is noticed that the subject, intent on hearing European strains within her, does not hear the rather loud indications of an African presence, indicated metonymically by 'atabales.'

The scrupulous, Parnassian etching of the second quartet in which the features of the woman are presented is evidence of the apt employment of an old style to convey an atavistic attitude. Nearly synonymous words – 'línea,' 'trazo,' 'raya' – and the contiguous paronomasia – 'trazo, trraza' – reflect effectively a fastidious attention to features that are the furthest removed from African ancestry. The hyperbolic character of the metaphor in the last two verses of the quartet maintains their compatibility with the Parnassian style of the stanza.

In the first tercet, the wise begins to address the foolish, as the speaker (proceeding from narrator to direct participant in the drama of the poem) addresses the woman with a tone of condescension indicated by the exclamation '¡Ah, mi señora!' This is accented by the following use of the familiar form of address, thus directing her on a voyage of self-discovery. It is an inner voyage into the past in which the imagery encountered – 'lirios, nelumbios, lotos, rosas' – conforms in the tercet with the best expectations of the 'mujer angélica.' In the final tercet, the contrasting values of the woman and the speaker are in open conflict. The imagery becomes disquieting for the woman while at the same time it is regarded affectionately by the speaker, the adjective 'dulce' reflecting his affective mood. But the black grandfather flees as a mutual embarrassment prevails arising from the unwillingness to acknowledge a parental relation. The image presented in the final verse reveals her full heritage and at the same time reveals the reason for the sharp, narrow focus on eyes, nose, and mouth in the earlier part of the poem.

The imagery of the tercets is reminiscent of 'Balada de los dos abuelos,' but in order to perceive the correct relation between these poems it is essential to appreciate the function of their respective speakers. In 'Balada ...' the speaker, the grandchild, unites the grandfathers with an attitude of frank, joyful *mulatismo*. He stands with full authority, including moral authority, and there is nothing that diminishes the credibility of what he achieves with his two grandfathers. The role of the speaker in 'El abuelo' is a relatively diminished one. The focus is on the woman in her relation to her grandfather. From the perspective of the speaker, this relation is highly unsatisfactory and his disapproval of it is perceivable throughout the poem, both in the form and content of his descriptions in the quartets and in the character of his participation, the tone of his address, and the quality of his descriptions in the tercets. In all this it can be seen that the speaker's attitude to the grandfather in this poem is similar to that of the speaker to the two grandfathers in 'Balada ...,' the implied attitude to *mulatismo*, to harmony within the population being identical in both poems. Underlying the humour that results from the ironic unveiling of the absurdity of the obsession with racial purity is a deep sadness that is the counterpart of the joy shown in 'Balada ...,' a sadness caused by the lamentable state of consciousness represented by this 'Mujer angélica' and by the symbol it represents of continuing national disunity.[34]

One way to approach the long poem 'West Indies, Ltd.' is to relate it to 'Palabras en el trópico.' While the latter poem presented the West Indies in its pristine, natural, geographical state, the former shows it in the turmoil of its social life; and it may be seen as summarizing those elements of *West Indies, Ltd.* that reveal an unhappy choice of the options with which this social life has been filled. The poem carries an urgent call for rectification. The first verse of the poem: '¡West Indies! Nueces de coco, tabaco y aguardiente ...' ('West Indies! Coconuts, tobacco and rum ...') immediately establishes the style and the perspective on the subject that prevails in the rest of the poem. The things that are enumerated in metonymical relationship to the West Indies are plantation products, usually under the control of foreign enterprises. Juxtaposed in subordinate position are the people, self-negating and obliging: 'Este es un oscuro pueblo sonriente' ('This is an obscure and smiling people'). The problematic nature of their posture is evoked by the antithetical, even paradoxical, relation existing between 'oscuro' and 'sonriente.' The ensuring polysyndetic enumeration in verses of irregular length reveals and reflects the chaotic ramifications of the production intimated in the first verse and opens the way for the exploration of the situation of the people in relation to this production.

Many warped forms sprout from the dependency that typifies this relation. There are the mimicked and quite meaningless political designations of liberal and conservative, an absurd social order including a pretended nobility that is treated respectfully by the oppressed, and an abusive tourism that uses hospitality insensitively and that demands servility. A structural pattern observed in many Guillén poems, such as 'Caña,' 'Guadalupe w.i.' and 'El abuelo,' in which the speaker intervenes in the poem in the first person following an accumulation of 'objective' outrages is in evidence here. The pattern provides grounds for the inference that the speaker reaches a point where he can no longer repress the surge of resentment he feels and it is one of the techniques employed in the conveyance of intense and justifiable emotion. After having come near the surface in the lyrical and ironical tone underlying certain earlier exclamations, first-person singular usage begins in the last and the longest stanza of the first of the eight parts into which this poem is divided. It appears in the phrase 'Me río de' ('I laugh at') that serves anaphorically to introduce a polysyndetic listing of elements which, together with those mentioned earlier in the poem, cover almost all aspects of social life. The overt first-person singular is an important factor in raising the tone to satire in this stanza that deals with the idle and false obsession with racial purity and the deplorable relation between the classes, exemplified by people taking seriously absurd claims to aristocracy. Parts four, six, and eight are presented directly by the speaker with the same rhyme scheme used in part one, even in the note that follows the first stanza pointing metaphorically to a future in which the limits of tolerance will be exceeded. The rhyme scheme, variations on *aab cc bddb*, serves to emphasize the random mixtures making up the untidy conglomeration that is *West Indies, Ltd.* A telling variation is the use of internal rhyme to accentuate the words 'yes' and 'inglés' and thus reinforce the idea of subservience required by tourism:

> puertos que hablan un inglés
> que empieza en yes y acaba en yes.
> (Inglés de cicerones en cuatro pies.)

> *ports that speak an English*
> *that begins in yes and ends in yes.*
> *(an English of four-footed tourist guides.)*

Parts four and six reveal, at closer range than in part one, aspects of the reigning social disaster. Hunger (which is potently personified), alcoholism, prostitution, the activities of visiting sailors, illicit drugs are images of wasted human potential in part four and are made conspicuous by the placement of words like 'prostituta,' 'morfina,' and 'heroína' in the positions of greatest stress in their respective lines. In part six various manifestations of imperialism are in evidence. Words in the poem such as 'Chesterfield' and 'Lucky Strike' (U.S. brands of cigarettes) bear, from the point of view of the speaker, the symbolism of imperialist penetration, including linguistic imperialism. From the point of view of the native smokers portrayed here, they are symbols of prestige. The speaker perceives that such false prestige is nevertheless a form of social control, militating against change. Drug trafficking and addiction appear here again as evils to be attacked, and as symptoms of the general malaise. Meanwhile the humble people who carry the promise of change are victimized.

A feature of part six, where the imperialist relations of the United States and Britain with the West Indies are examined, is the use of English not only to denote the companies, products, and places centrally involved but also to describe the general state of affairs. This state is summed up in a quartet in which Guillén reveals yet another way of using English to emphasize a contrast. He creates an antithesis between English, used to denote the superficial, conditioned opinion on the one hand, and the native language, used to describe the harsh reality on the other. He emphasizes this antithesis by placing the key linguistic terms at the ends of the verses. Thus, although he dispenses with rhyme, a semantically determined *abab* scheme is created which is so marked that it supersedes the function of rhyme. The quartet, also containing the climactic usages of the 'Este es' anaphora in the poem, reads as follows:

> Este es el pueblo del all right
> donde todo se encuentra muy mal;
> éste es el pueblo del very well,
> donde nadie está bien.

> *This is the people who say all right*
> *where everything is very bad;*
> *this is the people who say very well,*
> *where nobody is well.*

These people have their direct representative voice in the poem in the person of the *sonero*, Juan el Barbero. His *sones* alternate with and illustrate the parts presented by the principal speaker. They are shorn of any touch of lightness in their negative coverage of a broad range of subjects. Their difference in tone with earlier *sones* may be observed while a comparison is made between different stages of the development of a technical detail noticeable in Guillén's poetry: his presentation of alternatives that both have negative impact. It will be recalled that in the poem entitled 'Hay que tené boluntá' this usage was encountered in the previously translated lines:

> cuando pongo un ojo así
> e que no hay na;
> pero si lo pongo así,
> tampoco hay na.

Although the reality described in that poem is grave, there is a certain comic aspect in its portrayal, in the envisaged gesture of the speaker and the accented final syllables. In 'West Indies, Ltd.' the labourer presents his situation in these terms:

> me matan, si no trabajo,
> y si trabajo, me matan:
> siempre me matan, me matan,
> ¡siempre me matan!

> *they kill me if I don't work,*
> *and if I work, they kill me:*

they always kill me, kill me,
they always kill me!

The chiasmus, which gives the verb 'matan' initial and final positions in the first two verses, and the intensive repetition of 'matan' in the last two verses, together with the relative earnestness provided by the accented penultimate syllables, overwhelm any jocular effect.

After such signs of injustice and impending conflict, the controlling speaker returns to close the poem. In this eighth part of the poem, there is at the outset a return to the kind of primeval setting established in 'Palabras en el trópico' and 'Calor.' Adjectives like 'inocentes' and 'ingenua,' the activity and posture of the black man, the razing of the primitive plantation barracks, all suggest the prospect of a new beginning. Conflictive imagery appears in the last lines of this stanza in the form of American cruisers with a heritage that has links to pirates, such as Sir Francis Drake, who have defiled these waters in earlier times. The image with which the final stanza begins:

Lentamente, de piedra, va una mano
cerrándose en un puño vengativo.

Slowly, a hand, made of stone,
is closing itself into a vengeful fist.

may be considered to be the fulfilment, in definitive fashion, of the demands that the speaker who unifies *West Indies, Ltd.* has been making throughout the book – of the 'negro imitamicos' ('black monkey imitator') of this poem, of Sabás, and of the downtrodden ones of 'Nocturno en los muelles' – that the open, victimized hand be made into a fist. It is this combative attitude that holds the promise of a joyful resolution of the present trauma. The positive images of nature with which the poem ends suggest a new beginning, a harmony that will arise when the natural setting of the West Indies finally accommodates a social system that will be vigilant in its defence of the legitimate interests of the area and when the West Indies, or Las Antillas, will exist free of the company designation, Ltd.

The 'Adivinanzas' are suitably considered last because, notwithstanding their apparent playfulness, they serve as important recapitulations of Guillén's principal poetic subjects and of his approach to poetry. In the first four of these riddles or resolved metaphors, the tenor represents in each case a subject – the black man, hunger, sugar, or alms – that occupies a great deal of Guillén's attention. The vehicle used in the one whose tenor is 'La caña,' for example, compresses into two verses of paradox a great span of history and an insight

into the vulnerability of imperialism such as was revealed in the poem
'Caña.' Crucially important among these riddles is the final one:

> Un hombre que está llorando
> con la risa que aprendió.
> ¿Quién será, quién no será?
>   – Yo.

> *A man who is crying*
> *with the laughter that he learned.*
> *Do you know, or don't you know?*
>   *– I.*

The paradox provides a magnificent image that confirms a central aspect we
have been noticing throughout Guillén's poetry. It is the tension in several
forms that exists between a surface attractiveness or playfulness and an ultimate sadness. It was noticed in the pre-1930 poetry, in 'Gustavo E.,' for
example, in the contrast between the apparently light-hearted use of the *romance* verse and the parodied Quijotesque imagery on the one hand, and the
elusiveness of success in the serious task dealt with on the other. A similar
tension appears in the counterpoint between music and poverty in *Motivos
de son*; and like usage may be found in 'Pregón' of *Sóngoro cosongo*, for
example, where the music and picturesque imagery highlight by contrast
the hunger that forms the core of the poem. In 'El abuelo' of *West Indies,
Ltd.* the poem, formally structured to comically mock a foolish obsession,
has an overall effect of profound sadness. Finally, these 'Adivinanzas' themselves, while being true in a formal sense to their tradition of youthful playfulness, deal with matters that are of the utmost gravity. This tension is the
consequence of a fine interplay between the use of forms whose attractiveness
yields broad accessibility, and a content whose sadness reveals a basic
reality – the absence of harmony in regard to the major constituents of Cuban
national life and, beyond that, of West Indian and other exploited and
warped colonial lives.

CANTOS PARA SOLDADOS Y SONES PARA TURISTAS

The poems published in *West Indies, Ltd.* were written for the most part
between 1932 and 1934. A rising tide of protest, organized chiefly by the
Cuban Communist Party, had led to the fall of the Machado dictatorship in
August 1933, an event regarded by Guillén as one of the most important in
his life.[35] It is possible to discern a more direct combativeness in his post-
Machado poems (like 'West Indies Ltd.') than in those written during

Machado's tenure (such as 'Palabras en el trópico' and 'Sensemayá'). The importance Guillén attributes to the fall of the dictatorship may well spring from his perception of an atmosphere that was more propitious to militant writing and political activity. But Machado's fall was significant in other respects. Several of those young writers whom Guillén had first known in earlier days and to whom he had not felt attracted because they had opted for a literary as opposed to a political participation in the national process, had come to play a role in Machado's downfall and were now showing a firm social commitment. In the ensuing period, in the turmoil of the rapid succession of presidents (some of whom were installed and later removed due partly to the machinations of the young armed forces chief, Fulgencio Batista), several among the young Cuban intelligentsia struggled to have Cuban institutions and political administration function in the national interest. Guillén's period of distance from this group had been fertile and beneficial both for his own development and for promoting the nation's better understanding of itself. The key idea he nurtured during that period, and which distinguished him from most of the rest of the intelligentsia, was that a high priority should be given to the resolution of the question of Cuban racial identity and to the decisive solution of racial problems. By 1934 he had established indelibly this Urrutian position and had combined a desire for harmony in this respect with the pursuit of the national harmony that would result from a victory over imperialism, poverty, and the destructive shallowness of upper class pretentions. By 1935, thanks to Guillén's contribution, it would have been impossible for the circle with which he came to collaborate to have omitted the question of racial discrimination from any manifesto they might have drawn up, as the Grupo Minorista had done in 1927. It was important for Guillén to find a firm commitment to this basic issue not only in the leaders of the revolutionary movement in Cuba, such as Rubén Martínez Villena, but also in a genuinely dedicated core of comrades with whom he could associate. Two main factors determined his scepticism about political associations. The first was his belief that his father had shown inappropriate enthusiasm for politics by giving his life to a cause that was not worthwhile, in a meaningless quarrel between liberals and conservatives. Second, Guillén would have been justified in believing early in his career that his direct predecessor as an outstanding black Cuban poet was Plácido, whose sorry fate was recounted in the first part of this study. When, therefore, in 1935 Guillén began to work with the Communist Party of Cuba, he had already made a strong impression on progressive thinking in the country, and he was satisfied that the Party represented the best channel for the realization of the many-faceted harmony whose absence he had lamented. Guillén's position in the Ministry of the Interior was terminated when Machado fell and he continued to occupy himself in the fields of printing and journalism. He served as editor of the newspaper *Información* and was in charge of printing the journal *El Loco*. In 1935, thanks to the influence of José Luciano Franco, the historian to whom I have referred earlier and who was then head of the Havana City Council's Department of Culture, Guillén was given a position in that department. However, he was fired in the following year due to his increased political activity against the government. The subsequent period, when he and his colleagues built *Mediodía* into one of the leading literary and political journals in Cuba, was among the most fruitful in Guillén's career as an editor and a journalist.

This period of resolute political activity was also a time of incubation for Guillén's next book, *Cantos para soldados y sones para turistas* (*Songs for Soldiers and 'Sones' for Tourists*) (1937). Yet the logical progression generally noticeable in Guillén's work remains evident in the points of contact between this book and *West Indies, Ltd.*, particularly in the title poem of this book which, in turn, was tied to 'Palabras en el trópico,' as I have pointed out earlier in this study. In 'West Indies, Ltd.,' solidarity had been expressed with 'los que ante el máuser exclaman: "¡Hermanos soldados!"' ('those who facing the mauser cry: "Brother soldiers!"'). This is precisely the concept, in its many ramifications, that underlies the *Cantos para soldados* with its dedication: 'To my father, killed by soldiers.' The thirteen poems focus on the soldier, the most lethal agent and victim in a system devised by oppressors of using the oppressed against the oppressed. The aspect of this subject explored in most of the poems is that of the soldier's need to identify correctly his class interests and rectify his sense of loyalty. The soldier is treated without rancour. Guillén explained his attitude in an interview he gave in 1937: 'I address myself to the soldier because he is a potential revolutionary element, provided that he isn't converted, due to his own ignorance, into an instrument of the dominant class; and even in this case, there is no reason to condemn him, because he is only a man with blindfolded eyes: to remove that blindfold from him could be a beautiful artistic responsibility.'[36]

The central way in which the artistic nature of the project is manifested and a sense of comprehensiveness given to it occurs in the means used to convey the variations on the subject of the potential positive contribution of the soldiers. The variety of verse forms – the Alexandrine sonnet, the tercet, the elegy, the *romance*, the *redondilla*, in addition to the *son* (with the enormous flexibility with which Guillén has endowed it) – is crucial in this. It allows the various points of view and tonal effects to be fully realized within the different poems. Thus, a first-person speaker addresses a soldier instructively in entire poems such as 'Soldado, aprende a tirar' ('Soldier, Learn to Shoot') and 'No sé por qué piensas tú' ('I Don't Know Why It Seems to You') and, with the reveille used metonymically, in 'Diana.' In others, the first-person speaker describes a condition that elicits his later address to the soldier involved, as in 'Yanqui con soldado' ('Yankee with a Soldier'), 'Elegía a un sodado vivo' ('Elegy to a Living Soldier'), and 'Canción' ('Song'). At other times, the soldier is the sole speaker, as in 'Soldado así no he de ser' ('I Won't Be That Kind of Soldier') and 'Soldado libre' ('Free Soldier'). The poems 'Soldado muerto' ('Dead Soldier'), 'Fusilamiento' ('Shooting'), 'Riesgo y ventura de dos soldados' ('Risk and Good Fortune of Two Soldiers'), and 'Balada del policía y el soldado' ('Ballad of the Policeman and the Soldier') are dramatic in their presentation and include dialogue among third-person participants. In 'Soldados en Abisinia,' a poem that demonstrates the universality of Guillén's subject, the third person is used throughout to bring to notice the contemporary invasion of Abyssinia ordered by Mussolini and the situation of the soldiers dispatched by the Fascist leader.

Subtle points of appropriateness in the use of specific forms are in evidence, such as the formality of the Alexandrine representing the rigid physical and mental attitude of the soldier who is on unthinking guard duty in the sonnet 'Yanqui con soldado.' So too is the *son* with its lively familiarity aptly employed in poems such as 'Soldado, aprende a tirar' and 'No sé por qué piensas tú,' which depict the speaker's communality of class interests with the soldier. In the first of these poems, the soldier is instructed in the pursuit of his key function – shooting. Profuse rhyme plays an important part in suggesting the inextricable linking of speaker and soldier at the bottom stratum of society, from which position the soldier should take his aim:

> Soldado, aprende a tirar:
> tú no me vayas a herir,
> que hay mucho que caminar.
> ¡Desde abajo has de tirar,
> si no me quieres herir!
>
> Abajo estoy yo contigo,
> soldado amigo.
> Abajo, codo con codo,
> sobre el lodo.

> *Soldier, learn to shoot:*
> *You shouldn't want to wound me,*
> *for we have a long way to go.*
> *You will have to shoot upward*
> *if you don't want to wound me!*

I am at the bottom with you,
soldier, my friend.
At the bottom, elbow to elbow,
in the mud.

   The poem in which this linking is most elaborately explored is 'No sé
por qué piensas tú.' The usually alternating (*abab*) and sometimes enclosing
(*abba*) monorhyme, with all but three verses in the poem ending in 'yo' or
'tú,' in the context 'yo y tú,' musically reveals and cements the notion of
common identity. The notion is rivetted onto the reader's or listener's
perception by the fact that the monosyllabic 'tú' and 'yo' are stressed at the
ends of the verses (*versos agudos*) where they appear:

NO SÉ POR QUÉ PIENSAS TÚ

No sé por qué piensas tú,
soldado, que te odio yo,
si somos la misma cosa
yo,
tú.

Tú eres pobre, lo soy yo;
soy de abajo, lo eres tú;
¿de donde has sacado tú,
soldado, que te odio yo?

Me duele que a veces tú
te olvidas de quien soy yo;
caramba, si yo soy tú,
lo mismo que tú eres yo.

Pero no por eso yo
he de malquererte, tú;
si somos la misma cosa,
yo,
tú,
no sé por qué piensas tú,
soldado, que te odio yo.

Ya nos veremos yo y tú,
juntos en la misma calle,

hombro con hombro, tú y yo,
sin odios ni yo ni tú,
pero sabiendo tú y yo,
a donde vamos yo y tú ...
¡No sé por qué piensas tú,
soldado, que te odio yo!

I DON'T KNOW WHY IT SEEMS TO YOU

I don't know why it seems to you,
soldier, that I hate you,
since we are the same thing
I,
you.

You are poor, so am I;
I am kept down, so are you;
how has it occurred to you,
soldier, that I hate you?

It hurts me that sometimes you
forget who I am;
caramba, since I am you,
the same as you are me.

But not because of that I
am going to dislike you;
since we are the same thing,
you,
me,
I don't know why it seems to you,
soldier, that I hate you.

We will soon see each other, you and I
together in the same street,
shoulder to shoulder, you and I,
free of hatred I and you,
but knowing you and I,
where we are going I and you ...
I don't know why it seems to you,
soldier, that I hate you!

Here again there is a speaker who is aware of the fact that his political and social consciousness is more developed than that of the public he addresses. The soldier is inattentive to his true condition, to those features of his socio-economic life that place him squarely with the people. He is unaware, too, that the hostility he anticipates and reflects comes not from his real social self but from the role he plays in the superstructure of a system whose base is unjust. The speaker's understanding of the present enables him to foresee in the last stanza the kind of change in the base that would allow for a new relationship between soldier and people.[37]

In January 1952, during a long journey on the Trans-Siberian Railway that formed part of a longer trip he took from Moscow to Peking, Guillén wrote the extended poem entitled 'El soldado Miguel Paz y el sargento José Inés.' Written in décimas, and marking only the second time that Guillén had used what is probably the most frequently used verse form in Cuba in his serious compositions, the fifty-one ten-verse stanzas present the developing consciousness of two soldiers. They both speak in the first person and their attitudes and opinions are shaped by their honest reflections on their life histories. The principal external event, to which they react dissentingly, is the Korean War and the idea that they should participate in it. They are both concerned about conditions as they are and speculate on how they might be. They are thus at once preoccupied with the present and the future. Hence Miguel Paz, forced by poverty to join the army, declares:

> Nunca en verdad me ha gustado
> en mi país el cuartel,
> porque el soldado es en él
> instrumento ciego y mudo
> de un generalote rudo
> que al rico y no al pobre es fiel.

> *In truth I have never liked*
> *the barracks in my country,*
> *because in it the soldier is*
> *the blind and dumb instrument*
> *of a crude general*
> *who is loyal to the rich rather than to the poor.*

He looks forward to an alternative society in which the soldier enjoys real admiration:

> En los pueblos que han vencido
> a su cruel explotador,

de soldado es la mejor
manera de andar vestido.

Among those peoples who have conquered
their cruel exploiter,
the best way to go dressed
is as a soldier.

The sergeant José Inés, the only congenial spirit encountered by Miguel in
the camp, displays his experience (wider than Miguel's) by citing a broad
range of present ills – racial discrimination, poverty, imperialist exploitation, Truman's policies in Korea. All this provokes in him a concept of the
desired future similar to that found in the final stanza of 'West Indies,
Ltd.' His metaphor conveys the idea that the future is fashioned by man:

El futuro es una puerta
por la cual sólo se cabe
si el que quiere abrirla sabe
encontrar la cerradura
y en ésta con mano dura
a tiempo mete la llave.

The future is a door
through which one only goes
if wishing to open it one knows
where to find the lock
and in it with firm hand
in good time place the key.

The temperament and sensitivity needed to fashion the desired future are
displayed by the *sonero* José Ramón Cantaliso in the *Sones para turistas*.
After being introduced in a *son* by the poet as possessing 'Duro espinazo
insumiso' ('Hard unsubmissive backbone') and as being observant of matters of inequality and suffering, he contributes three *sones*. The guitar-heart
parallel established in the introduction predisposes the listener to hear his
songs as truth and his views receive corroborative support from the interventions of the sufferers of whom he sings. The *sonero*'s principal topics, the
absence of basic human needs – employment, food, housing and health care,
come steeped in irony, the harshness of which may be appreciated at this
stage in Guillén's poetry if we recall, for purposes of comparison, an earlier
usage. In the poem 'Búcate plata' of *Motivos de son*, the speaker contrasted
her poverty with the luxuries that were to be found in other parts of the

society. In that case, there was a simple irony in the contradiction between her poverty and that wealth. Here Cantaliso gives the cause of the illness of one of the poverty-stricken characters he presents:

> La muy idiota pasaba el día
> sin un bocado.
> ¡Qué tontería!
> ¡Tanta comida que se ha botado!

> *The silly woman would go without eating*
> *for a whole day.*
> *What foolishness!*
> *With all the food that has been thrown out!*

In addition to the ironical tone found in the earlier poem, there is a further dimension of irony in the presentation of hunger with phrases like 'La muy idiota' and the use of exclamations that do not mean what they readily seem to mean, thus compelling – by their extravagant inappropriateness – serious reflection on the real causes of hunger and disease. This dimension of irony is also apt when José Ramón's immediate audience is considered – for the ironical explanation he gives might well represent the genuine view of the tourists, whose contented affluence is unwilling to be disturbed by any contemplation of the real causes of the existing misery. The reader's awareness that the immediate audience is made up of tourists who are typically self-centred seekers of gratification intensifies the tension of these *sones* 'que no se pueden bailar' ('that cannot be danced'). Notwithstanding their powerful musicality, they have this non-danceability in common with Guillén's *sones* in general, resembling particularly those of Juan el Barbero of 'West Indies, Ltd.' in their use of an identified speaker. In the last of these *Sones para turistas* we find yet another variation in Guillén's presentation of alternative possibilities that offer no real solution within the existing system, but point rather to an inevitable unfortunate outcome. Thus to the person who cannot pay the rent:

> Si el dueño dice: 'Lo siento,'
> te tienes que mudar;
> pero si no dice nada,
> te tienes que mudar.

> *If the landlord says 'I'm sorry,'*
> *you've got to move;*
> *but if he doesn't say anything,*
> *you've got to move.*

The strong rhythmic trochaic stress of the refrain underlines masterfully the idea of compulsion inherent in the refrain.

Cantos para soldados y sones para turistas has its roots in *West Indies, Ltd.* and, thanks to Guillén's dominance of poetical forms, it reaches a heightened level of maturity. It grows, first by exposing in its rich variety of facets, the tense, unresolved situation of the soldier. Second, in confronting the tourist with the revolutionary *sonero*, it reveals the antithetical situation existing between those who have in excessive abundance and those in need of what is basic for subsistence. The two subjects have their immediate application to pre-revolutionary Cuba, but their universal implications are clear.

ESPAÑA: POEMA EN CUATRO ANGUSTIAS Y UNA ESPERANZA

Cantos para soldados y sones para turistas was published in Mexico in 1937 on Guillén's first trip outside Cuba. He had been invited by the 'Liga de Escritores y Artistas Revolucionarios de México' to attend its conference in January of that year. The Fascist rebellion led by Francisco Franco against Spain's republican government by then had been in progress for six months and was occupying the attention of people interested in politics, society and essential human dignity. While a poet like T.S. Eliot was proclaiming his neutrality, and others such as Neruda and Aragon were jolted into an openly social approach to poetry, the circles in which Guillén (and Marinello, who had been in exile in Mexico) moved were prepared by their firmly established political views to respond to the Spanish Civil War. *Mediodía*, edited by Guillén, was converted into a news magazine and much of its space was devoted to the war. Guillén's prompt and lasting response to the conflict was the production of his poem *España*: *Poema en cuatro angustias y una esperanza* (*Spain*: *Poem in Four Anguishes and a Hope*) in May 1937. In June he was invited along with Marinello to be a delegate to the Segundo Congreso Internacional de Escritores para la Defensa de la Cultura in Valencia, Barcelona, and Madrid. The Cubans, joined by the Mexican delegates Octavio Paz and José Mancisidor, travelled to Montreal by train and thence by boat and rail to Barcelona. Also participating in the congress would be other prominent Spanish-American poets such as Pablo Neruda and César Vallejo. Meanwhile many Cubans, mainly from the Cuban Communist Party, had joined together on the battlefields of Spain with volunteers from several other countries, in an effort to fend off the Fascist menace.

The fact that Guillén wrote his Spanish Civil War poems before arriving in Spain is indicative of the ideological, rational basis of his inspiration. Rather than a lyrical speaker seeing the disaster from the point of view of one who has suffered a change in his individual situation, the conception evident in the poem is historical in a broad, profound, and even serene sense. This is what

basically distinguishes Guillén's poem from the civil war poems of his other
great Spanish American contemporaries: Neruda's *España en el corazón* and
Vallejo's *España, aparta de mí este cáliz*. Neruda's collection of poems bears
the mark of a speaker to whom Fascist activity is a jolting revelation, and
Vallejo's response to the horror is related to his metaphysical view of un-
ending human suffering. Guillén, on the other hand, in order to apprehend
the full historical significance, needs to make no major adjustment from, for
example, the 'Soldados en Abisinia' of his previous book *Cantos para soldados y sones para turistas*, to *España* ...

The Spanish people and the Spanish-speaking peoples in their original
contacts are considered at the beginning of the poem. The tensions inherent
in these origins are not overlooked. There is here no selective viewing of
history such as is observable in Darío's 'A Roosevelt,' where the exploitative colonial phase of the Spanish presence in America is avoided. Guillén
instead applies class criteria to the conquest, distinguishing between Cortés
and Pizarro on the one hand and the serving soldiers on the other, and embraces the latter in their descendants who are:

> aquí al fin con nosotros,
> lejanos milicianos,
> ardientes, cercanísimos hermanos.

> *Here at last with us,*
> *distant militiamen,*
> *ardent, very close brothers.*

Their old armour comes to serve the present defenders of Spain whose horri-
fying beleaguerment by Fascist attackers is presented in an intense imagery of
desolation in which anaphora plays an important part. This intensity, assisted by the same anaphora, continues to the end of the stanza where, in the final
lines, the imagery comes to represent defiance. The resulting juxtaposition
of horror and defiance is an exceptional poetic achievement. The nature of
the relation of past to present established in the 'Angustia primera' serves as
the foundation for another kind of relation, that of blood, featured in the
'Angustia segunda' through the emphasis on 'raíz' ('root'). The first-person
singular used here is readily blended into a common Hispanic identity;

> Yo la siento,
> la raíz de mi árbol,
> de tu árbol,
> de todos nuestros árboles.

I feel it,
the root of my tree,
of your tree,
of all our trees.

In the third 'Angustia' the authentic Cuban identity, African and Spanish, makes a solemn declaration of solidarity with Spain. The 'Angustia cuarta' is dedicated to, and marked by usages – symbols and verse forms – that recall Federico García Lorca. Hence the *romance*, the *redondilla*, the tercet, the gypsy, the lily, Granada, the olive, the carnation are featured; and the image 'ambiguous limoneros' ('ambiguous lemon trees') serves as a particularly fertile allusion to the imagery of the Andalusian poet whose life was snuffed out during the first weeks of the war. All these usages combine to suggest a delicate sensitivity which, though crushed by 'el fascismo y su bota,' endures in its spirit.

The final section of the poem, 'La voz esperanzada,' is a pledge to a better future, and its stanzas as well as the section in its totality are structured to suggest a movement from setbacks to victory. The first stanza, for example, begins with images of Spain's destruction, the body of a mother set on fire by matricidal bullets. A purer rebirth is envisaged in the images at the end of this stanza. The second stanza, beginning with an image of lifelessness followed by a resurgence of life, also introduces another subject, the speaker, in the same pattern of progressing from a low to a high point. The first stage of the self-portrait reads:

Yo,
hijo de América,
hijo de ti y de Africa,
esclavo ayer de mayorales blancos dueños de látigos coléricos;
hoy esclavo de rojos yanquis azucareros y voraces;
yo chapoteando en la oscura sangre en que se mojan mis Antillas;
ahogado en el humo agriverde de los cañaverales;
sepultado en el fango de todas las cárceles;
cercado día y noche por insaciables bayonetas;
perdido en las florestas ululantes de las islas crucificadas en la cruz del
     Trópico;
Yo, hijo de América,
corro hacia ti, muero por ti.

I,
a son of America,
a son of Spain and of Africa,

a slave yesterday of white overseers and their choleric whips;
today a slave of red, sugary, voracious Yankees;
I splashing about in the dark blood in which my West Indies are soaked;
drowned in the bittergreen smoke of the canefields;
buried in the mire of all the prisons;
encircled day and night by insatiable bayonets;
lost in the howling woodlands of the islands crucified on the cross of
*   the Tropics;*
I, a son of America,
run to you, I die for you.

It leads to the projection of a new life with which this part ends:

otra vida sencilla y ancha,
limpia, sencilla y ancha,
alta, limpia, sencilla y ancha,
sonora de nuestra voz inevitable.

another life, simple and broad,
clean, simple and broad,
high, clean, simple and broad,
resounding with our every present voice.

Further comments need to be made on these passages. The first has to do
with the nature of the 'I' used here by Guillén. As is characteristic of his
practice, the 'I' is not limited to an individual existence; it is not singularly
lyrical but collectively representative. It is an image of historical Cuban
and West Indian experience; one can notice in the lines connecting the two
quoted passages imagery reminiscent of the representative 'I' of 'Palabras en
el trópico.' The second observation concerns the composition of the first
passage. Its power is due in no small part to the fact that it consists of four sets
of parallelly constructed verses. The first of these parallel constructions is
bound by 'hijo de,' establishing maternity; the second bound by 'esclavo de,'
is followed by imagery indicating a reaction of livid abhorrence; the third is
initiated by a participle, one of a series of five of which the speaker is the
subject, followed by a preposition that introduces metonymic aspects of
anti-human conditions, continuing through time, in which the speaker is
submerged. This series is capped by the *paronomasia* of archetypal suffering, 'crucificadas en la cruz,' applied to the West Indian islands. Following
this climactic, long verse, accentuated by the repetition of 'Yo, hijo de
América' (a statement now charged with meaning), comes the final, interior,
parallel construction briefly expressing determined solidarity reflected by

the prominent, initial, position of the verbs 'corro' and 'muero.' The third comment concerns, once more, Guillén's concept of simplicity. The context in which the adjective 'sencilla' appears in the second of the above passages is particularly enlightening, since the adjectives with which it is used compatibly, particularly 'alta' and 'ancha,' clearly enable 'sencilla' to embrace the connotation of unlimited development, thus confirming the view that Guillén's concept of simplicity is a progressive one.

The next stanza, too, begins with a glimpse of an unfavourable element, 'brazos conquistadores / ayer' ('conquering arms of yesterday'). In this later stage of the poem, however, negative elements yield quickly to positive ones and to an insistence on unity. These verses are structured so as to stress the active character of this unity. The anaphoric 'para' is later enlarged to form the phrase 'para pasear en alto' and rises to the exclamatory tone in the final line of the series;

¡para pasear en alto la llama niveladora y segadora de la Revolución!

to carry aloft the levelling and cleansing flame of the Revolution!

This tone prevails for the rest of the stanza. The subsequent eruption into a choral song continues the urging to battle in unity with the ultimate goal of a larger unity. In this image of telescopic effect, unity marching towards unity, lies the meaning of the following image of the soldier's boots announcing to the trembling woods: 'Es que el futuro pasa' ('The future is passing'). All this constitutes an elegant demonstration of how a poet deals at the same time with the present and the future, something that as a theoretical proposition seemed impossible to Peter Demetz, as we saw in the first part of this study. The basis on which this and the whole effectiveness of the poem depends is the firm historical core that exists in the poem.

Guillén's civil war poem, then, seems to develop naturally from his previous work, particularly from *West Indies, Ltd.* and *Cantos para soldados ...* The emphasis on unity found in those books and in this poem is reflected in the articles Guillén wrote for *Mediodía* during his stay in Spain. In these articles, he was constantly concerned that the anti-Fascist forces should work together and he was particularly critical of what he saw to be the divisive activity of the Trotskyists. The coincidence of his journalistic and poetic interests is in keeping with what was said earlier of the rational character of his inspiration; but his poetic mastery provides an expressiveness that invests his work in the latter medium with lasting attractiveness and renewable relevance. For example, the speaker in *España* ..., an authentic Cuban, a son of Spain and of Africa who in the situation of the poem is so eloquent about the need to defend Spain in its hour of danger, makes at the same time by inference an eloquent case for the defence of Africa in its hour of danger. This latent meaning of the poem has been uncovered by recent historical events such as Cuba's response to the South African regime's aggression against Angola, and has been reasserted in the bonds of the heart that are shown to bind Cuba and Angola in Guillén's poem 'Son de Angola' from his recent book, *Por el mar de las Antillas anda un barco de papel* (1977).

EL SON ENTERO

Guillén returned to Cuba in June 1938. He had changed boats in Guadeloupe where he wrote his poem entitled 'Guadalupe w.i.' which I have examined earlier. We learn from Augier[38] that he was in such financial straits that it took him a week to muster the means for the journey from Santiago de Cuba, where the boat had docked, to his mother's house in Camagüey. He had formally become a member of the Communist Party of Cuba in Valencia in 1937, and on his return to Cuba the Party had set up its daily newspaper *Hoy*. He worked in several editorial capacities with the paper and contributed articles and poems to its pages. In the general elections that Batista had permitted and won in 1940, Guillén ran as a candidate for the position of mayor of his native Camagüey and in addition campaigned with other candidates of his party, particularly Jesús Menéndez, the sugar workers' union leader. A feature of the Menéndez campaign was the reading of Guillén's poetry to workers in various parts of Cuba. In 1942, Guillén visited Haiti at the invitation of Jacques Roumain, and in November 1945, he visited Venezuela at the invitation of Miguel Otero Silva. This was to be the start of a prolonged tour of Latin America during which Guillén visited Colombia, Peru, Chile, Argentina, Uruguay, and Brazil, giving lectures and poetry readings in all these countries. He returned to Cuba in February 1948. *El son entero: suma poética 1929–1946* (*The Complete 'Son' ...*) was published in Buenos Aires during Guillén's stay there in February 1947. The book was made up of selections from his previously published poetry in addition to poems he had been writing since the early 1940s, some of which had appeared in *Sóngoro cosongo y otros poemas* of 1942. Several of those contained in the collection were written during Guillén's travels, expecially in Venezuela and Colombia. Thus the title *El son entero*, which has come to be applied to all these new poems, was intended originally to apply to a broader span of his work. Nevertheless, the twenty-six new poems, particularly in the use of the *son* in them, do show many points of contact with his previous work, and they touch on a wide range of subjects.

The initial poem, 'Guitarra,' an *arte poética*, reveals a view of poetry and some techniques that are consistent with his earlier work. The guitar as an instrument with which the people are familiar serves as a symbol of popular poetry; but this popularity involves serious responsibility. The guitar is presented in the early morning hours, the conventional time of clear-headed alertness and is modified by the adjective 'firme,' indicating an attitude of ready combativeness on behalf of the authentic interests of the people. It eschews, therefore, some of the accustomed haunts of the guitar, especially those associated with the cabaret and with impaired levels of perception. Here again, as in 'West Indies, Ltd.,' it is indicated that a lucid, sober, developmental viewing of society is one effected without 'opio, ni mariguana, ni cocaína.' The stanza:

> ¡Venga la guitara vieja,
> nueva otra vez al castigo
> con que la espera el amigo
> que no la deja!

> *Let the old guitar come*
> *anew to the punishment*
> *with which the friend who doesn't leave it*
> *awaits it!*

is of particular interest. The 'vieja'–'nueva,' 'castigo'–'amigo' paradoxes in it, both indicating a constant willingness to serve, relate stylistically to the main character of a kind of poetry that has the effect of producing the 'risa' (laughter) and 'llanto' (weeping) that are later referred to in the poem. The *redondilla* – with the final line of each stanza reduced to five syllables – gives way to the more strongly accentuated rhythm of the *son*:

> El son del querer maduro,
> tu son entero;
> el del abierto futuro,
> tu son entero;
> el del pie por sobre el muro,
> tu son entero ...

> *The* son *of the mature desire,*
> *your complete* son;
> *that of the open future,*
> *your complete* son;
> *that of one foot over the wall,*
> *your complete* son ...

It is quite evident that the *son* is associated here with central national issues, with serious aspirations, a democratic future, and an escape from the social and political constraints that have distorted national life. Here the conjuncture of playful popular music and sober social message that we have seen to be characteristic of Guillén's use of the *son* is again displayed.

The total effect of suggesting a contradiction that is to be corrected is conveyed by diverse procedures in the poem 'Mi patria es dulce por fuera ...' ('My Country is Sweet on the Outside ...'). An explicit form of presenting contradiction appears in the first verses of the poem where the title is continued:

> Mi patria es dulce por fuera,
> y muy amarga por dentro.

> *My country is sweet on the outside,*
> *and very bitter on the inside.*

This sharp antithesis prepares the way for the later developed contrast between the superficial natural attractiveness and the lived experience of oppressive social conditions. Another contradiction lies within the social realm itself, between the cheerful disposition of the people and the brutality of the economic base. This contradiction is at the core of the poet's *Weltanschauung* and determines substantially the form of his poetry. A clear example of the formal reflection of this world view comes in the following stanza:

> Hoy yanqui, ayer española,
> sí señor,
> la tierra que nos tocó,
> siempre el pobre la encontró
> si hoy yanqui, ayer española,
> ¡cómo no!
> ¡Qué sola la tierra sola
> la tierra que nos tocó!

> *Today Yankee, yesterday Spanish,*
> *yes, sir,*
> *the land that belongs to us,*
> *poor people have always found it*
> *today Yankee, yesterday Spanish,*
> *of course!*

> *How lonely the land lonely,*
> *the land that belongs to us!*

The lament over the long imperialist hold on Cuba comes interspersed with
the refrains 'sí, señor' and '¡cómo no!' – refrains that are commonly heard
in the popular musical compositions of *soneros* like Miguel Matamoros in his
'El que siembra su maíz,' for example. The use of such devices widens the
appeal of the poetry; and at the same time the reader who is attracted by such
familiar forms is forced to ponder the serious content with which they are
associated. The final contribution is a dramatic one between the speaker and
the American sailor. The speaker, characterized in the poem as concerned
about Cuba's identity and sensitive to the suffering inherent in its colonial and
neo-colonial condition, has his antagonist in the American, here characterized as a physically aggressive symbol of the intrusive, oppressive system.
This contradiction is resolved with the triumph, in the intense last stanza of
the *son*, of the speaker who exemplifies 'La mano que no se afloja' ('the firm
hand'), dealt with in the previous stanza. The poem is impressive for the
way in which it presents forms of contradiction and their resolution. But the
resolution here is exemplary only. It comes from one alert consciousness
and is not general. Accordingly, in the subsequent poems there are many
examples of further contradictions. The 'risa'/'llanto' opposition, for example,
is continued in 'Cuando yo vine a este mundo' ('When I Came into This
World'); and contradictions involving slavery in 'Sudor y látigo' ('Sweat and
Whip') and Elegía'; others involving poverty appear in '¡Ay, señora, mi
vecina! ... / ('Oh, Lady, My Neighbour! ...), set in Cuba, 'Barlovento,' with its
charming five-syllable tercets set in Venezuela, and 'Una canción en el
Magdalena' ('A Song on the Magdalena') set in Colombia. Set in Venezuela,
too, is the contradiction involving British and American imperialism treated
in 'Son venezolano.'

On the other hand, there are poems in which, as in earlier books, a solution
to racial divisions is projected. This is done in 'Un son para niños antillanos' ('A *Son* for West Indian Children'). But the image still remains of
a West Indian population adrift without a guide in a poem in which the
prominent elements of fantasy are matched by a delicate, unusual *romance*
verse form, the fourth verse of each stanza being a shortened, five-syllable
one with final stress. The other poem in which harmony is projected is the well
known 'Son número 6' ('*Son* number 6'). A comparison of this poem with
'Un son para niños antillanos' can provide an indication of the enormous
versatility of the *son*. In 'Son número 6,' fantasy and delicacy give way to
a vigorous message of integration that is served by a superb array of integrative techniques. The first person, used in only one stanza of 'Un son para

niños ...,' is ubiquitous in this poem, exercising a firm, unifying command of
the poem. To this basic support are added other binding features, many of
them appearing in the first lines of the poem:

> Yoruba soy, lloro en yoruba
> lucumí.
> Como soy un yoruba en Cuba,
> quiero que hasta Cuba suba mi llanto yoruba,
> que suba el alegre llanto yoruba
> que sale de mí.
>
> Yoruba soy,
> cantando voy,
> llorando estoy,
> y cuando no soy yoruba,
> soy congo, mandinga, carabalí.

> *I am a Yoruba, I weep in Yoruba*
> *Lucumi.*
> *Since I am a Yoruba from Cuba,*
> *I want my Yoruba weeping to go out to Cuba,*
> *my happy Yoruba weeping that comes from me*
> *to go out.*
>
> *I am a Yoruba,*
> *I go singing,*
> *as I weep,*
> *and when I am not a Yoruba,*
> *I am a Congo, Mandinga, or Carabali.*

Binding internal rhyme is evident in the first line, since 'Yor,' 'llor,' and
'yor' are pronounced identically in most forms of spoken Spanish. The
phenomenon is repeated within the third line with 'yoruba' and 'Cuba' and
again in the fourth ('Cuba,' 'suba') where it is continued by the end rhyme
'yoruba.' Besides, in this fourth line there are two sets of reinforcing alliteration, 'quiero que' and '*ll*anto yoruba.' 'Suba' appears with 'yoruba' again
in the fifth line so that in five lines of poetry the 'uba' ending occurs nine times.
The other rhyme used in the stanza is strengthened by stress, 'lucumí,' 'mí.'
Besides, oxymoron, the figure that most desperately seeks to resolve
contradictions, is employed in the fifth line. The strongly centripetal nature
of the poem is affirmed by the following monorhyme as well as by a special
trait shown here in the speaker, that is, his inclusiveness. He first identifies

himself as a Cuban with African ancestry, as a Yoruba originally from the Lucimí region. But now he indicates that at times he is also a Congo, a Mandinga originally from West Africa north of the equator, or a Carabalí, originally from the Calabar area of Nigeria. This readiness to dissolve himself into other identities represents a large measure of his suitability for conveying this 'alegre llanto,' this crying in pursuit of the happy end to racial disharmony in Cuba. The following stanza is presented as a riddle whose solution, not provided, is the unified, mulatto identity of the Cuban people. It demonstrates the aptness of the riddle as a device in poetry that bears an important social message. The riddle invites the reader to contribute to the message itself by providing the correct solution. The poem continues with a variety of rhythmical patterns and with a variety of further devices, such as repetition and extended chiasmus, that demonstrate the substitutability of Santa María and San Berenito, the African equivalent. In the final stanza the message of unity is again assisted by monorhyme. The rhyme employed in the final seven lines is particularly ingenious. In the first of these lines is the ten-syllable line ending with the three-syllable word 'separe.' The next five five-syllable lines end with the same word 'pare' and the final, ten-syllable line also ends with a word that counts for three syllables, 'parar.' Thus, in the first place, rhyme is a part of a symmetry of syllabic pattern; and second, the words that participate in the rhyme are very closely interrelated. In fact, they constitute *paronomasia*. By such devices does Guillén harmonize form and content to convey a message of harmony. Allusions to Africa are also made with unifying effect in the poem 'Una canción a Stalin' ('A Song to Stalin') (1942) in which the Lucumí deities Changó and Ochún are invoked to protect Stalin, presented here as the anti-Hitlerian leader of free men everywhere.

The dramatic characteristics that we have been observing throughout Guillén's work are developed into full-fledged theatre in the work 'Poema con niños' ('Poem with Children'). In the tradition of the morality play, it is an effort against racism. Its characters are representative types of different races – a white mother, her twelve-year-old son, and his three playmates who are black, Chinese, and Jewish. Reviving a specific interest Guillén had shown in the young in the poem 'Dos niños' of *West Indies, Ltd.*, the work is structured to move from representing spontaneous co-operation to showing explosive divisiveness to providing a final basis for informed co-operation. The enlightening role is played by the mother who, in order to bring the play to its happy dénouement, begins as the stage directions indicate, 'autoritariamente.' Thus her intervention because of her correct social views makes possible the suggestive pattern of chaos–authority–general enlightenment.

A lyrical tone that is new to Guillén's published collections appears in *El son entero*, mainly in relation to three subjects: nature, love, and death. As has been shown earlier, all three topics were treated in several of Guillén's pre-*Motivos de son* works. He does not now simply return to that stage of his poetry. The topics are treated within the context of his mature social preoccupations and are firmly related to the other topics treated in *El son entero*.

The poems that may be said to deal lyrically with nature are 'Ebano real' ('Royal Ebony'), 'Acana' ('Acana Tree'), and 'Palma sola' ('Lonely Palm Tree'). The reader is best guided to them by an attitude to nature in relation to man that Guillén had indicated in his previous book, *España ...* In the closing lines of that poem the image was presented of the woods trembling in the face of the soldiers marching to create a better future. The implication there of nature as being subordinate to man, particularly to man in his progressive mode of behaviour, applies to these poems. In them, objects of nature, trees in all three cases, are pondered from a perspective in which man's needs are pre-eminent. Thus in 'Ebano real,' the friendly relation between the speaker and the tree and his admiration for it have a practical goal – the use of its lumber for improving the conditions of his life. This goal can be realized only with the felling and death of the tree. A poignancy results in the poem from the admiration of the tree and the mutual friendliness between it and the speaker on the one hand, and man's overriding need to exploit it on the other. One of the ways in which the subordinacy of the tree is shown is by the unchanging response formed by its speech, while underlying all the man's plans is his confidence in his power to transform basic material to his various purposes. The refrain, comprised of *jitanjáforas*, 'Arará cuévano/arará sabalú' indicates the link between Africa and Cuba, a link symbolized by the ebony tree itself.

In 'Acana' the relation between man and nature is based, too, on the latter's potential to serve the former: as shelter, to assist mobility, and ultimately in death. The implications of this last usage are the most developed in the poem. Instead of the individual tree, we have here the abundant forest with tree upon tree shrouded in and contributing to darkness. That the trees portend sadness, or rather, are viewed from the perspective of a sad existence, is indicated by the emotive 'ay' preceding the speaker's repeated naming of them. The two verses indicating their location in darkness are repeated in the stanza where the final use of the tree is given:

> Allá dentro, en el monte,
> donde la luz acaba,
> tabla de mi sarcófago,
> allá en el monte adentro ...

> *Over there, in the woods,*
> *where the light ends,*

> *board for my coffin,*
> *over there in the woods ...*

The effect of this is to cause the verse 'donde la luz acaba,' because of its juxtaposition with 'tabla de mi sarcófago,' to serve at the same time as a metaphor for the death of the speaker. Two darknesses are subtly combined to suggest nature's function of serving man.

In the poem 'Palma sola,' the emphasis given to the adjective 'sola' produces an effect of the kind of alienation that was seen in the verses '¡Qué sola la tierra sola/la tierra que nos tocó!' from 'Mi patria es dulce ...' remarked on earlier. This view is consistent with the first line of the later poem, 'Elegía cubana' ('Cuban Elegy'), 'Cuba, palmar vendido' ('Cuba, sold-out palm grove'). Given the established associative tendency between man and nature, the abnormal solitude of the palm tree that exists apart from and without any point of contact with the speaker forms an image of discontent. It suggests the unfulfilled possibility of an interaction between the speaker and the traditionally representative Cuban tree. The distance between the speaker and the object that he desires to see integrated into a truly Cuban life is also evident in the poem 'Turiguanó.' Because the distance from which the islet, situated off the Camagüey coast, is viewed makes only its natural features prominent, 'Turiguanó' may be considered to be one of the nature poems in *El son entero*. That is to say, it is one of those poems in which the interrelation of man with nature is sought that is socially beneficial to man.

The love poems are characterized by sadness. In 'Glosa' ('Gloss'), for instance, an epigraph consisting of a *redondilla* of love poetry written by the Venezuelan poet Andrés Eloy Blanco is developed, in keeping with the *glosa* tradition, in four *décimas* (Guillén's first serious use of this popular verse form). Guillén infuses his verses here with melancholy by introducing and dwelling on the idea of illusion. In 'Agua del recuerdo' ('Water Remembered'), the sugar-cane metaphor is used at length to represent the beauty he saw in a girl of whom he had had a fleeting glance. He imagines her destiny, the crushing of her beauty in the course of the life offered by the society in which she lives. Haunting images of death, which the speaker himself does not want to see, predominate in 'La tarde pidiendo amor' ('The Afternoon Begging for Love'). The *romance* 'Rosa tú, melancólica,' a poem dedicated to Guillén's wife, Rosa Portillo, and written, as Augier informs us, during the poet's stay in Venezuela, is an artful exploration of nostalgia. Matching melancholy is achieved by the repeated characterization of Rosa as 'melancólica' because there is present, too, the unspoken melancholy of the speaker, which is indicated by his very act of evoking the absent loved one, and by images such as 'mi estrecha sábana' ('my narrow sheet'), with their suggestion of loneliness. Further, because of the way in which absence is captured in the present of the poem, with images of Rosa at

dawn, noon, and night, the melancholy seems to be an ever-present sentiment. It is nevertheless a sentiment that, as the bright name symbolism of the
poem suggests, is not inherent in Rosa and seems determined by changeable
social circumstances.

In addition to the state of sadness evident in these poems dealing with
nature and love and the intimations of death in several of them, like 'Acana'
and 'La tarde pidiendo amor,' there are other poems that have death as their
main subject. In the poem 'Pero que te pueda ver,' there is a materialist desire
to be conscious of the approach of death, to identify it and see how it behaves, to have it not be mysterious. A fearlessness of death pervades the poem
'Iba yo por un camino' ('I Went Along a Road'); while in 'Apunte' its shadow
haunts the gaiety of Havana's night life.

All these poems dealing with the principal traditional lyrical subjects, when
read in the context of the whole of *El son entero* and with some consideration of their place in the historical development of Guillén's poetry and of
Cuban social life, seem to bear, in their despondent tone, a relation to
Guillén's dissatisfaction with the pace of change in Cuba. They reflect the
notion that seemingly eternal lyrical subjects are conditioned by the historical situations from which they arise.

ELEGÍAS

That Guillén's perception of the historical situation was indeed negative may
be seen from all the works of the period following the publication of *El son
entero* both before and after his return to Cuba in 1948. Prior to leaving Brazil
for Cuba he had written his 'Elegía a Jacques Roumain.' The immediate
cause of his return to Cuba was the murder in Manzanillo, Oriente, in January
1948, of his comrade and friend Jesús Menéndez, the general secretary of
the National Federation of Sugar Workers. This provided a motive for another elegy, and during the long period of its gestation his other poetic
activity – he continued to write copious articles for *Hoy* and other progressive
publications – consisted of a series of political satires. The first set of these,
mainly *décimas*, appeared almost daily in the newspaper *Hoy* between January and March of 1949. Published anonymously, they constituted biting
attacks on members of the administration of Carlos Prío Socarrás for their
corruption, their brutality and their incompetence. It would not have been
difficult for a competent administration to detect the author's identity because
of the extraordinary sophistication with which the *décima* was used (Guillén
achieves enormous variety within the form) and because publication of the
satires ceased when Guillén left the island in March for a conference in
New York. Other conferences in Paris and Prague followed in quick succession, as did a visit to Moscow. In 1951 he visited the German Democratic

Republic, Romania, Bulgaria, Czechoslovakia, Austria, Poland, and the
Soviet Union; in 1952 he left the latter country for visits to China, Czechoslovakia, and Austria. He returned to Cuba in May of that year. In the meantime, Batista had overthrown the government of Prío Socarrás two months
earlier. Upon returning to Cuba, Guillén began to attack the new dictatorship
in a series of satires, *Las coplas de Juan Descalzo*. The regime soon began
to close in on him. He was detained and photographed, and for a period his
passport was seized. When he left for a conference in Chile in May 1953,
his departure was to be the beginning of a long exile. With the attack led by
Fidel Castro on the Moncada barracks on 26 July 1953, a new stage of
confrontation had arrived. The regime outlawed the Communist Party and its
publications and intensified the persecution of its leaders and members.
Consequently, Guillén had to endure the rigours of exile for six years. During
these years he travelled extensively (much of it enforced travel) and produced a collection of elegies and the other poems that constituted his book *La
paloma de vuelo popular* (1958).

It will have been noticed that the elegiac mood is prevalent in Guillén's
poetry, in the sadness, the 'llanto,' provoked by historical and continuing
social outrages that frustrate the realization of inalienable human aspirations.[39]
This causes the feeling of absence, loss, or deprivation that is germane to the
traditional elegy, whether heroic or intimate, to be a pronounced feature of
his work. We may recall, for example, his poem entitled 'Elegía' of *El son
entero* and notice the consistency of its content and temper with so many
earlier Guillén poems. It is also closely related to these later elegies, particularly to 'El apellido.' But the *Elegías* in their artistic elaboration reveal yet
other aspects of his poetic skill.

The first of the six *Elegías*, 'Elegía a Jacques Roumain,' was written, as
we have seen, in late 1947. The 'Elegía a Jesús Menéndez' was written
between 1948 and 1951, with substantial later revision; the 'Elegía cubana' in
1952; 'El apellido' between 1951 and 1953; the 'Elegía a Emmett Till' in
1955 and 1956; and the 'Elegía camagüeyana' in 1958. The first characteristic
to be observed about these poems is that the sense of intimate, personal
deprivation in them is so interwoven with a sense of public deprivation as to
invalidate any distinction between the heroic and the intimate, or between
the epic and the lyric. The speaker therefore plays in them a special representative role. The 'I' is translatable into a legitimate Cuban, West Indian,
and universal perspective. This is one of the ways in which the sentiment of
loss or absence is readily universalized. Another prominent aspect of these
poems is that, beyond the contemplative and resigned melancholy prevalent in
the traditional elegy, there is in them, as in Guillén's poetry in general, evidence of a combative attitude, of a will to create a future in which the factors
underlying the disaster that is the immediate motive of the poem will be

eradicated. Hence regret leads to resolve. And since the deprivation, brutal as it often is, is of something that is a basic right, the vision of a triumphant struggle for change is the ultimate message.

The 'Elegía a Jacques Roumain' is one of the three poems in which the death of a person is the motive of the poem. A comprehensive characterization of the Haitian writer is presented in the ingenious sonnet with which the poem opens. This sonnet's simple seven-syllable lines are raised to loftiness by a superbly inventive rhyme scheme, hyperbaton and metaphor, including the Dantesque metaphor 'A mitad del sendero' ('In the middle of the path'), followed by the concrete 'sentóse y dijo: – ¡Muero!' ('he sat down and said, "I am dying"'), which reflects at once the dignity and simplicity of the subject. The reiteration of 'muerto' following the initial 'Ay' on the next page conveys the grief at the loss. Free verse is next used for random personal recollections leading to the main task of Roumain's life: his struggle to end the bloodiness – indicated by the lengthy series of anaphoras beginning with 'Sangre en' ('Blood in') – of dictatorial politics in Haiti. The emphasis on 'sangre' links a Haitian reality to a Cuban one, for 'sangre,' as we have been seeing, is one of the leitmotifs of Guillén's poetry. The prospect is raised that Jacques Roumain will yet lead his people, by his example and his inspiration, to victory over oppression. Here, as in the poem *España* ..., a song is a part of the strategy for arousing determination and confidence.

'El apellido' ('The Family Name') carries a lament about the absence of balance in Cuban identity resulting from the abrupt break with the African past imposed by slavery. The name 'Nicolás Guillén,' which represents the blotting out of much of the provenance of the person who bears it and arouses curiosity about the void and indignation at the cause of the void, is scrutinized as a symbol of the inequitable status. In the first of the two parts of the poem it is already clear that the 'Yo' is broadly representative, for the investigation of 'Mis raíces y las raíces / de mis raíces' ('My roots and the roots / of my roots'), the citing of his 'sangre navegable' ('navigable blood'), and the enquiry after his 'abuelo nocturno' ('nocturnal grandfather') with 'una gran marca hecha de un latigazo' ('a great mark made by a lashing') all suggest a general experience. The generalization inherent in these symbols is made explicit in the second part of the poem with usage of the first-person plural. Here in the present time there is common feeling with all those with 'fragmentos de cadenas / adheridos todavía a la piel' ('fragments of chains / still sticking to the skin') and who are targets of

> los insultos como piedras
> que nos escupen cada día
> los cuadrumanos de la tinta y el papel.[40]

insults like stones
that four-handed manipulators of ink and paper
spit at us each day.

A spirit of defiance is signalled in this part by reference to a common 'sangre combatiente' ('combative blood'); and ultimately the question:

¿Ni el mandinga, bantú,
yoruba, dahomeyano
nombre del triste abuelo ahogado
en tinta de notario?

Can't I even have the Mandinga, Bantu,
Yoruba, Dahomeyan
name of the sad grandfather drowned
in notary's ink?

referring to the many whose identities were snuffed out by the inhuman administrative procedures, evokes the affirmation of a forthright, unifying, and enduring African presence and contribution.

It is precisely the total involvement of the speaker in the experience he conveys that most importantly distinguishes 'El apellido' from Neruda's 'Las alturas de Macchu Picchu' in which there is also a quest for a people's roots, but with the speaker extending solidarity from a self-aware position of poet and observer. The painful nature of the question examined in 'El apellido' makes apt the semblance of lack of formal control suggested by the employment of free verse of a wide range of lengths as well as of such figures as synaesthesia. Puzzlement and indignation are reflected in the frequent use of questions and exclamations; and the imaginative probing of substantial areas of uncertain knowledge prompts the frequent use of metaphor.

The 'Elegía cubana,' with its seven- and eleven-syllable verses forming the *silva* that was used often by José María Heredia for similar purposes, is a lament for the nation. Metonymy is used extensively here, as is anaphora, to elevate the poem's intensity; and imagery emphasizes the desperate state of the country. The controllers with enormous wealth are set against the humble people. The latter invoke Martí and Maceo in whose spirits lies the promise of a better future.

In 'Elegía a Emmett Till,' the Mississippi River is personified as an ally of the blacks, as witness to the racist murder of the fourteen-year-old boy, and as a judge that must decree vengeance. Here again metonymy and anaphora contribute to creating the solemn and intense tone of the poem.

A friendly evocation of Camagüey appears in the 'Elegía camagüeyana,' '¡oh suave / comarca de pastores y sombreros!' ('oh gentle / region of shepherds and sombreros!'). The youthful recollections, some of which use an *ubi sunt* motif, cover a wide range of emotions and experiences, and make this an unusually intimate elegy. The poem is informed by the situation of exasperating personal exile and comes to reflect the prevailing forbidding national situation. The speaker in his distant space cannot speak; he can only dream. A sense of desperate longing is suggested by his vicarious presence in Camagüey: 'Vengo de andar y aquí me quedo, / con mi pueblo' ('I am back from travelling and I am staying here / with my people'). This together with the use of the *décima*, on three occasions, to convey scenes that are at once intimate and broad endows the poem with a poignant sorrow that verges on being overwhelming. Yet here, too, there is the ultimate expression of hope, which cannot be regarded as being simply personal, since an end to exile must coincide with a change in the national situation.

The 'Elegía a Jesús Menéndez' is one of Guillén's major works. His reputation as a great contemporary poet could rest on it alone. In this seven-part poem the enormous range of forms of which he is master is used to make of the murder of his fellow worker in the cause of change and justice for the masses of the Cuban population an elegy that embraces the essential national topics; and he pursues their links to some of the broadest issues of our time. The range of forms includes those developed within the broad tradition of Hispanic poetry and those that Guillén himself has contributed to this tradition. The national topics are those conflictive ones in which the forces of progress are in combat against the forces of reaction and their external mentors. As is customary in Guillén's work, there is a projected time of triumph for the former. In fact, the revolution is envisaged here with remarkable clarity. The highly affective usage throughout the poem, particularly appropriate to the elegy as a genre, substantiates the view that the speaker within the poem is himself committed to the goals of which Jesús Menéndez is representative.

At the outset of the first part the intimate association of sugar-cane plants with Jesús and their anxious concern for him are indicated by personification:

> Las cañas iban y venían
> desesperadas, agitando
> las manos.
> Te avisaban la muerte,
> la espalda rota y el disparo.
>
> *The cane plants were coming and going*
> *desperate, waving*

> *their hands.*
> *They were warning you of death,*
> *the torn back and the gun shot.*

Jesús is represented only by the familiar personal pronoun, which communicates a closeness between him and the speaker. The elements of the warning are given in reverse chronology, the effect of which is to juxtapose 'disparo' with its agent 'el capitán,' the subject of the next five lines, who is treated with contrasting distance and is described by a series of metonymic nouns pointing to his metallic and animalistic characteristics. His low spatial situation contrasts with the upright manliness of the advancing Jesús in the line 'sentado en su pistola el capitán' ('seated on his pistol, the captain'). This line, by forming a chiasmus with the one that begins the description of the captain, heightens the sense of menace posed by the captain, as does the use of hyperbaton, which permits 'pistola' to be juxtaposed with 'el capitán.' All this intensifies the idea of the restricted identity of the captain who is related to Guillén's archetypal unenlightened soldier who has not benefitted from the *Cantos para soldados* ... The epigraph from Góngora borne by the first part of the poem – 'armado / más de valor que de acero' ('armed more with courage than with steel') – can now be read as applying to Jesús, since an understanding of the antithetical values that are attached to courage and steel reveals steel to be consonant with the metallic identity of the captain. The ensuing five-line exclamation underlying the participation of the cane plants indicates the epic proportion of the consequence of their failure to communicate to Jesús the imminent disaster. The line 'sentado en su pistola el capitán' subsequently becomes a refrain, finishing off passages of the elaborated animal imagery that confronts Jesús. The two antithetical paradigms are so skilfully developed that in the final verses of this series,

> el ojo fijo en tu pulmón,
> el odio recto hacia tu voz,

> *his eye fixed on your lung,*
> *his hatred aimed at your voice,*

the first hemistich of each line seems to apply to a bestial person, the second to Jesús.

The imperfect tense with which Jesús is described in the last stanza of this first part of the poem suggests not one single appearance in the cane fields, but his frequent presence there. In this there is a justification of the persistently protective attitude shown by the cane plants on his final appearance. He used to walk among them with his smile, his robust stature, and his voice which

– stern and sweet as the oxymoron 'violento azúcar' ('violent sugar') suggests, 'de yanqui en yanqui resonando' ('resounding from Yankee to Yankee') – would guard against the exploitative use of their product. Thus their concern is an act of reciprocity, and their personification is validated. The synaesthesia 'su luz de relámpago nocturno' ('its light of nocturnal lightening'), applied to Jesús's voice is in this sense a master stroke, for it at once suggests the power to change the aspect and nature of the cane field and Jesús's exceptional lucidity. Then suddenly comes the fatal 'pólvora' (gunpowder) which is transported metaphorically and with synaesthesia to the animal world as 'El zarpazo / puesto en la punta de un rugido' ('the claw blow / placed on the tip of a roar'). This image, apart from situating 'pólvora' clearly within the paradigm of 'plomo' (lead), 'diente' (tooth), and 'cuero' (hide), is keenly reminiscent, especially with the lexical usage 'zarpazo,' of the image used by José Martí in his essay 'Nuestra América' to convey the idea of surreptitious imperialist attack. Yet the immediate victim of the shooting is, paradoxically, the captain. The focus is on him submerged in the vital, national blood of Jesús Menéndez.

The number and potency of the adjectives preceding and modifying 'sangre' in the last two verses of the first part combined with the anaphora 'ya en tu' and the alliteration 'sangre sumergido' serve to magnify the image of blood. The image, used metonymically to represent Jesús, fulfils a linking function by appearing immediately in the first verse of the second part of the poem; and as 'agrio charco sobre azúcar' ('bitter pool covering sugar'), and therefore in oxymoronic association with sugar, it makes its way to Wall Street where the antagonism to Jesús of imagery evoking surreptitious animal life is continued after his death. The ticker tape taking into account the spilled blood of Jesús Menéndez indicates stock quotations in serpentine fashion. The metaphor and then the simile that comprise the image:

> esa cinta vertiginosa
> que envenena y se arrastra como una
> víbora interminable de piel veloz marcada
> con un tatuaje de números y crímenes.

> *that dizzy tape*
> *that poisons and crawls like an*
> *endless viper with agile skin marked*
> *with a tatoo of numbers and crimes.*

are variations on Guillén's use in the poem 'Sensemayá' of the snake as a symbol of imperialism and are linked, too, to the 'zarpazo' metaphor used in the first part of this poem. The epigraph of this second part, purportedly taken from the financial pages of the *New York Herald Tribune*, suggests the positive effects on the stock market of Jesús's murder. Generally favourable company news precedes the quotations, in uniform rhythm, of the share prices of those companies that have particular interests in Cuba and the West Indies; and all these make gains. The phenomenon underlying these advances, the blood of Jesús, introduced apocalyptically, appears finally as being itself marketable and is designated bullishly by the serpentine ticker tape. In the face of this horror, the focus is turned on the devilish traders who are characterized in one-word verses of four, then three, then two syllables, the changing positions of stress in these words creating a contrapuntal musical pattern. The traders are ultimately juxtaposed with 'la abierta espalda / de alto atleta vegetal' ('the open back / of the tall plantlike athlete'), with the physical wound and the Cuban spiritual essence of Jesús, commercializing him totally, selling and hawking his spiritual properties. But this skilful usage – vendiendo ... angustia, pregonando ... aquella descuartizada rebeldía (selling ... anguish, hawking ... that quartered rebelliousness) – suggests the impossibility of containing a people's anguish and the example of rebelliousness set by Jesús. An extension of the system of contrasts on which the poem is structured follows these images with the appearance of the captain in the same setting, decorated and in fawning posture, seeking his reward and speaking subservient English.

The other contrast involves the use of the term 'suspiro de angustia' ('sigh of anguish'), indicating the personified reaction of a New York daily, to classify and introduce an item concerning the stock market. The item itself is at first glance the least artful of the several prose passages contained in the poem, but it rewards careful reading:

> Aunque las ganancias ayer fueron impresionantes,
> el volumen relativamente bajo de un millón seiscientas
> mil acciones da motivo para reflexionar.
> A pesar de la variedad de razones expresadas,
> parece muy probable que la mejoría haya sido de
> naturaleza técnica, y puede o no resultar de
> un viraje de la tendencia reciente, dependiendo
> de que los promedios logren penetrar sus máximos
> anteriores ...

> *Although the gains were impressive, the relatively*
> *low volume of one million six hundred thousand*
> *shares gives cause for concern. In spite of the*
> *variety of reasons given, it seems very probable*
> *that the advance was of a technical nature, and*

it may or may not result from a break out from the
recent trend, depending on whether the averages
manage to penetrate their previous highs ...

The passage (actually taken from the Cuban newspaper *Información*, 18 March 1951) represents so accurately the terminology and attitude of a Dow stock market theorist that it seems unlikely as part of a poem. Business executives who have such specialized knowledge and who are poets, Wallace Stevens for example, have not offered this kind of material in their poetry. Earnest about both activities, they keep their 'worlds' separate and distinct from each other, or they use the one as compensation or therapy for the other. Guillén, by contrast, perceives relations between and assesses all forms of social activity. Balzac in his time possessed an understanding of aspects of the world of commerce and finance that enabled him to reveal the inimical social effects of acquisitive obsessions in novels such as *Eugénie Grandet*. Guillén knows how to fit the world of profit and speculation into his poetry with his daringly innovative formal techniques to convey powerful images of the functioning of imperialism. Thus, in the passage the two sentences are structured to suggest worry. The first one begins with what from the point of view of the implied writer is a positive development, but then comes a negative factor. In the second the burden of the preoccupation is revealed as whether or not the technical market rally will carry through to new highs. Given the earlier grave context of the word 'angustia,' its usage to introduce this passage sets up a case of bathos and, given the relation that has been established between the stock market and Jesús's murder, the preoccupation of the writer takes on the semblance of utter callousness. Thus, Cuba and the United States come in this second part to occupy antagonistic places in the pattern of opposition established in the poem.

In the final three verses of the second part, the focus is placed again on the captain, now in Cuba and marked by the blood of Jesús. The third part is devoted entirely to his doomed flight from the people's revenge. There is a regularity of metre here, the nine-syllable *romance* being used throughout the seven eight-line stanzas. The longer-than-usual *romance* verse lends sobriety to the description, while the regularity of the form throughout the seven stanzas is appropriate for and supports the reiterative pattern of the content of this part. Each stanza contains images of the resources for defence or escape at the disposal of the captain and each closes with the refrain 'pero tras él corre la Muerte' ('but Death runs after him'), which undermines those resources. The idea of pursuit rather than of blocking or encirclement contained in the refrain permits the flight to include a wide variety of imagery and movement representing possible though ultimately futile means of escape. The nature of this openness is well captured by the oxymoron 'libre prisión' ('free prison') and the catachresis 'metálico viento lo envuelve'

('metallic wind envelops him'). In the first stanza 'el odio' encountered in part
I achieves designatory value, as the captain becomes el Capitán del Odio.
The image of the vulture is now added to that of the serpent with which he was
earlier associated. In the image 'amargo gemido lo busca' ('a bitter moan
searches for him'), the personification, representing the people in general, is
an answer to the question posed in the epigraph to this part, taken from
Lope de Vega, and an affirmation of the people's indignation. The concept of
the captain made victim by his act of villainy finds new metaphorical expression in the image:

> En una ráfaga de pólvora
> su rostro lívido se pierde.

> *In a puff of gunpowder*
> *his livid face is lost.*

With most of this stanza devoted to the growing repugnance of the captain
in the popular imagination of which the speaker is representative, the opposition between the attempt to flee and its futility is limited to the last two
lines of this stanza. It becomes the substance of the next three stanzas. In
the second, the protection afforded by weapons and military life ends in the
verse '¡Oh capitán, el bien guardado!' ('Oh captain, the well guarded one!'),
the ironical meaning of which is made clear in the refrain that follows it.
In the third stanza, the mother's intervention brings a series of oppositions: 'nueve lunas' ('nine moons') suggesting hope and high expectation
is contrasted with 'terrestre' ('earthly'), suggesting the harsh engendered
reality, the violent son. In the following chiasmus 'lo maldice' ('she curses
him'), is opposed by 'lo llora' ('she weeps for him'). The tears with which
she builds the bridge that might help him are accusatory red tears. The first
two lines of stanza four reverse the order of the antithesis found at the beginning of the preceding stanza. Disillusionment becomes her reality, and
an effort to hide her son, with 'cubil seguro' ('secure lair'), her favoured
hiding place revealing her recognition of his wild, animalistic nature, leads
also to futility. The fifth stanza introduces a young Cuban who, like Jesús,
is in harmony with nature, as the metaphorical description of him, intensified
by internal rhyme and chiasmus, indicates. He exhibits the anguish felt by
the people over Jesús's spilled blood to the point that he is ill at ease with his
own blood. This is alarming for the captain, who again flees. The sixth
stanza (printed as two quartets in some editions of the poem) presents first the
mother, yet again in the context of imagery representing childbearing that
moves from expectancy to dissillusionment. In contrast to this anticlimax,
the second quartet begins with an image of the shining heart of Jesús as the
symbol of his renaissance; and in the rest of part III the frantic, violent,

hate-filled, and doomed captain is contrasted with the calm, gleaming Jesús. The symbolic meaning of this grows with the additions made in the course of the poem to the two paradigms, with the cluster of attractive associations around Jesús on the one hand and the disagreeable ones around the captain on the other.

Part IV is in praise of Jesús; the terms of praise are rooted in Cuban historical reality and in the personality and day-to-day experiences of the trade union leader. It is presented in a series of psalm-like stanzas of varying lengths, all but one of them ending in the consonantal rhyme 'ida.' The rectitude and loftiness of this black man, suggested in the epigraph from Plácido, is conveyed by the simile 'como un bastón / de ébano' (like an ebony walking stick'), 'bastón' in the vehicle providing an element of usefulness that is consistent with Guillén's position in the poem 'Ebano real' ('Royal Ebony'). In the following image, 'los dientes blancos y corteses' ('white and courteous teeth'), the catachresis produced by the adjective 'corteses' gives metonymic value to 'dientes' in an elegant example of concentrated expression. Other such examples come in the form of synaesthesia in the following stanza, not only in 'tristes y dulces' ('sad and sweet'), reminiscent of a prominent César Vallejo image embodied in his *Trilce*, but also in the verse 'a veces óyese bramar en sus ojos un agua embravecida' ('at times there rages in his eyes an angry water'), together indicating the duality of gentleness and firmness. Jesús's use of the guttural rather than the apical 'rr' is atypical in Cuban pronunciation, but this superficial idiosyncracy is outweighed by his lineage, which is profoundly Cuban through his paternal contacts with Maceo and the struggle for Cuban independence. Explicit internal confirmation of the closeness between the speaker and Jesús comes in the following stanza with the first-person usage:

> alguna vez anduve con Jesús transitando de
> sueño en sueño su gran provincia.

> *I went sometimes with Jesús criss-crossing from*
> *dream to dream his great province.*

The metaphor 'de sueño en sueño' suggests action spurred by the dream of a better Cuba and has its source in Guillén's participation in Jesús Menéndez's campaign for electoral office in the 1940 general elections in Cuba.[41] The undercurrent of allusion to Jesus Christ is made quite overt in the following stanza dealing with the welcome given to Jesús by his followers. Yet it is already clear in his dialogue with them, in his breaking bread with them, that any such allusion has a contrastive function. For this Jesus is entirely of the earth and his mission is solely among the people. Thus, when in the final stanza the people are exhorted to reach up to the level of Jesús and contemplate his life, the speaker implies that the benefit of that contemplation will be a demand for a better future; and the imagery with which that life is conveyed 'en ondas interminables' ('in interminable waves') is similar to the concept of breadth of life that was sought in *España* ... and that will be portrayed as having been acquired in the poem 'Tengo' of 1964. The optimistic view of the future, the promise of a better life through social actions, is Jesús's legacy.

An image of the constant renewal of life closes part IV; the prose passage that opens part V speaks in paradox of the immortality of great people who pass away but remain among us. The cycle of death, decay, and regeneration is represented graphically in a movement that goes from the person by way of simile to a plant and then by metaphor to a bird and the idea of reproduction, a process suggesting the fecundity of Jesús's immortal and ubiquitous voice. Communion with Jesús Menéndez is an everyday affair that involves neither anniversaries nor the trappings of ritual. But the real antithesis to Jesús is the captain. This is conveyed by a paradox that is antithetical to the earlier one concerning the immortal dead; it forms the leitmotif of the rest of the prose passage: 'El vivo es el muerto' ('The live man is the dead man'). Images recapitulative of part III, of the fleeing, voiceless captain are now combined with visual and olfactory images of death to represent his repulsive living death.

The stanza of poetry that follows provides evidence once more of Guillén's innovativeness and his sense of pace in poetry. The seven-line stanza directs the attention away from the confines of the captain to a general viewing of Jesús's murder, its associations and immediate consequences. The telegraphic style that has the effect of suggesting urgency is produced by the exclusive use in it of nouns with the site of the crimes, Manzanillo occurring as the middle word in every other line. The placing and repetition of Manzanillo indicates that it is the focal point of broad attention. The seventeen other nouns used in this stanza convey a great deal. The army's intervention to put down protests of sugar workers results in the bullet – fired on behalf of the owners of the sugar, the Americans – that felled Jesús. The crime results in a strike at the sugar estate and members of the party leading the strike are arrested. Despised money is offered as compensation to the widow. Jesús's parents and children attend the funeral. Vengeance is declared, affecting the sugar crop. The concentrated form in which all this is presented serves besides to reflect popular reporting, the words that may be most often repeated and overheard in the oral, agitated recounting by the broad public of what had happened. The at-first cryptic style of the stanza, then, is after all a device for lending authenticity to the presentation of the public reaction. It is to another manifestation of this popular reaction – by workers and some soldiers who show alarmed indignation at the crime and grief at the funeral – that the immediately following prose passage takes the reader.

Popular reaction ultimately achieves a new stage, one of profound reflection, when it finds expression in the poetic form that Guillén has created for it, the *son*. The singer of it is a soldier. Here, then, is a soldier who is the antithesis of the captain; he is representative of the people and is the realization of the labours of earlier Guillén poems such as 'No sé por qué piensas tú' ('I Don't Know Why You Think') and 'Soldado, aprende a tirar' ('Soldier, Learn to Shoot'). 'Soldado' and 'compañero de Jesús' ('Jesus's Comrade') are in harmonious juxtaposition. The wounded dove of the *estribillo* is a symbolic representation of the jeopardized advance of progressive ideology in Cuba signified by the murder of Jesús. The *motivo* beginning 'Nunca quiera' is the most complex and intense of this *son*. The soldier being pitted against the captain, challenging him to count his bullets, evokes first of all the conflict between the ordinary soldier and the captain as types in their relations with Jesús and consequently with the people who feel the anguish and loss caused by Jesús's murder. Second, there is ironic content in the fact that the only bullet that can be found missing in this context is the one the captain himself will have used. But the soldier's inference that it would be missing from his own cartridge belt is to be taken as indicating that as a soldier he feels a share of the responsibility for the crime. Also, there are extensions of the main paradigms of opposition in the poem: 'balas' ('bullets') and 'odio' ('hatred') as properties of the captain, the metonymy 'pecho puro' ('pure heart') and the metaphor 'flor' ('flower') representing Jesús. The opposition is climactic in the verse 'Las balas que a un pecho puro' ('The bullets that against a pure heart') in which the phonetic distinguishing feature of voice in the initial phonemes 'b' and 'p' aids the contrast between the opposing elements. The use of the present tense 'van' ('go') in the last verse suggests that this *son* is outside the dramatic chronology of the poem and points to its meditative character. The mood of the symbolism becomes positive at the end of the *son* where the replaced 'sinsonte' ('mocking bird') and 'barco' ('boat') suggest others appearing to continue the struggle left unfinished by Jesús. Thus in the final *estribillo* the dove is in sustained flight.

The epigraph to part VI, taken from Rubén Darío's 'A Roosevelt' with the lines referring to the cynicism of U.S. imperialism, signals the widening of Jesús's concern for those who need his consoling and rectifying hand both within Cuba and beyond, principally in Latin America and the United States. The opening sentence of the first prose passage: 'Jesús trabaja y sueña' ('works and dreams') reflects activity geared to creating a better future and is a further example of the meeting of present and future that is often to be found in Guillén's poetry. The temporal and spatial expansion of Jesús is a characteristic that adds to his epic stature. At the same time his preoccupation is here again shown to be with people's essential material existence. Echoes of the Cuban–Venezuelan parallels of suffering given in the 'Son venezolano' ('Venezuelan *son*'), of the hunger and oppressive conditions of labour portrayed in 'Una canción en el Magdalena' ('A Song on the Magdalena River'), and of the common Cuban and Haitain experiences in bloodletting shown in the 'Elegía a Jacques Roumain' ('Elegy to Jacques Romain') and many other abuses throughout Latin America are here presented as concerns of Jesús. His round of visits with the oppressed ends on a northward course; the preparation evoked by the description of the air in a series of four anaphorically structured phrases in which adjectives indicating disagreeableness are prominent. With the transition from the lands of the oppressed to the land of the oppressor, where the modern-day feast of Balthazar is in full swing, there is a change in versification from poetic prose to a more structured verse form. Now another unusual form of the *romance* is employed, this time in stanzas of eight lines, each with nine or eleven syllables and assonance in *á*. Since this assonance in all four stanzas ends in the chiasmus '¡Va por la muerte, por la muerte va!' ('He goes on behalf of death, on behalf of death he goes!') as a refrain, the assonance enhances musically the sense of aggressiveness that is rampant throughout the stanzas. Death is a constant feature of this section in which oppression is portrayed in its most lethal manifestations. In a subtle way the first verses are linked to the killing of Jesús. In the lines

> Ahí ve que de un zarpazo Norteamérica
> alza una copa de ardiente metal,

> *There he sees that with one claw-blow North America*
> *raises a goblet of ardent metal,*

the word 'zarpazo,' which was so tellingly applied to the captain's fatal act by a metaphor I have examined earlier, is juxtaposed with 'Norteamérica.' Also, the metallic identification of the captain has its obvious parallel here. The hydrogen bomb celebrated by Truman, who is represented by a metaphor in which (in keeping with a paradigm established in the poem) he is cast as a lower animal, the funereal men of the Klan, Jim Crow, Charles Lynch, and William Walker all appear as tools of carefully nurtured violence and oppression. Walker, for example, in images of precipitous anticlimax,

> Cultiva en su jardín rosas de pólvora
> y las riega con alquitrán.

> *Cultivates in his garden roses of gunpowder*
> *and waters them with tar.*

The final passage, devoted largely to racial crimes in the United States typified by Martinsville and then to the redeeming role of Jesús, is poetic prose at its most powerful. The lyrical lament with which the diabolical deeds are reported; the counterpoint, intensified by anaphora, between music and atrocities; the asyndetic series of rhyming adjectives; the crescendo effect, beginning with chiasmus and strengthened by hyperbaton, of verb usage in the sentence 'Todavía se oye, oímos todavía: suena, se levanta, arde todavía el largo rugido de Martinsville' ('It is still heard, we still hear: the long roar of Martinsville still sounds, rises, burns'); a second anaphoric series, beginning this time with 'le piden' ('they beg of him') and the reiteration to the point of symbolism of the number 'siete' ('seven') are some of the factors contributing to its power. In addition, the repetition, near the end of the passage, of an image used near its beginning at once effects the rounding off of the intervening content and indicates how this content had enlarged the meaning of the image on its second appearance. Finally, in the contrastive imagery of the negative / affirmative (not A but B) Gongoristic construction of the last sentence, the focus on Jesús as someone who by his work in the social rather than the religious field has acquired immortality causes the passage to display that movement from set-back to triumph that is at the heart of the meaning of several of the parts of the poem and of the poem as a whole.

Consonant with this movement toward triumph, the seventh and final part of the poem departs from the antithetical patterns prevalent in the earlier parts of the work, and images of the significance and future contribution of Jesús come to serve as metaphors for the revolution. The order of the images with which he is here portrayed reflects the positive resolution of the earlier conflicts in the poem and reveals him to be an agent of long-sought harmony. Thus in accordance with the sense of a new beginning indicated by the epigraph from the *Poema del Cid*, in which the cocks by their singing would create new dawns, the lustrous image of Jesús presented in the first stanza begins with the focus placed on his hands. After his initial appearance among the sugar-cane plants, a series of parallelisms in each case introduced by 'o bien' ('or') is employed to give him other locations, other missions. The alternatives are so joyfully imaginative that they seem almost surrealistic but are restrained from being so by their faithfulness to the central idea of Jesús as inspiration for practical social change. The indications of abrupt spatial changes are followed by a metaphor within a simile, then a metaphor and yet another metaphor containing a simile, then two synaesthesias, before the stanza ends with a final simile. The wealth of literary expression in itself suggests the host of possibilities represented by Jesús's inspirational presence.

This mood is continued in the second stanza with its interlocking and incremental structure. An indication of the defiant confidence in the new life is given in the use of the climactic part of this stanza of the words 'pólvora' ('gunpowder') and 'metálico' ('metallic'). We have already observed that to this point they have been used in association with the captain and with North America and have had decidedly negative value from the point of view of the speaker. Their use in this positive context, therefore, presents the kind of problem that exposes the limitations of a semiological approach to the analysis of Guillén's poetry. Their use here suggests the predominance of world view over words, that everything in the hands of the forces guided by Jesús's ideals can be turned into positive tools in the building of the revolution, symbolized here, in a way that relates it to the epigraph, by 'un gallo rojo' ('a red cock'). Since 'pólvora' and 'metálico' both modify 'gallo' they suggest in their striking oxymoron the proper use of arms by the revolution to ensure its triumph and then to protect itself. In the following stanza, the call to the people to join in and promote the lofty movement is combined with the need for arms and people – 'metal y huesos' ('metal and bones') – to nurture the revolution now represented by a series of nature metaphors that suggest tenderness, enlightenment, a general uplifting, liberty, a fresh harvest, beauty, and resoluteness. The images of the last lines of the poem are intimately bound to this projected achievement: Jesús, represented metonymically by his sabre and thus as the conquering fighter for justice in the cane fields; Jesús present ubiquitously with the basic elements of water and air; Jesús with his smile and his courtesy summarizing his personality, as the chiasmus suggests; and Jesús symbolizing the happy new relation between Cuba and its sugar. The words 'relámpago,' 'sonrisa' and 'lágrimas' ('lightening,' 'smile,' 'tears') used here have been associated earlier in the poem with Jesús; and the synthesizing role of this last part of the stanza is furthered by other means. The vehicles of the metaphors that were used in part v to suggest growth and revival and which illustrated the immortality of great people reappear here. They are now employed in the first person by Jesús in lines demonstrating his awareness of his own continuity of the revolutionary message that emanates from him and reveals his confidence in the imminent triumph of the revolution:

> Creció un árbol con sangre de mi herida.
> Canta desde él un pájaro a la vida.
> La mañana se anuncia con un trino.

> *A tree grew with blood from my wound.*
> *From it a bird sings out to life.*
> *Tomorrow is announced with a trill.*

An array of superb technical skills, exceptional knowledge, intelligence, dedication and imagination,[42] a consciousness devoted to justice, national integrity, and the uplifting of the population as a whole so that harmony may be attained all underlie the historic poetic achievement that the 'Elegía a Jesús Menéndez' represents.

LA PALOMA DE VUELO POPULAR

The title of the book *La paloma de vuelo popular* (*The Dove of Popular Flight*), containing poems written between 1947 and 1958 is taken from a verse in the final part of the 'Elegía a Jesús Menéndez' where it carried a meaning of positive augury for the revolution. The title is related to these poems by the dialectical implication that the matters with which they deal predominantly cannot remain for long in a state of unresolved tension. The only poems of the collection that do not submit to this classification are the 'Tres canciones chinas' ('Three Chinese Songs'), which deal with post-revolutionary China. For the rest, new aspects appear of the treatment of by now familiar attitudes and subjects. There is also a new emphasis on the subject of exile.

'Arte poética,' the initial poem of the book, is the second in Guillén's published collections to deal with his poetics as a subject (the first is 'Guitarra' of *El son entero*). In this poem he confronts what is often conceived of as the issue of a choice between romantic nature poetry and social poetry. The poem is written with an awareness of the fact that there are those who come to poetry predisposed to regard as secondary or impure a body of poetry that touches on man's material existence in more than a tangential way. Hence the speaker here affirms his poetic recognition of nature by presenting in the delicate simplicity of the *redondilla* some of the stock images of traditional nature poetry before counterposing these with images of human suffering, sometimes in settings where the insufficient observer would have his attention monopolized by nature:

> El cañaveral sombrío
> tiene voraz dentadura,
> y sabe el astro en su altura
> de hambre y frío.

> *The sombre cane field*
> *has a voracious set of teeth,*
> *and the star at its height knows*
> *of hunger and cold.*

The imminence of the revolution is suggested here, too. With imagery that makes nature serve metaphorically the high social achievement that the revolu-

tion will represent, with an irony that underlines the precedence of man's
social needs over nature, and in keeping with the practice noted in *El son
entero*, he ends the poem with the stanza:

Dile [al rosal] también del fulgor
con que el nuevo sol parece:
en el aire que la mece
que aplauda y grite la flor.

Tell it [the rosebush] too of the radiance
with which a new sun appears:
in the air that sways it
let the flower applaud and shout.

A variety of perspectives and forms is on display in the presentation of
the different subjects. This is demonstrable in the poems concerning exile, for
example. In the poem 'Exilio' ('Exile'), the topic is treated in such a way
that an open, profound sadness, not unlike that frequently found in César
Vallejo's poetry, results. As is done, too, in some Vallejo poems, numbers
are used in the evocation of this sadness;

Mi patria en el recuerdo
y yo en París clavado
como un blando murciélago.
¡Quiero
el avión que me lleve,
con sus cuatro motores
y un solo vuelo!

My country on my mind
and I stuck in Paris
like a soft bat.
I want
the airplane that will carry me,
with its four engines
and one single flight!

But, of course, the sense of 'patria' was less developed in Vallejo; another
difference between the two poets lies in the spirit of defiance found in the
closing lines of this poem where the speaker is firmly resolved to answer force
with force. In the poem referred to earlier entitled 'Pero señor' ('But Sir'),
the title serves as a refrain throughout the composition, effectively manifest-

ing the helpless indignation and incredulity of the speaker faced with the difficulty of finding even uncomfortable refuge in Mexico, France, and Venezuela. The poem 'Paloma del palomar' ('Dove of the Dovecote') queries Mexico's unexpected decision to deny him asylum.

An indirect approach to the general topic is represented by the poem 'Epístola.' The *silva* is employed here in a vivid recollection of Cuban dishes. The use of the formal second-person plural and other devices, such as incremental anaphora to inquire whether Cuban landscape and popular native Cuban dishes (of the kind now offered by Guillén's cherished Havana restaurant, the Bodeguita del Medio) are to be found in Palma de Mallorca, creates a charming atmosphere in the poem. But it is to be noticed that the poem conveys more than gastronomical memories. A poignant sadness ultimately results, because the obvious answer is 'no,' and the speaker, using verbs whose indication of declining pace suggests flagging anticipation, declares:

> Si lo hay, voy volando,
> mejor dicho, corriendo,
> que es como siempre ando.
> Pero si no, pues seguiré soñando.

> *If so, I'll come flying,*
> *or rather, running,*
> *which is how I always walk.*
> *But if not, then I'll keep on dreaming.*

It is clear that 'seguiré soñando' implies dreaming of Cuba and that the idea of exile underlies the whole poem.

The topic of exile is also treated with exquisite subtlety in the poem 'De vuelta' ('Return'), which reads:

> Por el largo camino
> me marché al azar,
> con un jarro de vino
> y un trozo de pan.
>   Me marché al azar.

> ¡Viento, viento – decía –
> contigo me voy¡
> (En el orto del día
> joven era el sol.)
>   Contigo me voy.

Tuve un prado con rosas,
que es mucho tener,
veinte y dos mariposas
y un solo clavel.
   Que es mucho tener.

Ardió el sol en mis manos,
que es mucho decir,
ardió el sol en mis manos
y lo repartí.
   Que es mucho decir.

Por el largo camino
regreso al azar,
con un jarro de vino
y un trozo de pan.
   Regreso al azar.

Taking the long road
I went on the whims of chance,
with a pitcher of wine
and a piece of bread.
   I went on the whims of chance.

Oh wind, oh wind – I said –
with you I will go!
(In the early dawn
the sun was young.)
   With you I will go.

I had a meadow with roses,
which is a lot to have,
twenty-two butterflies
and a single carnation.
   Which is a lot to have.

The sun blazed in my hands,
which is a lot to say,
the sun blazed in my hands
and I gave it away.
   Which is a lot to say.

> *Taking the long road*
> *I return on the whims of chance,*
> *with a pitcher of wine*
> *and a piece of bread.*
> > *I return on the whims of chance.*

Guillén demonstrates here once more his unsurpassed ability to invent a verse form that is of such appropriatness that it becomes an indispensable part of the meaning of his poem. The title suggests a return to a fixed base, while in the poem there is constant movement. The variation on the *redondilla* used here is a four-line stanza of dactylic seven-syllable lines with a refrain that repeats the second line. Consonantal rhyme is in force in the first and third lines while assonance in the stressed final syllable functions in the second and fourth lines and consequently in the refrain. The regularity of rhythm throughout the five stanzas and the consistency of repetition provided by the refrain assist the wandering, climaxless movement of the poem. Another factor contributing to the sense of aimless movement that is subtly evoked is the absence of a fixed *locus* for the speaker. In each stanza a new place or another aspect of a place is suggested, and to the repetition in each stanza effected by the refrain is added the repetition represented by the final stanza. These instances of repetition, however, are far from banal. The refrain, for instance, serves the additional function of confirmation, while, in the final stanza, the use of the verb 'regreso' instead of 'me marché,' the only divergence from the first stanza, suggests the idea of a return. In both cases there is ironic content; for confirmation, given the title that promises return, carries the idea that what is happening is not what should be happening, while the verb 'regreso,' which in view of the title would suggest a return to a firm base from which the departure was made, really suggests a continuation of wandering. Ultimately, then, the poem reveals a speaker in the rootlessness of exile; he has a minimum of subsistence and access only to what is in the unrestricted public domain; and he is obliged to continue on an apparently endless spiral of roaming. All this makes understandable the wish found in 'Exilio' for the decisive 'avión que me lleve / con sus cuatro motores / y un solo vuelo!'

Guillén's preoccupation at this time is not only with his own exile but with that of others who have sought refuge from other Latin American dictators. In the poem 'Hacia el Paraguay lejano ...' ('Towards Distant Paraguay'), dialogue is employed to evoke the pathos in the situation of the Paraguayan poet Elvio Romero and his compatriot the musician José Asunción who cannot invite the speaker to their country until they themselves are able to go there. The poems that are least obviously related to the idea of exile are the 'Tres poemas mínimos' ('Three Minimal Poems'). Indeed, they may easily be misread, as Iñigo Madrigal has done, as examples of Guillén's production of 'pure' nature poetry.[43] In these three short poems, 'Brizna, pequeño tallo ...' ('Blade, small sprout'), 'Brisa que apenas mueve ...' ('Breeze that hardly moves') and 'Punto de luz, suspenso lampo ...' ('Point of light, suspended lamp'), three subjects of Lilliputian dimensions are considered in their relations of possible usefulness to the poet. In each of them a marginalized, unfulfilled speaker longs for an end to his passivity, to his being placed in the doldrums of existence; and the sprout, the faint breeze, and the small distant light are disproportionate to the task of providing the required relief. The poems may be regarded as metaphors for a desire to end the prolonged absence from the vital tasks of Cuban national life. All these poems, together with the 'Elegía camagüeyana,' constitute one of the outstanding poetic treatments of the subject of exile. Here again, Guillén's inventiveness and subtlety are in evidence. His consummate mastery of a variety of forms has permitted him to present, in each case with telling effect, a variety of aspects of a subject. Given the priority he places on social action, it is not surprising that one of the principal notions arising from the poems should be that of exile as fruitless effort or inaction. It is seen as a dual hiatus, represented at home by the resistance to change on the part of the forces that made exile necessary and abroad by the restless languishing of a victim.

Cuba itself, with a concern for its future and for its population at large transcending pride in the accomplishments of some of its individuals, occupies four of the early poems of the collection. Cuba's shape on the map of the West Indies prompts, in the *romance* 'Un largo lagarto verde' ('A Long Green Lizard'), a consideration of its economic situation, with sugar viewed now as Cuba's 'corona esclava' ('slave crown'), a new oxymoron in the series associated with sugar in Guillén's poetry. A call for lifting the imperialist hold on Cuba, made climactic by the anaphora that leads up to it in the last stanza, is expressed in vivid metonymy in the verse 'Sacar las uñas del mapa' ('Remove the finger nails from the map'). 'Cañaveral' ('Cane Field'), written from the perspective of the cane cutter, constitutes in its *décima* an exquisite conceit founded on oxymoron and paradox and dealing with the worker's hostile relation to the product of his labour. In 'Deportes' ('Sports'), there is at one level pride in Cuban sportsmen – boxers, baseball players, and the chess champion Capablanca – who have excelled on the world scene. At the same time, particularly through the technique of disjointed dialogue with the speaker's insistent answers about Cuba to questions about Capablanca, the primary preoccupation is shown to be with the condition of the nation as a whole rather than with a few of its celebrities. Cuba, projected into a time of racial harmony, sets its criteria for friendship in the *son* 'La muralla' ('The Wall').

The police, as one of the tools of repression, are the subject of a number

of these poems. In 'La policía' ('The Police') the parallel identity between the
police force and a cat is astutely established by a technique of interchange-
able metaphor in which the police and the cat are used alternately as vehicles
for each other. In 'Canción de vísperas' ('Evensong'), a poem structured
on the basis of antithesis, the police are shown to form a part of an apparatus
of death; and the stigma properly attached to being a policeman in the
reigning socio-political circumstances is conveyed in *redondilla* verse with
exclamatory tone and hyperbole in the poem 'Doña María.'

New aspects of imperialism are explored in this book: the smothering of
West Indian initiatives, the fostering of a spirit of aimlessness and an
atmosphere of defeat and misery in a society where the 'Initial Judgment' is
still awaited, where people have not yet started to live. All these are exposed
in 'Casa de vecindad' ('Communal Yard'), a poem in which anaphora is
used in the presentation of a chaotic enumeration of images of woe. But the
poem closes with a strong indication of synthesis as a powerful image of birth
carries the promise of victory after strenuous struggle. In 'El banderón'
('The Big Flag'), the 'látigo en mano' ('whip in hand'), which throughout
Guillén's poetry has served to represent the slave master, is now applied to
U.S. imperialism in its Caribbean functions. The workings of imperialism
outside the Caribbean area also receive Guillén's attention in *La paloma de
vuelo popular*. In the poem 'Mau-Maus,' the clever perfidy of British propaganda is shown as it emits venomous allegations about the Mau Mau to cover
its own planned atrocities against the fighters for Kenyan independence.
Parenthesis and change of tone to give the confidential and authoritative view
that counteracts the British propaganda are effective devices in the poem.
Guatemala is viewed from two perspectives and in two different forms. In the
sonnet 'A Guatemala,' the parallel experience of Cuba and Guatemala
portrayed in the first two quartets are merged in the first tercet, the merger
sealed by metonymy and metaphor:

> Cañaveral y platanal, oscura
> sangre derraman de una misma herida
> de puñal, en la misma noche oscura
>
> *Cane field and banana plantation, spill*
> *dark blood from one same dagger*
> *wound in the same dark night.*

The other poem, 'Balada guatemalteca' ('Guatemalan Ballad') is a lament
for the country as the poet leaves it in its wounded state, expressed in imagery
recalling that depicting the jeopardized revolution in the 'Elegía a Jesús
Menéndez.'[44]

¡Guatemala,
verte en la calle tendida,
rojo el pecho, rota un ala
y entre la muerte y la vida!

Guatemala,
to see you sprawled in the streets,
your breast red, a wing broken
and lying between death and life!

The antithetical factor, as in 'Mau-Maus,' is presented in parenthesis, with a standard metonymy or symbol that has historical aptness in view of the actual role of the U.S. airforce in the set-back to Guatemala that was the occasion for the poem:

(Pareja con el avión
iba el águila imperial;
ojos de piedra, y el pico
como un sangriento puñal.
Hoy mata y mata, ¡mañana
ya no la verás matar¡)

(Level with the plane
went the imperial eagle;
eyes of stone, and its beak
like a bloody dagger.
Today it kills and kills, tomorrow
you will see it killing no longer!)

The final two verses, by the certainty of a better future expressed in them, continue a noted characteristic of Guillén's poetry. Cities, serving as metonymy for the general condition of national life, are looked at in the poem 'Ciudades' ('Cities') where the sub-section 'Madrid' is presented in the form of a riddle, the key to the solution of which lies in the image 'Un joven muerto, ya viejo, / se saca un árbol del pecho' ('A dead youth, now old, / a tree grows from his breast'). The image was encountered earlier in the final lines of the 'Elegía a Jesús Menéndez' and bears here a similar meaning of continuity and heightening of the struggle for change. In the section 'Kingston,' it is wondered for how long the colonial attitude exemplified by the earnest singing of 'God Save the King' would continue.

'Canción puertorriqueña' (Puerto Rican Song') reveals another kind of enquiry into the situation of a neighbouring country. The poem reads:

¿Cómo estás, Puerto Rico,
tú de socio asociado en sociedad?
Al pie de cocoteros y guitarras,
bajo la luna y junto al mar,
¡qué suave honor andar del brazo,
brazo con brazo del Tío Sam!
¿En qué lengua me entiendes,
en qué lengua por fin te podré hablar,
si en yes,
si en sí,
si en bien,
si en well,
si en mal,
si en bad, si en very bad?

Juran los que te matan
que eres feliz ... ¿Será verdad?
Arde tu frente pálida,
la anemia en tu mirada
logra un brillo fatal;
masticas una jerigonza
medio española, medio slang;
de un empujón te hundieron en Corea,
sin que supieras por quien ibas a pelear,
si en yes,
si en sí,
si en bien,
si en well,
si en mal,
si en bad, si en very bad?

Ay, yo bien conozco a tu enemigo,
el mismo que tenemos por acá,
socio en la sangre y el azúcar,
socio asociado en sociedad:
United States and Puerto Rico,
es decir New York City with San Juan,
Manhattan y Borinquen, soga y cuello,
apenas nada más ...

No yes,
no sí,
no bien,

no well,
sí mal,
sí bad, sí very bad!

How are you, Puerto Rico,
you an associate associated in society?
Under coconut trees and guitars
beneath the moon and beside the sea,
what a gentle honour to walk on the arm,
arm in arm with Uncle Sam!
In what language do you understand me,
in what language can I now talk to you:
in yes,
in sí,
in bien,
in well,
in mal,
in bad, in very bad?

Those killing you swear
that you are happy ... Is that true?
Your pale forehead burns,
the anaemia in your look
achieves a fatal gleam;
you mumble gibberish,
half Spanish, half American slang;
with one shove they plunged you into Korea,
without your knowing for whom you would fight,
whether in yes,
in sí,
in bien,
in well,
or in mal,
in bad, in very bad?

Oh, I know your enemy well,
the same one we have right here,
an associate in blood and sugar,
an associate in society.
United States and Puerto Rico,
that is, New York City with San Juan,
Manhattan and Borinquen, rope and neck,
just about, nothing more ...

> *Not yes,*
> *not sí,*
> *not bien,*
> *not well,*
> *yes mal,*
> *yes bad, yes very bad!*

Here the speaker, with marked authoritativeness, engages the personified Puerto Rico as a silent interlocutor. The initial question is apparently the simplest and most commonplace of openers: '¿Cómo estás, Puerto Rico …?'; but the speaker follows by demonstrating his special knowledge, adding the characterization 'tú de socio asociado en sociedad.' Within this *paronomasia*, which mocks the historical reality of Puerto Rico's special constitutional status as an associate state of the United States, is revealed the speaker's sarcastic attitude. It thus begins to be clear that the salutation is addressed to a Puerto Rico seen with concerned condescension. The following image reflects a stereotypic, romantic, touristic viewing of the island; and in this setting is placed the biting irony of the exclamation '¡qué suave honor andar del brazo, / brazo con brazo del Tío Sam!,' in which the idea of guidance inherent in the familiar name of the United States, the inequality of the two, and the attitude of close escort conveyed by the synecdoche in the described action all indicate that the 'suave honor' imputedly felt by Puerto Rico is a juvenile misperception. The mode of presentation of the poem, a thwarted dialogue that becomes a dramatic monologue, comes to have further internal justification when, by the speaker's questioning about language, it is revealed as doubtful that Puerto Rico is able to sustain a dialogue in Spanish. The sarcasm is intensified in the second stanza where a question is asked which, however it is answered, exposes an intolerable position that requires, for the sake of survival, urgent redress: 'Juran los que te matan / que eres feliz … ¿Será verdad?' A symptom of the unhealthiness is conveyed by the oxymoron 'brillo fatal.' The unequal, exploitative, and deforming relation is pursued through visual and auditive imagery and by historical reference to the Korean War in which Puerto Rico is shown to serve through compulsion and out of confusion, conveyed here by a subtle form of synaesthesia in which uncertainty over language is used to indicate the misapprehension of an ideological factor. The speaker and his subject are shown in the third stanza to share a common experience, that of imperialist exploitation. The *paronomasia* used in the first stanza now has the United States as its subject. Another modification in its use is that it now forms part of an anaphoric series in which the syntax determines that 'sociedad' is a synonym of 'la sangre y el azúcar' used as metonyms of suffering and expropriated national product. Thus when the coupling is effected between the United States and Puerto Rico either through the names of the countries, of their principal cities, or of the indigenous name Manhattan with Puerto Rico's indigenous name Borinquen, the national opposition between them stands out and is summed up in the antithesis 'soga y cuello.' In keeping with this definition of the relation, the *estribillo* with its alternating Spanish and English is no longer presented in the mode of a question but as a firm opinion in which the positive is denied and the negative affirmed. The speaker thus produces with his established authoritativeness a conclusive, negative, impatient assessment of Puerto Rico's condition.

A preoccupation with matters of racial hatred is shown in the poem 'Little Rock' where the outrages of the epoch of Orville Faubus are intensely conveyed. A viewing of servitude rising to rebellion is presented in 'Canción de cuna para despertar a un negrito' ('Cradle Song to Awaken a Black Child'). The word 'despertar' is dualistic in its meaning, with its more important aspect being the figurative one of an awakening from the sleep of social apathy. As such the poem's epigraph, taken from a poem by Emilio Ballagas, 'Dormite, me nengre, / mi nengre bonito ...' ('Sleep my black child / my beautiful black child ...'), is appropriate for its literal and figurative contrast. It illustrates once more the difference between Guillén and the *negrista* poets.

Guillén's travels yielded poems touching on yet other topics. The two contrasting faces of Rio de Janeiro, glamour and poverty, are shown in 'Canción carioca' ('Song of Rio de Janeiro') where the pivotal stanza is:

> Yo te hablo de otro Río:
> del Río de Janeiro
> de no-techo, sí-frío,
> hambre-sí, no-cruzeiro.

> *I speak to you of another Rio*
> *of Rio de Janeiro*
> *of no roof, yes cold,*
> *hunger yes, no money.*

The stanza displays Guillén's tyical skill at versification, a skill that is approached only by Rubén Darío in Hispanic poetry. Tightness of rhyme is achieved by the use of internal rhyme linking Río to Río de Janeiro and consequently the 'Río'–'frío' rhyme is tied closely to the 'Janeiro'–'cruzeiro' rhyme. At the same time the Portuguese words 'Janeiro' and 'cruzeiro' rhyme impeccably when pronounced either in Spanish or in Portuguese. Moreover, the rhyme is achieved coincidentally with a complex chiasmus in which the antithetical 'no-sí' pattern further intensifies the idea of deprivation.

The sadness of Chile in the first two of the 'Tres canciones chilenas' ('Three Chilean Songs') is relieved in the third by the celebration of its useful health-giving mineral water, intriguingly called 'Panimávida' (the name of the site of famous thermal baths in Chile; the word, though not Spanish, seems to mean in Spanish 'bread and more life,' reflecting the healthful nature of the place). The assonance in *é o* and *á a* in consecutive lines throughout the first and last of these poems respectively is superbly crafted to enhance their lyrical effect.

Love and death, two topics that were quite prominent in *El son entero*, appear in a minor role in this book and are again tied to Guillén's materialism. In the two versions of 'Muerte' ('Death'), for instance, the desire to recognize death, to be able to say to it 'Te vi primero' ('I saw you first') recalls the attitude shown in the poem 'Pero que te pueda ver' ('So that I may see you') of *El son entero*. Understandably, then, what is presented as the sudden disappearance of Paul Eluard is troubling to the speaker of the poetic obituary that bears his name. If the death of a famous poet is a notable loss, so too is that of the ordinary citizen who died without the opportunity to realize her talent and who is mourned in the poem 'Epitafio para Lucía.' On the other hand there is joy over a belated death in the 'Pequeña letanía grotesca en la muerte del senador McCarthy' ('Little Grotesque Litany on the Death of Senator McCarthy'). There is a fleeting moment of happiness in a spontaneous expression of love in 'La pequeña balada de Plóvdiv' ('The Little Plóvdiv Ballad'), a poem based on a pleasurable incident Guillén experienced in that Bulgarian town.[45] But love or, rather, the failure to communicate it, appears in the context of death in 'Ronda' ('Rondo') and thus in a mood that is characteristic of its manifestation in Guillén's poetry to this point. Finally, Guillén's growth-oriented outlook is reflected in his celebration in the *silva* 'Sputnik 57' of mankind's confidence in itself, its ability to achieve a more and more profound understanding of natural laws, and its evolution through serious effort to deeper levels of consciousness and higher forms of social organization.

The *Elegías* and the poems of *La paloma de vuelo popular* form a fitting climax to one phase of Guillén's poetry. The concentration of elegies represents the culmination of lament while it points the way to a different, improved future. The solution suggested by the poems of exile amounts to the positing of the idea of urgent basic change within Cuba, an idea reinforced in those poems having Cuba, imperialism, or racism as their principal subject. Those poems revealing a mood of contentment and celebration, the 'Tres canciones chinas' ('Three Chinese Songs'), 'Sputnik 57,' and 'La pequeña balada de Plóvdiv' derive from post-revolutionary societies. Away from such settings, love, for example, becomes a subject for negative treatment and has associations of death. All this, particularly with the tone of impatience that pervades the collection, indicates the end of the pre-revolutionary phase of Guillén's poetry – the phase in which the tone of condemnation is predominant and the common theme is that the basic conditions for harmonious relations among the Cuban population and between the Cuban and other workers and their products should be established. The triumph of the rebellious forces in Cuba within days of the publication of *La paloma de vuelo popular* brought about the coincidence of a national historical development with the internal imperatives of Guillén's work.

TENGO

La paloma de vuelo popular was published on 28 December 1958. The flight of Batista from Cuba in the early hours of 1 January 1959 marked the triumph of Fidel Castro's rebel army. Guillén returned to Cuba on 23 January 1959 and was given a welcome the size and warmth of which suggested that he was popularly regarded as one of the heroes of the revolutionary struggle. He immediately undertook a variety of new tasks on behalf of the revolution. The popular poetry readings he had given in the late thirties and forties during the course of usually unsuccessful political campaigns were repeated now as events of acknowledged national importance. At the same time, his administrative abilities were put to the service of helping to design a cultural policy for his country and, as was indicated earlier, of establishing the Union of Writers and Artists of Cuba. He resumed, too, his activities in journalism, and the diplomatic position of ambassador-at-large was soon added to his duties. Along with all this activity, he continued to exercise his high artistic gifts, and published, in 1964, the collection *Tengo* ('*I Have*').

The title itself, especially as it is elaborated in the title poem, reflects the satisfaction brought by the revolution. Yet while this satisfaction is expressed in several other poems of the collection, it would be erroneous to see *Tengo* as a book that is predominantly celebrative in tone. For Guillén's perception of the content that was now making its way to the surface of his society allowed him to use the word 'Tengo' not only to mean the realization of a long sought goal, but also to indicate a new sense of responsibility. What results, then, is a reaffirmation of revolutionary commitment from the new setting of a society that had made the decision to change its structure completely, to establish a new base. Thus in several poems, the preoccupation is with nurturing the revolution and defending it from the past and from a vast array of machinations. In others, those who died in its service are mourned. Beyond Cuba, there is a searching attack on racism in the United States, while solidarity is expressed with certain countries and people whose goals are viewed as admirable. The host of forms involved in their elaboration attest to Guillén's fecundity. The sixty-four poems of the collection are divided among an initial section of nineteen poems and three other sections: 'Sones, sonetos, baladas y canciones' ('*Sons*, Sonnets, Ballads and Songs') (eight poems), 'romancero' ('Collection of Ballads') (twenty-six poems) and 'Sátira' ('Satire') (eleven poems). In addition, there is the witty dramatic farce 'Floripondito,' Guillén's second contribution to the theatre genre. The poems of celebration are usually structured on a basis of antithesis, the significance of the revolution being emphasized by contrast with the past. The poem 'Canta el sinsonte en el Turquino' ('The Mockingbird Sings on Turquino Peak'), for instance, provides a wide-ranging retrospective viewing of Cuban life, the poet's exile, and his return in a new dawn. From this vantage point, there is a wave of reiterated, happy goodbyes to U.S. personnel: to governors of Cuba between 1898 and 1909 (Leonard Wood, Howard Taft, Charles Magoon), to the adviser on constitutional matters under Taft (Enoch Crowder), and to other prominent figures such as Charles Lynch and Richard Nixon. The promise of the new dawn is developed in the final section of the poem, which is preceded and followed by the salutation 'Buenos días, Fidel'; and 'buenos días' is the leitmotif of this section, greeting metonyms of a variety of aspects of Cuba's sovereignty. An impressive economy of usage results from all this due to the polyvalence of 'buenos días.' For example, the verse 'Palma, enterrada flecha, buenos días' ('Palm tree, buried arrow, good morning') recalls and integrates into the new life the 'Palma sola' of *El son entero*, making active the long-submerged potential for a decisive, vibrant Cuban presence. There is a vigorously etched image of Antonio Maceo:

> Buenos días, perfil de medalla, violento barbudo
> de bronce, vengativo machete en la diestra.

> *Good morning, medal profile, bearded violent one*
> *of bronze, vengeful machete in his right hand.*

The title of the poem appears in its penultimate line – the mockingbird singing on the highest peak of the Sierra Maestra, El Turquino – crowning the suggestion of triumph. A mood of exaltation is conveyed by the *sones* 'Soy como un árbol florido' ('I Am Like a Tree in Bloom'), in which *paronomasia* is developed with variations of the word 'flor,' and 'Se acabó' ('It is over') in which the lines

> Te lo prometió Martí
> y Fidel te lo cumplió

> *Martí promised it to you*
> *and Fidel delivered it to you*

serve as an *estribillo*. The power of these verses rests on the conveyance in them of history and poetry. Chiasmus plays a strong linking role here, allowing the juxtaposition through enjambment of the two great Cuban leaders 'Martí y Fidel' in this summation of their historical roles with the Cuban people.

Fidel Castro is also a central presence in the series of five historical *romances*, the verse form of the ancient Spanish epics, used here to convey the epic events in the early life of the struggle to establish the revolution.[46] The first of these, 'Son más en una mazorca ...' ('They Are More on a Corncob'), dealing with the arrival on the Cuban coast of Fidel and the nucleus of his guerrilla force in the Granma to later establish themselves, after severe losses, in the Sierra Maestra, is rich in metaphor, metonymy, personification, and zeugma. The first three of these figures are continued prominently in the rest of the series. In the second, 'Tierra de azules montañas ...' ('Land of Blue Mountains'), the simile 'como espumoso torrente' ('like a foaming torrent'), appearing four times in the poem, is the key image in suggesting the swell of support for the guerrillas. The pre-Columbian name of Santo Domingo is used in the next poem, 'Hacia la esclava Quisqueya ...' ('Towards the Slave Quisqueya'), as the destination of the fleeing Batista. The oxymoron 'jóvenes abuelos' ('young grandfathers') applied to the victorious guerrillas refers at once to their bearded visages and to the knowledge and experience they had acquired during their years of combat and study. Maceo and Martí are evoked metonymically by reference to San Pedro and Dos Ríos, the respective places of their deaths, and the image 'palmas baten los palmares' ('palm groves clap hands') is reminiscent of the action, in a different mood, of the agitated canes at the beginning of the 'Elegía a Jesús Menéndez.' In 'Abril sus flores abría ... / ('April was Opening its Flowers') the surreptitious and treacherous nature of the attack on the motherland at the Bay of Pigs (April 1961) is developed in the first part of the poem through usages like 'herir con fácil cuchillo / ... el gran pecho de Girón' ('to wound with easy knife / ... the great breast of Girón'). The firm response to this comes in the second part of the poem, where a profusion of verbs are structured in patterns that form incremental chiasmus, thereby underlining the idea of envelopment that is conveyed semantically:

> pero el pueblo los achica,
> los achica y los envuelve,
> los envuelve y los exprime
> y los exprime y los tuerce.

> *but the people humble them,*
> *humble them and envelop them,*
> *envelop them and squeeze them*
> *and squeeze them and bend them.*

In the last of these, 'Está el bisonte imperial ...' ('The Imperial Bison is ...'), another antithesis is developed, this time between imperialism and the revolution, symbolized by a bison and a dove respectively. The frustrated aggressiveness of the bison conveyed in the images of the first part of the poem gives way to the lofty militancy of the dove, which is supported materially and spiritually by the people:

> los milicianos la visten
> de pólvora y de ternura
> y de hierro y de esperanza
> y de granito y de espuma.

> *Militiamen clothe it [the revolution]*
> *with gunpowder and tenderness*
> *and with iron and with hope*
> *and with granite and with foam.*

The confidence expressed in the permanence of the revolution, found elsewhere in the poem 'Nadie' ('Nobody'), comes at the end of a series that shows a process of cause, leadership, struggle, popular commitment, and triumph. The poem celebrating this triumph from a popular perspective is the title poem of the collection, 'Tengo,' in which a representative ordinary Cuban pays homage to the revolution by showing the contrast between the past and the present. The speaker's identity is thus protean, covering the range of economic and social statuses occupied by the heretofore suffering classes: 'yo, campesino, obrero, gente simple' ('I, a peasant, worker, simple person'). With this mobility he can attest to the variety of new freedoms, rights, and opportunities in what is now seen as an open, democratic society. Besides, there is the perception of the revolution as an open-ended developmental force that sponsors the growth and fulfilment of the people:

> Tengo, vamos a ver,
> que ya aprendí a leer,
> a contar,
> tengo que ya aprendí a escribir
> y a pensar
> y a reír.

> *I have, let's see,*
> *I've already learned to read,*
> *to count,*
> *I've already learned to write*
> *and to think*
> *and to laugh.*

Here, then, is another instance of Guillén's allying the concept of improvement to his view of the simple man.

Closely linked to the idea of celebration is the idea of the defence of the revolution. This defence is undertaken in two principal ways: first, by retrospective viewings of the past in poems in which sarcasm and satire function conspicuously and, second, by exposing present dangers. The poem that most clearly spans celebration and defence is the *canción* 'Muchacha recién crecida' ('New Grown Girl') in which the 'paloma' as an object to be cherished is used as a symbol of the revolution. The retrospective views, carrying implicit warnings against the recrudescence of pre-revolutionary ills, and contained most prominently in the poems 'Allá lejos' ('Far Away') and 'Cualquier tiempo pasado fue peor' ('Any Past Time Was Worse'). As the titles suggest, the reality that has been superseded by the revolution is represented in them as being spatially and temporally distant from the new reality. This pattern appears in concentrated and acerbic form in the poem 'Como quisimos' ('As We Desired'), where the pattern in the first two quartets of three eleven-syllable lines and a final seven-syllable one yields in the final quartet to one eleven-syllable line and three seven-syllable ones, each with a marked caesura. This effects a slowing of pace to achieve affirmation precisely where the resolve to defend tenaciously the new status is being expressed. The poems 'Bonsal' and 'Frente al Oxford' ('Facing the Oxford') provide examples of the kinds of resistance the revolution must combat. In the former poem, the duplicitous diplomatic advances that would steer the revolution from its course are exposed by a technique in which the u.s. ambassador is shown as an animal clothed in charm and as seeking talks with a persistence that seems indecent. In the latter, the whole background to the immediate affront – the stationing of the warship Oxford outside Havana harbour to monitor the effectiveness of the u.s.-inspired economic blockade of Cuba – is articulated with serene anger in a poem in which the speaker addresses a friendly foreigner. The ship is seen as the embodiment of a paradigm of evils that includes Ben Johnson, Charles Lynch, William Walker, the Truman of Hiroshima, Joe McCarthy, u.s. military aggressiveness and economic exploitation. The poems '¡Míster, no!' and 'Como del cielo llovido ...' ('As if Rained Down from Heaven')[47] and the sonnets 'Abur, Don Pepe' ('So Long, Don Pepe') and 'Al mismo individuo' ('To the Same Individual') both dealing with the then Costa Rican president, José Figueres, form, together with 'Bonsal,' a paradigm based on diplomatic intrigue against the revolution. Forming a paradigm with 'Frente al Oxford' that involves aggressive military and economic acts are 'Son del bloqueo,' ('Blockade Son')[48] 'Touring for Trujillo,' 'Marines u.s.a.,' and '¡Oh, general en tu Pentágono!' ('Oh, General in Your Pentagon!').

There are also three poems in which the broad Latin-American problem of poverty and underdevelopment and approaches to them are considered. In 'Coplas americanas' ('American Verses'), a poem of studied simplicity, an intricate and appealing verse form is employed in which a five-syllable second line ending with a stressed syllable is in assonance with the final stressed eighth syllable of the fourth line of each quartet. This verse form serves to accent musically the intense presentation of the sad dependency of the Latin-American and Caribbean countries. The Alexandrine couplets of 'Crecen altas las flores' ('The Flowers Grow Tall') are presented by a speaker who establishes his knowledgeable authority by enumerating at the outset the eclectic components of his identity – as a thick-skinned alligator, as a Chinese, an Indian, a Soviet citizen, a black man, as one who understands the influence exerted by Charles Lynch and Jim Crow, and who knows in 1964 that the founder of McCarthyism, Joseph McCarthy (1908–1957) is not dead:

> Murió McCarthy, dicen. (Yo mismo dije: Es cierto, murió Mc-
> Carthy ...') Pero lo cierto es que no ha muerto.

> *McCarthy is dead, they say. (I myself said: 'It is true, McCarthy is*
> *dead ...') But the truth is that he is not dead.*

With these credentials he sets out to attack the 'Alliance for Progress' with images that suggest the inherent incompatibility of u.s. interests and attitudes with Latin American ones. In the *letrilla* 'Las dos cartas' ('The Two Charters'), two declarations concerning the future of Latin America with Cuba as the central preoccupation – the San José declaration of the Foreign Ministers of the Organization of American States of August 1960 and the Declaration of Havana made by Fidel Castro in September 1960 – are considered. Yet another form of antithesis is revealed here by Guillén. Each stanza consists of two *redondillas* as questions and is followed by an answer that alternately names one or the other declaration. And since the judgments are diametrically opposed, the images to which 'Con la Carta de la Habana' ('With the Havana Charter') is answered suggest, both in their visual and auditive aspects, what is desirable. These images are also predominant in the poem since the first and last stanzas have the Havana Charter as their subject.

The fate of individual countries is examined in other poems: 'Panamá,' where there is expectation of change; in the eleven-syllable tercets of 'A Chile' ('To Chile'), which express sad farewell and solidarity; and in the *décimas* of 'A Colombia' ('To Colombia'), where metonymy is used in the representation of this sad country of flowers: '¡Oh Colombia prisionera / orquídea puesta en un vaso!' ('Oh imprisoned Colombia / an orchid placed in a glass!'). With imperialism such a pressing concern, a view of relations with a big country that is not imperialistic is provided in the poem 'Unión Soviética' ('Soviet Union'). Long anaphorical series beginning with 'Ni' are developed to indicate the absence of the curses of imperialism and racism in Soviet–Cuban relations. That a poet should speak of this is a matter that is raised within the poem itself, and it is soon realized that 'poet' here is invested with all the fine perception of social and political questions that has been noticed throughout the course of Guillén's poetry. Thus verses like the following are spoken with comprehensive authoritativeness:

> En nuestro mar nunca encontré
> piratas de Moscú.
> (Hable, Caribe, usted.)
> Ni de Moscú tampoco en mis claras bahías
> ese ojo-radar superatento
> las noches y los días
> queriendo adivinar mi pensamiento.
> Ni bloqueos.
> Ni marines.
> Ni lanchas para infiltrar espías.
> ¿Barcos soviéticos? Muy bien.
> Son petroleros, mire usted.
> Son pescadores, sí señor.
> Otros llevan azúcar, traen café
> junto a fragantes ramos de esperanzas en flor.
> Yo, poeta, lo digo.
> Nunca de allá nos vino nada
> sin que tuviera el suave gusto del pan amigo,
> el sabor generoso de la voz camarada.

> *In our sea I have never found*
> *pirates from Moscow.*
> *(You can attest to that, Caribbean.)*
> *Neither from Moscow is there in my limpid bays*
> *that attentive radar-eye*
> *night and day*
> *trying to read my thoughts.*

Nor blockades.
Nor marines.
Nor launches for infiltrating spies.
Soviet ships! Very well.
They are oil tankers, look!
They are fishing boats, yes, sir.
Others take away sugar and bring coffee
together with fragrant branches of flowering hopes.
I, a poet, say this:
Nothing has ever come to us from there
that did not have the smooth taste of friendly bread,
the generous flavour of the comradely voice.

The poems '¿Puedes?' ('Can You?') and 'Tierra en la sierra y en el llano' ('Land in the Hills and on the Plain') develop one of the principal tenets of the praised 'Carta de la Habana': that people should have access to land. In '¿Puedes?' as in 'las dos cartas' questions play a central role. They show the preposterousness, readily acknowledged, of the private appropriation of elements such as air, water, and sky. This prepares the way for insistent questioning about the final element, land, which must evoke the response that is valid in the other cases. The *son* 'Tierra en la sierra ...' ('Land in the Hills'), in celebrating from the point of view of the hitherto landless peasant and the agrarian reform of 1959, furthers the notion of the justness of land distribution. Nor is the topic of defections from Cuba overlooked. In both poems touching on this topic, 'Responde tú' ('You, Answer') and '¡Ay qué tristeza que tengo!' ('Oh, How Sad I Am!'), the concern shown is not a sudden one related only to immediate developments. It has to do with some long-standing issues raised in Guillén's poetry and prose, with the 'convivencia' ('living together') and 'connivencia' ('connivance') advocated, for example, in the closing lines of the 'Son número 6': 'De aquí no hay nadie que se separe' ('No one will leave us'), a sentiment that has, of course, a new dimension in the post-revolutionary society, as the poem 'Prólogo' of *La rueda dentada* will show.

This topic has links with the treatment of the question of race in *Tengo*. In the poem 'Vine en un barco negrero' ('I Came in a Slave Ship'), for instance, a line of struggle by blacks for a dignified existence is traced, while the yagruma tree with its two-toned leaves forms an enduring Cuban symbol, from the days of slavery to the present, from Aponte through Maceo and Menéndez to the poet who writes in the period of full liberation. This state, as shown in the poems 'Está bien' ('It's alright'), 'Gobernador' ('Governor'), 'Escolares' ('Schoolboys'), and 'Un negro canta en Nueva York' ('A Black Man Sings in New York'), still eludes blacks in the United States.

A keen sense of history is evident in the finely crafted sonnets to Mella and Che Guevara. The images of the first vividly convey the daring and tenacity of Cuba's first communist leader. There is here, too, the idea of time that allows the grafting of a better future on to a past that was in dire need of change. A parallel between San Martín and Martí on the one hand and Che Guevara and Fidel Castro on the other is the basis on which the sonnet 'Che Guevara' is developed. The duality of firmness and gentle warmth that make them excellent guides is emphasized in the portraits of both Lenin and Martí. Lenin is at once 'tempestad y abrigo' ('storm and shelter'), while with Martí it is necessary to see beyond the voice that seems to be a sigh and hands that seem like shadows, that

> Su voz
> abre la piedra, y sus manos
> parten el hierro.

> *His voice*
> *breaks stone, and his hands*
> *split iron.*

Continuity in Guillén's poetry may be observed in his treatment, with new formal procedures, of certain other subjects with which he had dealt in earlier books, such as the soldier, nature, and death. In the poem 'Balada,' the loss of two soldiers in a national effort, indicated by the metonym 'bandera' ('flag'), is the cause of the sadness of the 'paloma,' the symbol of the revolutionary spirit. Two different kinds of fighters with two opposing motives for fighting are presented in the two stanzas of 'Canción.' The unreflecting, automatic soldier with an underdeveloped consciousness of the world and of the possibilities of military uses will die unremembered, while the battler against the banditry of soldiers will spawn an ineffaceable line of resisters.

Nature is subtly treated in two poems of the collection and in a way that is consistent with its treatment in other parts of Guillén's work. The poem 'Voy hasta Uján' ('I Am Going as Far as Uján'), one of five dealing with China, is presented as a dialogue, which on the surface resolves the question as to whether the speaker should go to Shanghai, where he is inclined to go, or to Uján, the destination of his interlocutor. The speaker finally opts for Uján. The poem, though, treats the question of man's precedence over nature. Shanghai is presented in the garb of nature. It is at the mouth of the Yang-tse-kiang – the river on which the two are travelling – the confluence of river and sea that had so entertained the imagination of the speaker as he admired the cloudless sky. On the other hand, Uján is given no other identity in the poem than the fact that his friendly interlocutor is going there. By outgrowing his attraction to nature and putting man in the ascendancy, the speaker shows an attitude consistent with views established throughout Guillén's poetry. The inadequacies of nature in the face of man's inhumanity to man that were shown earlier in Guillén's 'Arte poética' of *La paloma de vuelo popular* are demonstrated here in the Alexandrine sonnet addressed to the moon, 'Pascuas sangrientas de 1956' ('Bloody Christmas 1956'), one of the two poems dealing with a brutal night-time slaughter of twenty-one civilian opponents of Batista by his soldiers. In the precise case of the moon, its inadequacies, coupled with doubts about the real basis of its prestige, were evident in Guillén's poetry as long ago as 1931, in his poem 'Elegía moderna del motivo cursi' ('Modern Elegy of the Motif of Affectation'). The last four lines of the sonnet are:

> Luna grande del trópico, alta sobre el palmar,
>
> tú que despierta estabas aquella noche triste.
> Luna fija y redonda, tú que todo lo viste,
> no te puedes callar, ¡no te puedes callar!
>
> *Big tropical moon, high above the palm grove,*
>
> *you were awake on that sad night.*
> *Fixed and round moon, you who saw everything,*
> *you must not be silent, you must not be silent!*

The lines are complexly ironical, and they go beyond pathos to deep indignation. The big tropical moon appears here in anything but its stereotypic romantic role. It is the mute, insensate witness to a slaughter that has national reverberations, as is indicated by 'palmar,' and although it is a pathetic fallacy to expect it to speak, it is nevertheless the least likely of those who witnessed or participated in the atrocity to wish to withhold evidence against the criminals. Thus the moon bears a moral superiority to them; but ultimately, because it must remain frustratingly quiet, it is useless and irrelevant to a society that demands justice.

Death as a topic appears in the poems 'Camilo,' 'A Conrado Benítez' and 'La sangre numerosa' ('The Numerous Blood'). The first of these, considering the death of the revolutionary leader Camilo Cienfuegos, focuses, as did the poem 'Paul Eluard,' on the abruptness of the disappearance. This for the speaker is a troubling characteristic, since it frustrates the materialist desire to understand the how and the why of his death; but ultimately Camilo's death is transcended by the permanence of his contribution. This kind of transcendence is evident, too, in the poem dedicated to Conrado Benítez, the young teacher who was hanged by counter-revolutionaries in his school in the remote Escambray region of Cuba as he worked in the literacy program in 1961. In this poem, it is shown clearly that the link between present and future is a part of a revolutionary identity, a notion from which the idea of the immortality of the revolutionary follows:

> Maestro, amigo puro,
> verde joven de rostro detenido,
> quien te mató el presente
> ¿Cómo matar creyó que iba el futuro?
> Fijas están las rosas de tu frente,
> tu sangre es más profunda que el olvido.

> *Teacher, pure friend,*
> *green youth with well-cared face,*
> *whoever killed your present*
> *how did he think he could kill your future?*
> *Secure are the roses of your forehead,*
> *your blood is more profound than oblivion.*

This concept is developed powerfully in 'La sangre numerosa.' The poem is dedicated to the militiaman Eduardo García who was mortally wounded on 15 April 1961 in one of the raids carried out by U.S. planes on Cuban military and civilian airports in preparation for the Bay of Pigs invasion. Before dying, he struggled to a wall and wrote with his blood the name 'Fidel.' This information is contained basically in the dedication that accompanies the poem, the text of which is:

> Cuando con sangre escribe
> FIDEL este soldado que por la Patria muere,
> no digáis miserere:
> esa sangre es el símbolo de la Patria que vive.

> Cuando su voz en pena
> lengua para expresarse parece que no halla,
> no digáis que se calla,
> pues en la pura lengua de la Patria resuena.

> Cuando su cuerpo baja
> exánime a la tierra que lo cubre ambiciosa,
> no digáis que reposa,
> pues por la Patria en pie resplandece y trabaja.

Ya nadie habrá que pueda
parar su corazón unido y repartido.
No digáis que se ha ido;
su sangre numerosa junto a la Patria queda.

When with his blood
this soldier who dies for the Fatherland writes
FIDEL, *do not say miserere:*
that blood is the symbol of the Fatherland that lives.

When in pain his voice
seems not to find language to express itself,
do not say that he is silent,
since he resounds in the pure language of the Fatherland.

When his body descends
lifeless to the earth that ambitiously covers him,
do not say that he is at rest,
since upright for the Fatherland he shines and works.

There is now no one who can
still his united and shared heart.
Do not say that he has gone:
his numerous blood nurtures the Fatherland.

Here again Guillén has discovered a metrical form that merges impeccably with the other aspects of his poem. The four stanzas are symmetrically constructed except for the absence of the anaphoric 'Cuando ...' in the final one. In each case the initial seven-syllable verse is in effect prolonged into the following Alexandrine by enjambment. Besides, caesura occurs precisely after the seventh syllable in the two Alexandrines in each of the four quartets, thus providing a measured rhythm. But these pauses are subordinated to the sustained, taut, rhythmic pattern in the initial twenty-one-syllable sense period of each stanza. This in turn results from a rising intonation in these sense periods that is due to the fact that they end strongly, usually in verbs, and in two exceptional cases, in adjectives. Both of these adjectives attain special strength: 'ambiciosa,' because of personification and 'repartido,' because of its paradoxical function. The rising intonation in all the twenty-one-syllable sense periods is begun in each case in the first, seven-syllable line, which also almost invariably ends in a verb. All these musical features contribute to the high solemnity, dignity, and power of the content. These characteristics of content are supplied semantically from the outset by such items as 'sangre,' 'FIDEL,' 'este soldado,' 'Patria,' and 'muere.' They are furthered by the use of the formal second-person plural 'digáis' and the *cultismo*, or learned word, 'miserere' in the third seven-syllable verse. In the fourth verse of the stanza, the metaphor with 'sangre' as its tenor provides a vehicle, 'símbolo de la Patria que vive,' that maintains with clarity the elevated level of expression. The contrast created by this vehicle with the second verse of the stanza, 'este soldado que por la Patria muere,' underlines the power brought to 'sangre' by its associations.

The pattern of adverbial clause containing an act or attitude of the soldier, followed by a precluded incorrect interpretation and then by the correct interpretation, which occupies the three punctuated segments of the first stanza, is continued in the next two stanzas. Continued, too, is the loftiness of tone, which is contributed in the second stanza in the formal sense by hyperbaton and in the ideological sense by the relaying of the voice of the soldier to that of the Fatherland. In the third stanza, the adjective 'ambiciosa' serves as an example of the kind of subtle complexity that abounds in Guillén's poetry. It modifies and personifies 'tierra.' At the same time, by its semantic value it points to a double inadequacy: it shows the futility with which the earth attempts to contain the heroic soldier and it mocks the idea of personification itself, making conspicuous the fact that 'tierra' cannot really be personified and is of a lower order than man. The full effect of this is to keep unsullied the image of the soldier, as the verb 'resplandece' of the last line of the stanza confirms. The denial of the notion that the soldier's legacy can be contained is made categorical and the possible agents of its suppression raised to the human level in the final stanza. The adjectives 'unido' and 'repartido' used in this stanza pose a paradox in their immediate context; the paradox is resolved by taking into account the identity that by now has been securely established between the exemplary soldier and the people. Thus 'unido' evokes the idea of the bond between the people as a whole and the soldier created by his sentiment and his courage ('corazón'), while 'repartido' suggests the idea of the diffusion among the people of these qualities; and 'sangre numerosa' affirms the broad, salutary effect of his example.

It is important to notice that the speaker is here addressing, with the authority of a firm and wise teacher, an audience made up of the people in general, the unspecified subject of 'digáis.' Since their attitudes and impressions, which he corrects, are already sympathetic ones that needed to be refocused and refined, their silent acquiescence may be assumed and in this raised state of consciousness they may be regarded as joining the paradigm formed by the soldier, FIDEL, and the Fatherland. Besides, owing largely to the special function of the anaphoric 'Cuando ...' in the poem, the elevating effect of the soldier's act must be perceived as a sustained one; for 'Cuando' is not used here in a future conditional sense. The images it introduces are events that have taken place, but the broad public has not actually witnessed them as they unfolded. The images can only be seen as replays in the popular imagination of each of these events. The idea of recurrence suggested in this contributes to giving sustained effect to the exemplary behaviour of the national hero. While there is no explicit antithesis to this lofty unanimity in the poem itself, in the light of the dedication that accompanies it – 'To Eduardo García, the militiaman who wrote with his blood, upon dying machine gunned by Yankee aviation in April 1961, Fidel's name' – the forces that killed this soldier form the unstated antithesis. Thus two opposing silences, the non-representation of aggressive external force on the one hand and the silence of the determined, unified people on the other are operative in the poem, heightening its tension. With 'La sangre numerosa,' Guillén has made of a historical event an enduring lesson and a permanent work of art.

Finally, a prayer, 'A la virgen de la Caridad' ('To the Virgin of Charity'), that demonstrates in yet another form our poet's ability to combine piquant humour and serious social commentary. In this *décima* (the form appropriate for dealing with such popular matters as Cuba's patron saint), the speaker, functioning as the voice of the poor, touches economically on such subjects as poverty, class privilege, and inequality and on the failure of the religious approach to remedy them:

> Virgen de la Caridad,
> que desde un peñón de cobre
> esperanza das al pobre
> y al rico seguridad.
> En tu criolla bondad,
> ¡oh madre!, siempre creí,
> por eso pido de ti
> que si esa bondad me alcanza
> des al rico la esperanza,
> la seguridad a mí.

> *Virgin of Charity,*
> *who from your copper pedestal*
> *giveth hope to the poor*
> *and to the rich security.*
> *In your Creole kindness,*
> *Oh Mother! I have always believed,*
> *and so I beg of you*
> *that if that kindness extends to me*
> *give to the rich hope,*
> *and security to me.*

Tengo, then, as befits its place in Guillén's first book of the post-revolutionary period, contributes a mood of celebration, new in its prominence, to his poetry. It combines this with several of the preoccupations that produce the ironic, satiric, sarcastic, and elegiac moods of his earlier poetry. But whether the mood be new or old, the formal means he employs in evoking it displays constant innovation. He adapts here traditional forms such as the *romance*, the *redondilla*, Alexandrine and eleven-syllable sonnets to new realities, adjusts his previous innovations such as the *son* to give them new possibilities, or creates new forms, all to accommodate his revolutionary insights into historical reality. The breadth of the collection is a measure of the enormous scope of Guillén's poetic powers.

EL GRAN ZOO

El Gran Zoo (*The Great Zoo*) consists of poems that combine characteristic elements observable in the course of the development of Guillén's poetry with an increased role for metaphor and for compactness of design that in their concentration are new to his poetry. The book is a bestiary in which people, places, institutions, and abstract and concrete things are represented as animals. In the long literary tradition practised by such writers as Aesop, La Fontaine, Apollinaire, Valle-Inclán, Borges, and Neruda the overwhelming tendency has been to use animals as the subject of fables illustrating human attitudes, or to show a fascination with animal life, sometimes situating mankind in general in an unfavourable position relative to the animals. As will be shown, Guillén's concept and practice of the bestiary are unusual in their versatility. His animals are sometimes tenors and at other times vehicles of metaphors, which by their extension and ingenuity attract attention to themselves while they illuminate one or more conceits.

Antecedents to this kind of recourse to animal life for imagery date from Guillén's pre-1930 poetry, from 'El aeroplano' ('The Airplane') and 'Sol de lluvia' ('Sunny Rain') of 1927 and 'Reloj' ('Clock') of 1929. They are continued in 'West Indies, Ltd.' of 1934, 'Guitarra' ('Guitar') of 1942, in 'Un largo lagarto verde' ('A Long Green Lizard') of 1952 and 'Pequeña letanía grotesca en la muerte del senador McCarthy' ('Little Grotesque Litany on the Death of Senator McCarthy') of 1958. Guillén began to write the poems of *El Gran Zoo* in 1958, producing the first six or seven while he was in exile in Argentina.[49] He continued to produce them up to 1967 when the book was first published. There is a great deal of evidence in *Tengo* that the poet's imagination was engaged, while the poems of that book were being written, in the overlapping activity of composing poems of *El Gran Zoo*; for in the former book the usages of animal imagery become intensive. In the initial poem of *Tengo*, 'Bonsal,' the subject of the poem is described as

Animal
ojiazul, peliplúmbeo, de color
rojicarne, que hable un inglés letal.

Blue eyed, leaden haired
animal,
flesh red in colour,
that speaks a lethal English.

In the poem 'Frente al Oxford' the battleship is called

... aquella larga bestia de gris acero,
mojándose en mis aguas, mis tierras vigilando.

... that long steel-grey beast,
entering my waters, spying on my country.

In 'Canta el sinsonte ...' ('The Mockingbird Sings ...'), the erstwhile occu-
piers of Cuba are told, 'Podéis marcharos, animal / muchedumbre' ('You
can leave, animal / crowd'); and the poem 'Primero de octubre' ('First
of October') begins 'Recuerdo cuando China / era una bestia fina / y en-
démica' ('I remember when China / was a thin / and endemic beast'). The
entire poem 'Está el bisonte imperial ...' ('The Imperial Bison Is ...') is, as
we have seen, structured on the basis of antithetical animal imagery focusing
on the bison and the dove. But the dove ('la paloma') is an exceptional and
supremely positive image throughout Guillén's poetry. It symbolizes the revolution. This distinguishes it from mere animal imagery, which usually carries
a negative charge. And so it is that the cages of *El Gran Zoo* hold animals
not as curiosities to be explored, as in Neruda's 'Bestiario,' but as creatures
that have been judged and in most cases, as in Dante's 'Inferno,' condemned
with varying degrees of severity. They are sketched with a vividness that
belies the brevity of the poems. The concept of animal tends to be equated
with the levels of behaviour that are injurious to man in his normal quest for
improving his own life and the lives of others about him. An animal, then,
like nature, is at its best when it is serving that end, when as with 'paloma,' it
suggests the certainty of a new and just social order.

The range of the collection is due to the variety of subjects covered. Of
its thirty-nine poems, the largest group deals with various types of people.
Among them are 'Los usureros' ('The Usurers'), patricidal, cannibalistic
vultures that do not fly or sing and who do commerce in their feathers; 'Los
oradores' ('The Orators'), the compulsive practitioners of the inebriating

exercise of the cliché, who extend the paradigm of the 'En estos momentos críticos' ('In These Critical Times') found in 'West Indies, Ltd.'; the 'Gángster' belonging to the bulldog family and associated with illicit drugs and other imported objects that were shown to be the scourge of the West Indies in 'West Indies, Ltd.' Echoes of 'West Indies, Ltd.' precisely of the stanza of that poem beginning

> Me río de ti, noble de las Antillas
> mono que andas saltando de mata en mata
>
> *I laugh at you, nobleman of the West Indies,*
> *monkey that goes jumping from bush to bush*

are also heard in the poem 'Monos' ('Monkeys'). Other subjects that recall earlier Guillén preoccupations are 'El chulo' ('The Pimp'), which had been encountered in *Motivos de son* and *Sóngoro cosongo*, and '[Charles] Lynch' who, beginning with his appearance in the 'Elegía a Jesús Menéndez' of 1951, is a frequent target in Guillén's poetry and the police ('Policía') which became a hostilely treated group in *West Indies, Ltd.*

Only one of the above titles, 'Monos,' is normally denotative of the animal world. All the others support the view that the designation 'animal' in *El Gran Zoo* springs from the unworthy actions of the subjects in much the same way as the perpetrators of the crime in the earlier-examined 'Pascuas sangrientas de 1956' ('Bloody Christmas, 1956') are comparable to nature in its most handicapped aspects. This concept is developed further in those poems dealing with institutions or organizations in which certain mentalities congregate. In 'Policía,' for example, two strata in the hierarchy of policemen are presented: the pipe-smoking ones whose phobia is international communism and the beat-walking ones whose phobia is local communism. The 'KKK' is howling and dying from starvation in its Cuban cage, unable to obtain its normal fare of roasted black flesh. Another klan-like organization, the Haitian 'Tonton Macoute,' is an exhibit that is also conveyed in imagery that suggests intense savagery. The poem 'Gorila' ('Gorilla') deals explicitly with the concept of animal that I have been examining. It exploits the polyvalency of the word 'gorila,' meaning either the ape of the African bush or the Latin American military 'strongman,' known for his machismo, his massacres, and his medals. The poem reads:

> El gorila es un animal
> a poco más enteramente humano.
> No tiene patas sino casi pies,

no tiene garras sino casi manos.
Le estoy hablando a usted
del gorila del bosque africano.

El animal que está a la vista,
a poco más
es un gorila enteramente.
Patas en lugar de pies
y casi garras en lugar de manos.
Le estoy monstrando a usted
el gorila americano.

Le adquirió
nuestro agente viajero en un cuartel
para el Gran Zoo.

The gorilla is an animal
that is almost entirely human.
It does not have paws but almost feet,
it does not have claws but almost hands.
I am talking to you
about the gorilla of the African forests.

The animal now before you,
is almost
entirely a gorilla.
Paws it has instead of feet
and almost claws instead of hands.
I am showing you
the American gorilla.

It was acquired
by our travelling agent in a military barracks
for The Great Zoo.

This category also includes, in the poem 'Las águilas' ('The Eagles'), a survey of symbols of imperialism that ends in the bathos of Eagle Brand condensed milk.

Another category in which people as animals are the prime exhibits is one in which certain abstract qualities are portrayed. The presence of the abstract quality in such poems makes the imagery three-dimensional, presenting at once the person, the animal, and the abstract quality. Thus the severe and compact lines of 'Institutriz' sketch the instructress, the giraffe, and haughtiness as inextricable parts of one system. In the poem 'Tenor,' a consuming vanity is evoked in a cage in which the mirror is a purposeful prop, allowing the singer to be absorbed endlessly in himself, in his own glory and advancement to a degree that makes him less than a social being:

Está el tenor en éxtasis
contemplando al tenor
del espejo, que es el mismo tenor
en éxtasis
que contempla al tenor.

Sale a veces a pasear por el mundo
llevado de un bramante de seda,
aplaudido en dólares,
tinta de imprenta
y otras sustancias gananciales.
(Aquí en el Zoo le molesta
cantar por la comida
y no es muy generoso con sus arias.)
Milán Scala.
New York Metropolitan.
Opera de París.

The tenor is in ecstasy
contemplating the tenor
in the mirror, who is the same tenor
in ecstasy
who is contemplating the tenor.

Sometimes he goes travelling about the world
led by a silk leash
applauded in dollars,
printer's ink
and other profitable substances.
(Here in the Zoo it annoys him
to sing for his supper
and he is not very generous with his arias.)
Milan Scala.
New York Metropolitan.
Paris Opera.

Places are treated in another category with, again, striking versatility. 'El Caribe' is an animal composed inventively of seascape, while the landscape of the Andean peak 'El Aconcagua,' by its animalization and slow mobility, is endowed with a forbidding sense of distance and a coldness that is associated with the moon. The moon itself gets separate, characteristically harsh treatment in the three telegrammatic stanzas of the poem 'Luna' ('Moon'):

Mamífero metálico. Nocturno.

Se le ve
el rostro comido por un acné.

Sputniks y sonetos.

Metallic mamal. Nocturnal.

Its face can be seen
eaten by acne.

Sputniks and sonnets.

This cryptic last verse is decipherable by relating it to a pattern often observed in Guillén's writing in which military or scientific technology and poetry, such as the 'bazukas y poemas' of 'Crecen altas las flores' ('The Flowers Grow Tall'), are used as partners in combating a regressive element. In this case, sputniks and sonnets are enlisted in the task of demystifying the moon, of countering the magnetism it holds for the lazy imagination. The sputniks are those that enable scientific study of the moon and the sonnets are like the already-examined 'Pascuas sangrientas de 1956' ('Bloody Christmas, 1956'). Nature is shown in other poems to be ignorantly destructive. In 'Ciclón' ('Cyclone'), for instance, with the irresponsible innocence of its age of two days, a hurricane wreaks havoc as it smashes into one West Indian island after another; and in 'Los vientos' ('Winds') high winds ignorantly destroy huts, boats, farms – all those things carved out of nature by man in his struggle to satisfy his needs.

   The poems dealing with abstract things have a special significance in the bestiary, since they demonstrate a constant trait in Guillén's poetry, that of making phenomena concrete that are often referred to theoretically. We have seen this throughout, particularly in those poems dealing with death. The poems 'El sueño' ('Sleep'), 'La sed' ('Thirst'), and 'El hambre' ('Hunger') are examples of this. 'El hambre' is representative of the technique employed in these poems. The abstraction is made concrete not by its representation by one known animal but, through similes and metaphors, by being a composite of selected hostile characteristics of various animals. An intensification is thus achieved of the kind of personified hunger earlier encountered in 'West Indies, Ltd.' 'El hambre' reads:

Esta es el hambre. Un animal
todo colmillo y ojo.
No se harta en una mesa.
Nadie lo engaña ni distrae.
No se contenta
con un almuerzo o una cena.
Anuncia siempre sangre.
Ruge como león, aprieta como boa,
piensa como persona.

El ejemplar que aquí se ofrece
fue cazado en la India (suburbios de Bombay),
pero existe en estado más o menos salvaje
en otras muchas partes.

No acercarse.

This is hunger. An animal
all teeth and eyes.
It is not satiated at one sitting.
No one deceives or distracts it.
It is not satisfied
with a lunch or a supper.
It always announces blood.
It roars like a lion, squeezes like a boa,
thinks like a person.

The sample given here
was captured in India (outskirts of Bombay),
but it exists in a more or less savage state
in many other places.

Keep away.

Especially remarkable here is the culminating simile, 'piensa como persona.' It lifts the series of similes above the animal level to indicate the ingenuity, persistence, and irrepressibility of hunger. As such it is a defiant challenger of people and to be overcome requires their most calculating means of combat.

Finally, some of these poems contain reflections on literature itself. In the poem 'Escarabajos' ('Beetles'), for example, exhibits of that species taken from different countries and from pre-Columbian times to the present, have their special cage. The poem ends 'El de oro / (donación especial de Edgar Poe) / se nos murió' ('The golden one / (a special donation from Edgar Poe) / died on us'). The allusion is to Poe's story 'The Scarab,' and the death signifies the weakness of the fantastic when it is compared with the real. There are also allusions to Guillén's own earlier poetry. In the poem 'Al público. Avio-Mamut' ('To the Public. Aero-Mammoth') the specimen arousing curiosity turns out not to be the wreckage of an airplane but the skeleton of a mammoth. This plays on and reverses the order of identification presented in 'El aeroplano' ('The Airplane') (1927), where it was projected that in the distant future the wreckage of an airplane would be adjudged to be the remains of an extinct species of animal. 'Reloj' ('Clock') elaborates on the human attitude of embrace displayed by the hands of a clock that was first treated in his poem 'Reloj' of 1929. Of all the exhibits of *El Gran Zoo*, 'Guitarra' ('Guitar') receives the most favourable treatment. The animal serving as its metaphorical vehicle is the bird – not the flightless bird of 'Gángster,' but one that soars and swoops and is capable of song. It also has 'mulata' ('mulatto') associations and is inspired by *sones* and *coplas*. All this makes it suggestive of the 'paloma' ('dove'). The poem was written in 1958, in the period of the publication of *La paloma de vuelo popular*, and shares a close identity with the symbol embodied in that title, the revolution, which is its dream. It also displays the essential characteristics of the instrument used by Guillén to convey his 'arte poética' in *El son entero* and thereby has high significance in *El Gran Zoo*.

The titles of the poems seem to obey the following systems. Where a sustained metaphor used in the poem is developed in relation to one animal, the poem is named for that animal. For instance, 'El cangrejo' ('The Crab'), with its terrible voraciousness, represents cancer. Where the vehicle used to represent the phenomenon is a vague approximation of an unspecified animal or a combination of aspects of several animals, the phenomenon is named in the title, as in 'Bomba atómica' ('Atomic Bomb') where the danger posed by the undefined animal is exacerbated by the reckless attitude publicly shown in some quarters toward it. In a third case the titles are polyvalent, referring both to an animal and to something else as in 'Gorila' and 'La osa mayor' ('The Great Bear'). And there is one poem, 'El tigre' ('The Tiger'), in which the procedure playfully defies the above systems, fittingly so since the poem is structured as a riddle. The initial images

> Anda preso en su jaula
> de duras rayas negras.

El metal con que ruge
quema, está al rojo blanco

A prisoner in its cage
of hard black stripes.
The metal with which it roars
burns, it is white red

seem to conform to the title. But they are followed by a series of possible
tenors that have the effect of transforming the initial images into unstable
potential vehicles, conveying the idea of caged fury and illustrating one or
the other of these tenors:

(Un gángster.
El instinto sexual.
Un boxeador.
Un furioso de celos.
Un general.
El puñal del amor.)

A gangster.
Sexual instinct.
A boxer.
A man in a fit of jealousy.
A general.
Love's dagger.

Then, following the ironical use of the verb, comes the solution that corresponds to the title:

Tranquilizarse.
Un tigre
real.

Calm yourself.
A real
tiger.

The net result, then, is the economic achievement of a multiciplicity of
analogies to the impression given by the tiger.

   The collection contains, as is constant in Guillén's poetry, a variety of
metrical forms. Polyrhythmic lines are predominant, with frequent broken

feet, stressed final syllables, and occasional consonantal rhyme or assonance. This assists in the production of a wide range of tone in the book, from
the quietly narrative poems such as 'Los ríos' ('Rivers'), to the declamator-
ily hostile ones such as 'Lynch,' even when the overwhelming number of
poems are disapproving of their subjects. With all these features added to
the wide diversity of subjects treated, the thirty-nine short poems come, upon
careful reading, to represent a substantial body of work.

'Aviso' ('Notice'), the poem that introduces *El Gran Zoo* is to be read
(with its clear patriotic indicators) as suggesting that the collection is, for
all its attractive novelty and hyperbolic temper, a contribution to the revolution. This notion is confirmed by the poem 'Guitarra.' As in *Tengo*, the
focus is most often on what is to be guarded against, spurned, or condemned
from the standpoint of a new society that promises general social, economic, and cultural advancement. The poem 'Tenor,' for example, at first
glance a work of lively entertainment, attacks the individualism and vanity
that are to be deprecated in the new society in which the salutary approach is
one of co-operativeness. And so, being intensely serious but 'con la risa
que aprendió' ('with the laughter that he learned'), Guillén produces in *El
Gran Zoo* a work that coheres with the essential attitudes shown in his
earlier works. His regard for the broad literary tradition is shown in his
encouragement of projects to have the collection translated into Greek and
French (the languages to which the bestiary is most closely linked) almost
coincidentally with the book's original publication in Spanish.[50] But, essentially, he has adapted the bestiary to serve Cuban purposes in a way that
enriches the tradition.

LA RUEDA DENTADA

Guillén's next book, *La rueda dentada* (*The Gear-wheel*) published in
1972, reveals in yet other ways his ability to create new forms and adapt old
ones to a changed historical situation and while doing so to achieve a new
kind of poetry with no barriers between it and a developing people. The book
suggests that the changed historical situation determines new social responsibilities. At the same time it accommodates subjects that were not treated in
the years before the revolution and allows others to show a different face.

Throughout this new epoch Guillén contributes to the construction of the
national life with poems that in their formal aspects invite the reader to new
aesthetic experiences. In this regard, the counterpart of the attitude of showing what was to be avoided, such as the individualism in the poem 'Tenor,'
is revealed at once firmly and subtly in poems that point to what is to be done,
such as the poem that introduces *La rueda dentada* and bears the title
'Prólogo' ('Prologue'). What is immediately conspicuous about the poem is
the unusual indirectness of its mode of presentation. This is made intriguing by

the pronounced rhythmical and phonic features. The indirectness derives from the evident improbability that the poem deals primarily with the obvious subject. The poem reads:

La rueda dentada, con un diente
roto,
si empieza una vuelta se detiene
a poco.

Donde el diente falta (o mejor no falta,
sino que está roto),
la rueda se traba, el diente no encaja,
la rueda no marcha, no pasa, no avanza,
se detiene a poco.

Ni árboles de fuerza, ni engranajes, bielas,
coronas tal vez, brazos y poleas,
serán suficientes, pues como se sabe
no hay rueda dentada sin dientes que ande,
ni rueda que ande con diente que falle:
si empieza una vuelta se detiene a poco,
bien si el diente falta, o bien si está roto.

Pudieras, lector, pensar que yo busco
meterte en un cuarto cerrado y oscuro,
para calentarte de tal modo el seso
que exclames con rabia: ¡Demonios, qué es esto!
Mas yo me adelanto, y con voz tranquila
te digo: ¿Qué pasa, que vas tan de prisa?

No es nada
no es nada
no es nada
no es nada

no es nada
no es nada
no es nada
no es nada

¡Arriba y arriba la Rueda Dentada!
¡Arriba y arriba!
¡Arriba y arriba, dé vueltas y siga!

¡Arriba y arriba!
Sin que falte un diente, o esté un diente
roto.
Siempre mucho mucho
Nunca poco poco.

The gear-wheel, with one tooth broken,
if it starts to turn it soon stops.

Where the tooth is missing (or rather is not missing,
but broken)
the wheel labours, the tooth does not grab,
the wheel does not move, it does not go, it does not advance,
it soon stops.

Neither drive-shafts nor gears, connecting rods
or perhaps crowns, levers and pulleys
will be sufficient, since as is known,
there is no gear-wheel that works without teeth
nor any wheel that works with a bad tooth:
if it starts to turn it soon stops,
be the tooth missing or broken.

You could think, reader, that I am trying
to put you in a closed dark room,
to so heat up your brain
that you shout angrily: What the hell is this!
But I will go on and with a tranquil voice
ask you: What is the matter? Why are you in such a hurry?

It is nothing
it is nothing
it is nothing
it is nothing

it is nothing
it is nothing
it is nothing
it is nothing

Faster and faster, gear-wheel!
Faster and faster!

> *Faster and faster, turn and turn!*
> *Faster and faster!*
> *Without a tooth being missing, or a tooth being*
> *broken.*
> *Always more and more*
> *never less and less.*

The poem at first glance deals with a gear-wheel, with the functional dis-
ability of a defective gear-wheel, and suggests in the last stanza the happy
fulfilment brought by the working of a sound wheel. The poem begins with
anticlimactic lines, each presenting expectation and then frustration. The
gear-wheel of the first hemistich is shown to be defective in the second. Its
expectant beginning of a turn in the third hemistich is shown to be abortive in
the fourth. The key words effecting antithesis are presented as short lines
whose independence is mitigated by enjambment. The words themselves,
'roto' and 'a poco,' are linked by forceful assonance. The unproductive
consequences of the faulty tooth are developed in the second stanza and are
heightened by the use of the anaphorical 'no,' negating verbs that indicate
action and progress:

> La rueda se traba, el diente no encaja,
> la rueda no marcha, no pasa, no avanza.

The 'a' 'a' assonance in all these verbs complements internally the identical
end assonance that is dominant in this stanza. In the third stanza, hyperbolic enumeration is used to indicate the impossibility of any external force
making the wheel effective. So the conclusion:

> No hay rueda dentada sin dientes que ande,
> ni rueda que ande con diente que falle,

introduced by 'como se sabe,' comes when the idea has been well established. Its repetitious nature is underlined by the use of *annominatio* –
'dientes,' 'dentada,' 'diente' – and chiasmus – 'rueda sin dientes que ande'
followed by 'rueda que ande con dientes que falle.' The reappearance of the
third and fourth lines of the poem as well as the fifth and sixth, slightly
altered, to close this stanza and this first part of the poem further emphasizes
the inadequacy of a gear-wheel whose revolutionary capacity is limited to
an incomplete revolution. And all the while there is the rhythm of the verses,
skilfully accentuating starting and stopping, the anticlimactic direction of
the verses.

The subtlety with which Guillén uses music is demonstrated in the rhyth-

mic change he effects in the next stanza while using the same twelve-syllable
verse used in the previous stanza. The diminished caesura, the use of the
familiar second person and an easier level of language that includes colloquial
expressions make the lines now flow in familiar conversational cadences.
The indirectness of the presentation of the poem becomes an issue within the
poem itself as the reader is imagined to show premature exasperation at this
poem that is apparently going nowhere, that promises no solution to this
point. The effect of this is to arouse in the reader a curiosity about another
level of emerging meaning. The eight three-syllable verses of the refrain form
two twelve-syllable verses, but with yet a different rhythm. With their
quickened, regular pace they announce new life in the wheel. This smooth-
ness of movement leads to the final stanza which with its exclamations
exhorts the gear-wheel to productive action, which is achievable only when
the teeth of the wheel are sound and working in concert.

It thus becomes clear that the poem is an allegory, an extended metaphor,
carrying a message aimed at furthering the process of reconstruction. The
message is that there can be no weak link in the human chain of participants in
this process. The primary audience to whom the poem is addressed is, of
course, the Cuban people, but it may have relevance to other situations. The
allegory is a universal and perennial device for imprinting a message on the
minds of those who have ears to hear by presenting the message engagingly,
and it presumes in the listeners the capacity of transposition, of constructing (on the basis of experience) a paradigm that parallels the given metaphor.
Guillén enriches the tradition here as in the earlier examined 'Sensemayá,'
with musicality that is warmly inviting to his public. This poem, with its
demonstration first of the cause of futile effort and then of the correction
that leads to fruitfulness, shows his ability to place poetry at the service of
cohesive reconstruction.

Another principal manifestation of social responsibility to the new society
is to be found in those poems that treat various aspects of the concept of
defence. There is a vigilance against the evils of the old times expressed
occasionally in recollections of those times. In the poem 'Burgueses' ('The
Bourgeoisie'), for instance, the speaker, a battler in the class struggle, re-
members with passionate denunciation the conditions of deprivation that until recently were rife in his country. Their persistence and comprehensiveness are indicated by parallelism within which things of utilitarian and spiritual value are coupled and racial discrimination is exposed:

Pienso en mis largos días sin zapatos ni rosas.
Pienso en mis largos días sin sombrero ni nubes.
Pienso en mis largos días sin samisa ni sueños.

Pienso en mis largos días con mi piel prohibida.
Pienso en mis largos días.

I think of my long days without shoes or roses.
I think of my long days without a hat or clouds.
I think of my long days without a shirt or dreams.
I think of my long days with my prohibited skin.
I think of my long days.

Nor is the defence of the principles of the revolution limited to internal Cuban matters. In the poem '¿Qué color?' ('What Colour') devoted to Martin Luther King, Guillén points out a faulty perspective on the question of race and colour shown by the Soviet poet Evgeni Yevtushenko in his attempted tribute to the black civil rights leader. Yevtushenko's words, 'His skin was black, but his soul as pure as white snow,' quoted as the epigraph to Guillén's poem, are ridiculed and rectified. The ridicule extends to the idea of the colour of the soul, as well as of the images conventionally used to represent it as pure, images that would be appealing to semiologists:

Su piel tan negra, dicen,
su piel tan negra de color,
era por dentro nieve,
azucena,
leche fresca,
algodón.

His skin so black, they say,
his skin so black in colour,
was on the inside snow,
lily,
fresh milk,
cotton.

The poem, by linking King's heroic and lofty deeds to his blackness, challenges a hackneyed fallacy that has acquired the status of symbolism: the association of goodness with whiteness.[51]

Absence of balance, of fullness of vision, is treated in another way in the poem 'Noche de negros junto a la catedral' ('Night of Blacks Next to the Cathedral'). The first stanza presents an image of costumed blacks depicting a mood of celebration in an eighteenth-century scene. This distanced presentation includes the detail that all this is taking place by moonlight.

The reader, by now accustomed to the negative symbolism of the moon in Guillén's poetry, suspects that this is not an entirely satisfactory scene. The suspicion is confirmed by the speaker who at the end of the stanza intrudes with the question '¿y el cañaveral?' ('and the cane field?') which exposes the reductionist, idealized nature of the scene that has omitted the basic reality of the depicted times. This structure is repeated in the second stanza where this time a nineteenth-century scene excludes the overseer, a metonym for slavery and wielder of the whip. The exclusion of other makers of nineteenth-century history as resisters, commanders, and victims is brought to notice by allusions to Aponte, O'Donnell, and Plácido, respectively. And the real horror of what is being veiled by giddy pageantry is ultimately exposed in the speaker's portrayal of the unrepresented ordinary slave:

> Y nada se sabe del negro Santiago,
> con la llaga viva, tremenda,
> que en nalgas y espalda le abrió el bocabajo.
> (La cura fue orine con sal.)

> *And nothing is known of Santiago, the black man,*
> *with the tremendous raw sore,*
> *which a whipping opened up on his buttocks and his back.*
> *(The medication was urine and salt.)*

In the poem 'Ancestros' ('Ancestors') the speaker, the descendant of a slave who is addressing the descendant of a slave owner, restores balance to the viewing of slavery, balance in all the real violence that typifies the institution. The hostile interacting of the black grandfather with the white grandfather leads to the stark ending of the poem: 'El tuyo murió de un garrotazo. / Al mío lo colgaron' ('Yours died strangled. / They hanged mine'). Guillén once more shows his affinity for a broad perspective in the poem 'Digo que yo no soy un hombre puro' ('I Declare that I Am Not a Pure Man'), which is a hymn to life, to vibrant living, to sensuous attitudes, at the same time as it attacks ascetic pretensions. This vigorous humanizing position is present too in the poem 'El cosmonauta' ('The Cosmonaut') where the demystification of outer space and the removal of signifieds for the baggage of vocabulary that was employed in fashioning the myths that hitherto filled the unexplored space now permit an improved understanding of man's wide environment. (A copy of this poem was taken into outer space by the Cuban cosmonaut Arnaldo Tamayo.)

As in *Tengo*, the question of the defections from Cuba is again troubling to Guillén here, particularly in the poem 'La herencia' ('The Legacy'), where the long backward jump to the racism, prostitution, and marijuana use of

Miami is decried. The topic is given another aspect in the poem 'París,' where the seductions of that city are shown to prompt the alienation of the indigenous Latin American student from the issues facing his country. This general question is taken to another stage in the poem 'Problemas del subdesarrollo' ('Problems of Underdevelopment') in which cultural imperialism is shown to be a menace, calling for a defence based on the promotion of national values. The poem reveals, through metonymy, some national propensities of developed imperialist cultures of which the addressed student is a victim. In the antithetical second part, the student is counselled on how to confront those attitudes, countering with affirmations of his own cultural landmarks, heroes, and expression. The act of confrontation is in itself the resolution of the problem. The poem is:

Monsieur Dupont te llama inculto,
porque ignoras cuál era el nieto
preferido de Víctor Hugo.

Herr Müller se ha puesto a gritar,
porque no sabes el día
(exacto) en que murió Bismarck.

Tu amigo Mr. Smith,
inglés or yanqui, yo no lo sé,
se subleva cuando escribes *shell*.
(Parece que ahorras un ele,
y que además pronuncias *chel*.)

Bueno ¿y qué?
Cuando te toque a ti,
mándales decir cacarajícara,
y que dónde está el Aconcagua,
y que quién era Sucre,
y que en qué lugar de este planeta
murió Martí.

Un favor:
que te hablen siempre en español.

Monsieur Dupont calls you uneducated
because you don't know which was
the favourite grandchild of Victor Hugo.

Herr Müller has started shouting
because you don't know the day
(the exact one) when Bismarck died.

Your friend Mr. Smith,
English or Yankee, I don't know,
becomes incensed when you write shell.
(It seems that you hold back an 'l'
and that besides you pronounce it chel.)

O.K. So what?
When it's your turn,
have them say cacarajícara,*
and where is the Aconcagua
and who was Sucre,
and where on this planet
did Martí die.

And please:
make them always talk to you in Spanish.

The defence against the more physical form of imperialism is pointed to in the tender portraiture of firm determination in the poem 'Angela Davis,' in the physical toughness evoked in the war metonyms of the poem 'En el museo de Pyongyang' ('In the Pyongyang Museum'), and in the unbending will of the Vietnamese people represented in the 'Pequeña oda a Viet Nam' ('Little Ode to Vietnam'). The decline of U.S. imperialism is heralded in 'A las ruinas de Nueva York' ('To the Ruins of New York') and 'Papel de tapizar' ('Wall Paper') where the collapsed dollar is used with relish as wallpaper.

The new subjects treated in *La rueda dentada* are closely related to the idea of defence, primarily the defence and praise of Cuban cultural reality. Cuban birds, the sparrow, the mockingbird, and the hummingbird are exhibited in charming portraits that include aspects of their social usefulness and their role in the people's leisure. Our poet's artistic ingenuity is in full force in the series of five poems in which he deals with the works and personalities of five renowned Cuban painters. Each poem has its distinctive stanza pattern, rhythm, and semantic features, which are employed to evoke the personalities of the different artists and the temper of their works. Thus the works of Carlos Enríquez (1901–1957) are characterized, in the images that form the first two stanzas of the poem devoted to him, as consisting of

---

*A Cuban place name, which has come to be used as an exclamation of approval.

spacious and randomly peopled landscapes that are representational and closely controlled by the painter. In the final stanza, the comparison of Carlos with
historical Carloses and the frequent repetition of the name suggests the pre-
possessing and irrepressible nature of the painter, while his Bohemian traits
emerge in lines such as 'Carlos Fálico y Diablo' ('Carlos Phallic and Devil').
The irregular lengths of the lines and stanzas, together with the variety of
rhythms, form the appropriate musical accompaniment to the exuberance that
typifies the artist.

By contrast, the dactylic octosyllabic *redondillas*, with the artist's name
forming a shortened line in each stanza and with the same set of images repeated in each stanza suggest the stylized, tightly organized work of Víctor
Manuel García (1897–1969) with its variations on a small range of subjects.
The poem also suggests the orderliness and austerity of the painter himself.
The work of Eduardo Abela (1889–1965) is shown to be rooted in the gua-
jiro-peasant sector and to favour portraits. The speaker's expressions of
surprise throughout the poem are a reflection of the daring use of colours and
the element of suspense in the compositions. These qualities are matched by
Abela's eccentric personality, as is indicated by the skewed dialogue at the
end of the poem.

Verbs indicating rapid movement and violent transpositions aided by technical figures such as the strident synaesthesia 'Son colores que rugen en la
noche' ('They are colours that roar in the night'), all in the lively trochaic
metre, lead the reader into the explosive world of Amelia Paláez del Casal
(1896–1968). It is a world best rendered by oxymorons – 'flores terribles,'
'montes fragmentados' ('terrible flowers,' 'fragmented mountains') – and
the related figure, paradox, is used to convey the total and lasting impression
of the artist's works: 'Amelia pasa en un gran soplo, y queda' ('Amelia
passes in a gust of wind and stays'). Finally, the formidable Fidelio Ponce
de León (1895–1949) who, usually viewed in his large sun hat, speaks of
himself in the third person. His mercurial temperament (suggested throughout
the poem by the irregularity of its stanza and verse forms), his tendency to
delve into styles of different periods, and his particular susceptibility to El
Greco are all agilely represented in the narrative ending of the poem:

> Un sábado del siglo XVI,
> mientras lo buscaban en Camagüey,
> pasóse todo el día en Toledo
> viendo pintar al Greco, su maestro.
> Hizo bien.
>
> *One Saturday in the sixteenth century,*
> *while they were looking for him in Camagüey,*
> *he spent the whole day in Toledo*

watching El Greco, his master, paint.
He did well.

In each of these cases Guillén does not merely build a story on the basis of a painting as is done, for instance, by Robert Browning in 'My Last Duchess,' or describe a work of art to celebrate its immortality as with John Keats's 'Ode to a Grecian Urn,' or interpret a painting impressionistically as Apollinaire does in 'Les Fenêtres,' or make of a painting a motive for the outpouring of religious sentiment as Unamuno does in his long poem 'El Cristo de Velásquez.' With the economy that is characteristic of his work, Guillén puts all the aspects of each poem to the service of capturing the artistic and personal essence of each of these five artists who have played important roles in building the national culture.

Just as Guillén uses poetry as a medium for rendering the essence of paintings, so too does he use it to render playfully a certain style of piano music in the poem 'Ejercicio de piano con amapola de siete a nueve de la mañana' ('Piano Exercise with Poppy at Seven A.M.'), one of a series of sonnets contained in *La rueda dentada*. Several of these sonnets continue to show the spirit of defence of national institutions. Thus in 'A la Bodeguita' ('To the Bodeguita'), dedicated to Angel Martínez (its former owner who gave it to the revolution and who now manages it), the restaurant famous for its typical Cuban dishes and as a meeting place for writers and artists is praised. Likewise, in the sonnet 'A Retamar' the bond between two of Cuba's foremost cultural institutions, the Unión de Escritores y Artistas de Cuba and the Casa de las Américas, is celebrated and strengthened. The dedication of the sonnet to the poet Roberto Fernández Retamar is an acknowledgment by the president of the former institution of the successful guidance given to the latter one by the multifacetedly productive Retamar. The mood of praise for authentic Cuban values is continued in the prose poem 'Nancy' of the section entitled 'Ex corde' ('From the Heart'). The poem extols the poetry, the manner, and the beauty of the distinguished and captivating poet Nancy Morejón, one of the vital forces in post-revolutionary writing.

The poems of 'Ex corde' are, in the main, love poems, and a discussion of them may also conveniently include commentary on the section of the *Obra poética* entitled *Poemas de amor* (1933–1971), largely republished in the book *El corazón con que vivo* (1975). It has been shown throughout this study that love, a frequently treated subject in Guillén's poetry, beginning as (we have seen) with such early poems as 'La balada azul' ('The Blue Ballad') and 'Tu recuerdo' ('Memories of You'), can usually be related in its mood to his social perceptions. The oppressive bearing of social conditions on the manifestations of the emotion was observed in the study of *Motivos de son*. From then onwards, whenever love poems have appeared in Guillén's pre-revolutionary poetry they have been clothed in sadness, primarily in *El son entero* and *La paloma de vuelo popular*. In fact, the one poem to this point that provides relief from the persistent mood of sadness is 'La pequeña balada de Plóvdiv' ('The Little Plóvdiv Ballad'), which belongs to the latter book. This exception points to the fact that the mood governing the portrayal of love in Guillén's poetry is determined not merely by his disposition to be 'un hombre que llora' ('a man who weeps'), or by the broad inclination of poets to find more substance in the hardships than in the joys of love, but more so by the effect on love of the social and political environment in which it strives to exist. It is significant in this regard that 'La pequeña balada de Plóvdiv' has for its setting a gentle Bulgarian town whose people, in 1951 (when the poem was written), were seen by Guillén to be enjoying the kind of social system that he was struggling to bring into existence in Cuba. So it is that in the post-revolutionary period, poems that accent the positive aspects of love begin to make their appearance in his poetry. Among the *Poemas de amor* (1933–1971) the idea of disrupted love is in the forefront in such poems as 'Un poema de amor' ('A Love Poem') (1953), 'Nocturno' (1948) and 'Piedra de horno' ('Kiln Stone') (1944). They are poems of lament that show the disillusioning force of love. In the first of these are verses such as:

> Es un amor así,
> es un amor de abismo en primavera,
> cortés, cordial, feliz, fatal.

> *It is that sort of love,*
> *it is an abysmal love in spring time,*
> *courteous, cordial, happy, fatal.*

The speaker in 'Nocturno' begs the vision of his lost love: 'Déjame el llanto, déjame a solas con mi voz' ('Leave me tears, leave me alone with my voice'). In the atmosphere of 'Duros suspiros rotos, quimeras calcinadas' ('Hard broken sighs, charred dreams') scenes of deception rather than of love are recalled. On the other hand, in such poems as 'Alta niña de caña y amapola' ('Tall Girl of Sugar Cane and Poppy'), written in Moscow in 1957, and in post-revolutionary ones like 'Ana María' (1962) and 'Teresa' (1961), the positive attributes of the woman who inspires love are emphasized. In the latter poem, in an atmosphere of light-heartedness contributed to by sprightly *redondillas*, the enchantment of Teresa's eyes are celebrated. Similarly, in 'Ana María' the poet selects for praise her finest graces and the extent of the positiveness of his attitude is measurable by his use of the serpent as an image in the poem. That image, as we have seen, has had heretofore consistently negative value in Guillén's poetry and is often associated with an imperialist *modus operandi*. Here, however, the simile 'como una lente y suave serpiente suspendida' ('like a slow, gentle, suspended serpent') functions as part of the admired essence of Ana María.

Among the poems of 'Ex corde' in *La rueda dentada*, there are several that reveal the old mood of sadness, caused by the absence of the loved one as in 'Solo de guitarra' ('Guitar Solo'), by failed attempts at communication as in 'Pas de téléphone' ('No Telephone') and 'Una fría mañana' ('One Cold Morning') or by loneliness felt in distant travels as in 'Nieve' ('Snow'). On the other hand, there is the above mentioned encomium to 'Nancy' (1972), with verses such as

Yo amo su sonrisa, su carne oscura, su cabeza africana

I love her smile, her dark flesh, her African head.

and the poem of 1970, 'El árbol' ('The Tree'), with its powerful images of renewal, reveals a speaker who feels a new enthusiasm in matters of love paralleling the enthusiasm felt by the speaker of 'Tengo' for the new society.

Death is also an important topic in *La rueda dentada*. It is examined unmetaphysically in the poem 'Sobre la muerte' ('Concerning Death') where, although no solution is encountered to the materialist inquiry into its general character, it is at least demystified by being shown to be the common experience of all living things and is heavily featured, for instance, in any restaurant menu.[52] Nevertheless, gradations of its significance and impact are illustrated in several poems of the collection. In the 'Elegía a Martín Dihigo' the passing of a good man who is of a calibre that is not greatly different from that of his numerous friends and who excelled as a baseball pitcher is mourned with deep funereal grief. One detail of the poem may be cited as evidence of the flexible semiotic system that functions in Guillén's poetry. The image 'una blanca pelota' ('a white ball') is used here to represent the worthy goal of Dihigo's life, thus contrasting diametrically with the image 'La pelotilla blanca' ('The Little White Ball') of the poem 'Little Rock,' which symbolized the golf-playing Eisenhower's presidential indifference to the racist outrages dealt with in that poem. In the 'Balada por la muerte de Gagarin' ('Ballad on the Death of Gagarin'), with its rhyme scheme based skilfully throughout on two consonantal rhymes, 'ida' and 'erte,' tears are shown to be inappropriate. This pioneering cosmonaut, having forged a permanent identity with the stars, is beyond death. Immortality has also been won by the Vietnamese leader in the poem 'Ho Chi Minh,' where in another demonstration of Guillén's flexible symbol system, white, Ho's habitual dress, is used to represent his candidness and simplicity.

The poems 'Che Comandante' ('Commander Che'), 'Guitarra en duelo mayor' ('Guitar in Grief Major'), and 'Lectura de domingo' (Sunday Reading') are all devoted to the death of Che Guevara. The first of these poems is an elegy providing, in the first of its five parts, the fact of the death of Che together with the denial, in anaphorically structured verses that give solemnity to the poem from its outset, of any possibility of his being confined by death. In the second part, the immediate and contrasting reactions of his enemies and his comrades are shown. In the third, his living and ubiquitous presence (similar to that of Bolívar's in Neruda's poem 'Un canto para Bolívar') is affirmed. The particularly intimate Cuban knowledge of him in the various manifestations of his purity and his genius is conveyed in part four. The poem ends with the pledge to aspire to the quality of life, death, and immortality that he achieved.

'Guitarra en duelo mayor' is addressed to the not yet developing simple man. Its ten numbered stanzas, each with seven lines, contain so many repeated lines that only three of them in each stanza yield new content. The appropriateness of this structure is appreciated when it is realized that the speaker's immediate audience is the Bolivian soldier who in his naïveté has been duped into having been Che's killer. Hence the frequent repetition of 'soldado boliviano' is indicative of the forebearance of the speaker who gradually imparts to the soldier, with the guitar in its usual musically didactic role, the meaning of his deed. The poem by exceeding the spirit of forebearance even of the *Cantos para soldados* becomes a measure of the egregious error of the soldier and of the patience with which he can be regarded by the speaker who now speaks from the superior historical position of post-revolutionary Cuba. 'Guitarra en duelo mayor,' like the 'Coplas americanas' of *Tengo*, also highlights the fact that the strategy of devising a simple structure for conveying a message to the Cuban population is abandoned in this new stage of its development in favour of the kind of sophisticated enterprise that a poem like 'Prólogo' or the poems of 'Salón independiente' of *La rueda dentada* represent.

'Lectura de domingo' is the account of a reading of Che's *Bolivian Diary*, containing the ultimate perils faced by the guerrilla leader. The text of the poem is:

> He leído acostado
> todo un blando domingo.
> Yo en mi lecho tranquilo,
> mi suave cabezal,
> mi cobertor bien limpio,
> tocando piedra, lodo, sangre,
> garrapata, sed,

orines, asma:
indios callados que no entienden,
soldados que no entienden,
señores teorizantes que no entienden,
obreros, campesinos que no entienden.

Terminas de leer,
quedan tus ojos fijos
¿en qué sitio del viento?
El libro ardió en mis manos,
Lo he puesto luego abierto,
como una brasa pura,
sobre mi pecho.
Siento
las últimas palabras
subir desde un gran hoyo negro.

Inti, Pablito, el Chino y Aniceto.
El cinturón del cerco.
La radio del ejército
mintiendo.
Aquella luna pequeñita
colgando suspendida
a una legua de Higueras
y dos de Pucará.
Después silencio.
No hay más páginas.
Esto se pone serio.
Esto se acaba pronto.
Termina.
    Va a encenderse.
Se apaga.
    Va a nacer.

I have spent a whole soft Sunday
reading in my bed.
I in my tranquil bed,
my smooth pillow,
my nice clean bedspread,
touching stone, mud, blood,
cattle-ticks, thirst,
urine, asthma:

silent Indians who do not understand,
soldiers who do not understand,
gentlemen theorizers who do not understand,
workers, peasants who do not understand.

You finish reading,
your eyes remain fixed
on what part of the wind?
The book blazed up in my hands,
I placed it open,
like a pure live coal,
on my chest.
I feel
the final words
rise up from a large black hole.

Inti, Pablito, el Chino and Aniceto.
The belt of encirclement.
The army's radio
telling lies.
That small moon
hanging suspended
a league away from Higueras
and two leagues from Pucará.
Then silence.
There are no more pages.
This is getting serious.
This will soon end.
It is over.
    It is going to ignite.
It is extinguished.
    It is going to be born.

In the drama developed within the poem, the speaker as reader is drawn by the
book away from his initial comfortable circumstances, which are distant
and distinct from those being revealed to him. Drawn by his solidarity with
Che, he becomes immersed in that world, detailed aspects of which make
their deep impression on him. Che's isolation in a hostile milieu, in which
disagreeable things and people who do not understand come to form parts of
the same paradigm, is underlined by the anaphoric 'que no entienden.' This
together with the troubled state of his health, his self-discipline, his four
comrades with whom the speaker is familiar, the tightening noose, the ever-

useless moon, and the remote geography are images that engage firmly the speaker's imagination. The pregnant silence that follows the end of the reading yields the speaker's perception of a synthesis of rebirth, a triumph of the revolutionary spirit championed by Che and with which the speaker is to be identified. Hence his retrospective self-consciousness about what comes for him to be the culpable physical comfort in which he carried out the reading.

Three technical procedures contribute markedly to the poem's strength. The sweep of time in it goes from the past to the future, the present coinciding with the presumed time of writing. This heightens emotion in the poem, baring the process by which the speaker moves from ease to desperate helplessness to the calming concept of rebirth. Secondly, tension is enhanced in the poem by movement from long, asyndetically structured sentences in the first stanza, to the short, sometimes verbless, sentences that convey stylistically the tense, climactic antithesis effected in the last stanza. Finally, the transition from first to second person at the point of finishing the reading adroitly broadens the perspective to which the subsequent charged silence and interpretation are applicable.

The poems devoted to Che Guevara emphasize the idea of his example and by doing so contribute to the concept of defence, which is prominent in *La rueda dentada*. This prominence, in turn, reflects the general attitude revealed in Guillén's post-revolutionary collections. On the one hand, they show a spirit that is accommodative of aspects of life in general and of Cuban life in particular that indicate satisfaction and pride in areas of experience and achievement that were earlier overlooked. Yet at the same time they are attentive to the challenges brought by the new historical stage and to the need for vigilance against the recrudescence of past conditions. So consummate is the ease with which Guillén produces the forms appropriate to the representation of a variety of perspectives on several subjects that the considerable artistic challenges with which he is faced are scarcely noticeable.

EL DIARIO QUE A DIARIO

Guillén's most recent book of new works, *El diario que a diario* (1972) is in several senses a culmination and synthesis of his total expression and ideological vision. The two principal areas of writing in which he has been engaged throughout his life – poetry and journalism – are publicly wedded here. The union is governed by a keen historical perspective, with irony and satire determining its predominant mood. The format of the book is modelled on the Cuban newspaper of times past and its content is a collection of representative news items, official proclamations, a wide range of advertisements and society notes – all presented in a way that exposes the absurdity, disorder, immorality, injustice, insecurity, and mimicry of Cuban colonial society from the beginning of Spanish rule to the flight of Batista and the triumph of the revolution. This large historical span is represented in language that ranges from the quaintly anachronistic to the raucously colloquial. The presentation of chaos is effected by a semblance of chaos in the presentation itself. The newspaper format with its scope for randomness provides the general frame for this semblance, and it is achieved by a variety of further measures within the individual items. But this semblance is always ultimately superseded, at the level of the individual item, by its hidden coherence and, in the work as a whole, by the contribution of its parts to a subversively though carefully delineated chronological portrayal of consistently viewed historical reality. Thus the mode of presentation, by being other than it appears to be on the surface, contributes in the realm of form to the irony that abounds in the work.

The impression of chaos is created from the outset, in the self-characterization of the speaker in the 'Prologuillo' ('Little Prologue') both as 'el notario / polvoriento y sin prisa' ('the dusty and unhurried notary') and as the all-accommodating and all-dispensing 'diario que a diario' ('daily paper which everyday') who receives and distributes a varied stock ranging from smiles to dromedaries. The 'Epístola' ('Epistle') that follows the 'Prologuillo' introduces and characterizes the whole collection as something that has gone awry. Intended to be a rapidly flowing stream, it has inundated the meadow. This metaphor of failed intention is the concretization of the motive for the apologetic tone in which the collection is offered to the reader:

> Estos viejos papeles que te envío,
> esta tinta pretérita, Eliseo,
> ¿no moverán tu cólera o tu hastío?
> …
> Juro por los sinsontes y las flores
> que en aquesta ocasión no he pretendido
> provocar con mi verso tus furores.
>
> Torpeza y no maldad más bien ha sido.

> *These old papers that I send you,*
> *this ancient ink, Eliseo,*
> *will probably stir up your anger or your disgust.*
> …
> *I swear in the name of mockingbirds and flowers*
> *that on this occasion I haven't tried*
> *to provoke your fury with my verses.*
>
> *It has been due to clumsiness rather than to wickedness.*

The dedication of the book to the poet Eliseo Diego should not be treated merely as a cordial, non-literary gesture. Diego, apart from being a friend and close associate of Guillén, is (as I have described him earlier) a poet of exquisite control who is being evoked in the poem as one who is therefore unlikely to tolerate the book's supposed unwieldiness. Besides, the people in general are held to react hostilely to the book and its author:

> Con chicotes tremendos, con puñales
> exigen voceando mis lectores
> que me vaya a otro sitio a mear pañales.

> *with tremendous whips, with daggers*
> *my readers demand, shouting,*
> *that I go elsewhere to wet napkins.*

But all this is an irony of modesty, alerting the reader playfully to the relative obscurity of the book, just as he was alerted by the imagined reaction 'exclames con rabia ¡Demonios qué es esto!' ('You exclaim with rage, what the hell is this!') to the relative obscurity of the poem 'Prólogo' of *La rueda dentada*. In its obscurity, the book is in keeping with the observation made earlier about the tendency in Guillén to assume a growing level of sophistication in his post-revolutionary readers. The rest of the poem treats, in sober terms, more specific aspects of the content of the book, with occasional descent to a level of language appropriate to the harsh activities later to be described. The change of tone is most marked in the apostrophes in parallel construction that lament the suffering of blacks and of patriots in general, ending with fitting Gongoristic *cultismo*, ellipsis, and hyperbaton in the apostrophe

> ¡Oh Reino de la Muerte, tiempo España,
> charcos de sangre tus provincias eran!

> *O Kingdom of Death, in Spain's times,*
> *your provinces were pools of blood!*

The period of economic exploitation of Cuba by the United States is referred to with usage that is less classical and strongly satiric:

> Luego el castrón del Tío, cuya maña
> usual en sus atracos de usurero
> ni al sobrino más fiel turba o engaña,

> salvo si el tal sobrino es un madero.
> Y maderos tuvimos es el caso.

> *Then there was the ass of an Uncle, whose usual*
> *cunning in his racketeering swindles*
> *did not bother or deceive even his most faithful nephew,*

> *unless such a nephew were a dunce.*
> *But we had dunces, that is the truth.*

This leads to the positive pole in the antithesis, to those who forged a new future out of these circumstances and brought about the revolution:

> y a quienes hubo que cortar el paso
> para abrirnos el nuestro hacia adelante
> como el pueblo acostumbra: de un trancazo.

> *and there were those who had to clear a path*
> *to open our way to the future*
> *as is usual with the people: in one great stride.*

When the speaker returns to the initial mood of the poem in the final stanza, which serves as an *envoi*, it has already become clear that the interaction between the playful and the profoundly serious (a principal characteristic of Guillén's poetry) has been in force here. 'Epístola,' with its skilfully composed eleven-syllable tercets, plays a shrewdly controlling role in *El diario que a diario*, intimating the content and the chief features of style that are to follow.

The periods of Cuban history into which the book is divided are a) the Spanish conquest and occupation up to b) the English occupation of Havana, c) the period of French influence, d) the Ten Years War, and e) the final years of the struggle for independence from Spain and the period of U.S. presence and influence from the defeat of the Spaniards to the triumph of the revolution. Each transition is marked by a 'Paréntesis' ('Parenthesis') a poem that evokes the atmosphere of the ensuing period. The poem 'Final' with which the book ends is in effect the last 'Paréntesis,' pointing joyfully to liberation.

The harsh satire with which the first period is represented is immediately displayed in the 'Pregones' ('Street Cries'). These official proclamations are constructed so as to reveal their function to have been robbery by decree. In such a context, the phrase, 'según uso e costumbre' ('in keeping with custom and habit') used in both proclamations is at the formal level a *topos* of commencement, while it conveys the idea that official robberies were habitual. Satire is muted by pathos in those items dealing with the rifeness of diseases, which in men and beasts are combated by religious processions and the glorifying of saints.[53] Following the announcements of such festivities is the sonnet that is entitled simply 'Soneto,' in which the unhealthy disease-incubating conditions are enumerated in their stark repulsiveness.

A special emphasis is given to the representation of slavery in this period. Guillén adopts yet another strategy for exposing the inhumanity of the institution, this time portraying the victims as being white. The newspaper advertisements that are the medium for this portrayal are in effect items of third-person verse or narrative. But concerning as they do European slaves, they are not allowed to stand autonomously. They arouse the Spanish newspaper editor to intrude in the first-person to remark on their resemblance to normally carried announcements concerning African slaves and, therefore, to declare his reluctance to publish them: 'Forzados por la costumbre general aceptamos su publicación, no sin consignar la repugnancia que tan infame comercio produce en nuestro espíritu' ('Forced to do so by the general custom we allow its publication, not without stating the repugnance that such infamous commerce produces in our spirit'). This expression of disapproval is based on a double standard that disqualifies the editor's view for being unjust and subjects it to correction by the reader. For a crime against humanity is to be perceived whether the victim be black (which was the historical case) or white in for-sale advertisements such as 'Blanca de cuatro meses de parida, sin un rasguño ni una herida, de buena y abundante leche, regular lavandera, criolla cocinera, sana y sin tacha, fresquísima muchacha: EN 350 PESOS LIBRES PARA EL VENDEDOR' ('One white girl who gave birth four months ago, without a scratch or a wound, with good and plentiful milk, fair laundrywoman, creole cook, healthy and without defect, very sweet girl: FOR 350 PESOS CLEAR FOR THE VENDOR'); or in those for-exchange advertisements, with pointed anachronism such as: 'Se cambia un blanco libre de tacha / por una volanta de la marca Ford / y un perro ...' ('We will exchange a white slave with no defects / for a Ford buggy / and a dog'); or in those announcing escape such as: 'Ha fugado de casa de su amo / un blanco de mediano estatura, / ojos azules y pelo colorado, / sin zapatos ...' ('A white slave has run away from his master's house. / He is of medium build, / blue eyes and reddish hair, / barefooted'); or in the ironically titled 'Acto de justicia' ('Act of Justice') in which it is announced that the white Domingo Español, for having wounded his masters, will face the full fury of the whip. The placing of whites in the roles lived by blacks is not a question of substituting racially the oppressor for the oppressed. The fact that there is no indicated change in the Spanish control of the institution causes the image to picture an oppressed class rather than an oppressed race.

The loyalty of the colonized to the colonizers is parodied in the poem 'Llanto de las habaneras' ('Lament of the Women of Havana') from the period of the English occupation. The prayer device used here is not unlike that found earlier in the poem 'A la virgen de la Caridad' ('To the Virgin of

Charity'), but here the irony is at the expense of those doing the praying, the ladies of Havana who pray that the English colonial masters be kicked out and that the Spanish ones be returned to power. The language of the prayer is skilfully managed to achieve the ambivalence that makes it tensely unclear whether it is aimed at a divinity or a man – the King of Spain.

The period of French influence, which came second hand to Cuba through the strong French influence in Spain, is marked by the inferiority complex that pervades the colony, especially with regard to cultural matters. Native products are supposedly dignified by linking them in advertising to French landmarks. Bogus art is given appeal by invoking its French origin as are pharmaceuticals, which are as magical and of as suspect efficacy as those encountered earlier in the dramatic farce 'Floripondito.' Some items that at first glance seem to be unequivocally direct are revealed to allude to significant historical matters on careful reading. The section covering the arrival of ships in Havana harbour regularly includes the detail that in the cargo are several hundred 'sacos de carbón' ('bags of coal'). This is an allusion to the fact that this was a period in which clandestine trafficking in slaves was widespread and slaves were sold to many territories as 'sacos de carbón,' a euphemism of telling callousness.

The period covering the Ten Years War is represented by two antithetical positions. The first is the Spanish viewpoint conveyed by the Captain General Francisco Lersundi, who paints a picture of a peaceful and prosperous society being threatened by a small group of lawless trouble-makers. Ranged against this view are several of the essayists and poets, mentioned in the first part of this study, who began to develop a staunchly nationalist ideology and who understood Antonio Maceo's determination to fight without truce for full independence. The subtle undermining irony of the first puts the weight of credibility on the earnestly expressed second pole of the antithesis.

An enormous variety of topics is dealt with in the intensive final period. The independence struggle itself is shown to be tainted by racism and, with the death of Martí and Maceo, the u.s. finds the divisiveness opportune for excluding Cuban representation from the Conference of Paris that settled its fate. Large print is used to indicate the slight, and symbols of radically different interpretations of the new status of Cuba emerge. The machete – the key weapon of the insurgents and a metonym for Maceo – in a case made of selected national woods on the one hand, and on the other, a copy of the Platt Amendment with an eagle, its wings spread wide on the cover are exchanged as gifts between Cuban veterans of the war and Leonard Wood, respectively. The flood-gates are thenceforth open and the oil companies, the language, the social register, the motor vehicles, the dishes, the newspapers, the medicaments, the banks, the utility companies, the status symbols, the racial discrimination, and one model for two political parties, the

Liberals and Conservatives, pour in from the north to monopolize the pages of *El diario que a diario*, which in itself has grown to be a barometer of the influences on Cuban cultural life. In this period the excuse of ignorance does not exist and satire is not mitigated by pathos. Satire is ever present, imparting its acerbic flavour to all the subjects; and in partnership with it, irony here realizes its central role of undermining what poses as desirable. Thus the 'Miami Club' advertises itself in terms that betray racism and the distortion of the national culture:

> Diviértase cada noche bailando con las mejores
> orquestas de la Habana. Estrictamente privado.
> Clientela distinguida en su mayoría norteamericana.
> Aviso importante: la Administración o su delegado a
> la entrada del local se reservan el derecho de
> admisión, sin explicaciones. Buffet frío y platos
> criollos. Show especial a las 12, con la negra
> Rufina y el negrito Cocoliso, los mejores bailadores
> de la rumba cubana.

> *Enjoy yourself every night dancing to the best*
> *orchestras in Havana. Strictly private. Distinguished*
> *clientèle, for the most part North American. Important*
> *note: the management or their delegate at the*
> *entrance of the club reserves the right to deny*
> *admission, without explanation. Cold buffet and*
> *creole dishes. Special show at 12, with the negress*
> *Rufina and the negro Cocoliso, the best dancers of*
> *Cuban rumba.*

Classical allusions mix with modern references in the advertisement for 'Sanitube:' 'Visite a Venus sin temer a Mercurio. El preventivo oficial del ejército norteamericano. En todas las farmacias' ('Visit Venus without fearing Mercury. Use the official prophylactic of the u.s. army. Sold in all pharmacies'). Other advertisements reveal, in their humiliating address, a lack of respect for the people as in 'Ya ... yo ... ya: Pruebe la píldoras vitalinas, y cambiará de opinión. También la cambiarán sobre usted' ('Ya ... yo ... ya: Try vitamin pills and you will change your mind. People will also change their minds about you'). A society of such attitudes requires its special code for living, its ten commandments or 'Decálogo,' the first of which recognizes the extent of the difference between the two political parties: 'Si te agrada ser liberal, no hay problemas: puedes seguir siendo conservador' ('If you want to be a liberal, no problem: you can go on being conserva-

tive'). There follows a series of rules of opportunism, which contain incidentally many glimpses of severe social problems – high infant mortality, for
example.

A 'high society' wedding provides another area for satire. The reporter
uses a large number of journalistic hyperboles, with the implied narrator
exposing the affectation in them. The reporter's pretensions of elegance,
revealed, for example, in his attribution of isolated French words to Baudelaire
and Montesquieu, are undermined. At the same time the standing of the
families involved in the wedding is shown to be based on the emptiness of
social snobbery. Point of view is also skilfully exploited in the statement put
out by the National Police regarding the impending visit of u.s. President
Calvin Coolidge to Cuba. The many prohibitions contained in the statement,
including those of topics such as the Platt Amendment, the Guantánamo
Naval Base, and the ownership of the sugar crop contradict and outweigh the
clichés of friendship between the two countries. The ideological confusion
revealed here is soon followed by 'La quincalla del ñato' ('The Snub-nosed
Man's Hardware Store') the description of the contents of a hardware store
in which the technique of chaotic enumeration with no punctuation is used to
represent the jumble of imported junk that is one important consequence of
the special relation with the 'coloso del Norte' ('colossus of the North'). The
theatrical announcement that follows this enumeration is a hidden metaphor for the overthrow of the dictatorship of Gerardo Machado.

The struggle between colonialist and liberationist attitudes continues
with the book's penultimate announcement indicating (now with calm earnestness replacing irony and satire) that the ideas of Martí are gaining currency
among the people. The new mood is evident too in the final announcement,
which advertises the general distribution of Fidel Castro's speech, *La historia
me absolverá*, in which he upheld the ideas of Martí in defending the attack
he led on the Moncada army barracks and so started the new state of revolutionary struggle. The poem 'Final' heralds the happy conclusion to a long historical process. The momentousness of this achievement is measurable by a
detail of technique in the poem. The woods, it will be recalled, trembled at the
advance toward projected victory of the progressive militiamen in the
closing lines of the Spanish Civil War poem *España* ... In this poem the
achievement of revolutionary victory also causes nature to be submissively
responsible to man, to reflect the ardent glory of the moment of his triumph
over a range of persistent social and political systems that had always
signified one or another form of oppression: 'Su gran frente sombría / sintió
arder el Turquino' ('Turquino felt its great sombre forehead burn').

The coverage of large sweeps of history in their favoured genres is one of
the features of the work of foremost twentieth-century Spanish-American
writers and artists like Pablo Neruda, Alejo Carpentier, Juan Rulfo, Gabriel

García Márquez, and Diego Rivera. In *El diario que a diario*, Guillén does not simply adapt his principal genre, poetry, to suit such representation. He has again shown new resources and broadened his formal range by inventing a newspaper – always potentially the medium *par excellence* for conveying with lively authenticity social and political history in the making – which permits him to offer the kind of authoritative knowledge of the period that the best historians possess and the emotional richness of a powerful literary experience. Guillén has combined narrative, journalistic, and poetic arts with a deftness that has enabled him to achieve a constant interpretive vision by showing rather than by telling. The power with which he has effected this owes a great deal to his versatile and at the same time economical means of producing irony and satire, and to his unerring judgment in selecting from his array of techniques those best suited in each case to convey a mature vision based on a profound and many-faceted knowledge of history.

3

Conclusions

The continuity and steady development of social perceptions in more than fifty years of Guillén's poetry has its mainstay in a world view that is constantly fixed on historical reality. Within this sphere, Guillén's primary focus is on man, seeing him as entirely responsible for lifting the level of his condition. This is complemented by a democratic outlook that firmly combats economic exploitation and racial discrimination, that is hostile to any tradition that does not foster the general advancement of mankind, that impedes an understanding of the intimate as well as the wider environment of man, and that obscures the relation of an individual's life to the basic organization of the whole society.

Involvement with historical reality is manifested in Guillén's progressively enlarged embrace of time and space. From his earliest poetry, which showed individual discontentment, he began in 1929 to represent aspects of national life, soon emphasizing the deprived black sector of the Cuban population. He proposed a Cuban identity based on the true composition of this population and on the promotion of harmony. Subsequently, Guillén turned his attention to the West Indies, illustrating his diagnosis of imperialism as the root cause of the hardships common to the region. Cuba, meanwhile, was the locus of the strategy for revolutionary change that in the mid 1930s became based on a recognition of the oppression and opportunity inherent in the class structure. This recognition is reflected in Guillén's two books of 1937, *Cantos para soldados y sones para turistas* and *España ...*, and is expanded to represent elaborately a materialist consciousness in *El son entero* and *La paloma de vuelo popular*. In the *Elegías*, a current that runs through much of his poetry is given prominence in poems lamenting persistent abuses or extolling those who won immortality by attempting to relieve their fellow men of heavy burdens.

Guillén's poetry since 1959 suggests that the revolution has offered enlarged scope for creativity. Celebration has been tempered by the idea of defence; new opportunities have disclosed new responsibilities at home and abroad; and the new stage of history has prompted new critical examinations of the past. It is a past during which racism, apart from victimizing blacks to different degrees of intensity, from slavery in the colonial period to racial discimination in the neo-colonial, colluded with imperialism to hinder the cultural and economic development of Cuba. In the sobering light of this history, the new opportunity for harmony is seen to be rooted in the common ownership of the national assets, in the sharing of work, and in the building together of all the aspects of superstructure. The world view from which Guillén's poetry springs is insistently rational, sophisticatedly social. By a process observable in the progression of his books, Guillén's early national interest (reflecting the views of Gustavo E. Urrutia and others who have toiled to implement the Maceo–Martí ideals) converged with Marxist ideology. Guillén has attributed to this ideological formation and development (and not to any magical, seer-like gifts) the fact that his interpretation of social reality has consistently needed no revision and that history has borne out his postulates.[1] Because in retrospect his books are milestones along the path taken by the progressive sector in Cuba and because this has been increasingly recognized within that country as more and more of its people have joined in its cultural life, he has come to be regarded there as Cuba's national poet. The reader will distinguish between the concept of national poet so derived and the other apparently related concepts such as that implied in the term 'poet laureate,' the celebrator of, among other things, such regal accomplishments as births, marriages, and coronations. Guillén's poem entitled 'Poetas' (*La rueda dentada*), in which he distinguishes between three historical stages and types of poet – the feudal, the bourgeois, and the democratic – is itself enlightening in this regard. That a keen appreciation of his work ranges afar is attested to by the honorary University degrees and other tokens of public acclaim that have come to him in recent years in the English-speaking West Indies, several Spanish-American, African, Asian, and European countries. These complement his most valued early award, the International Lenin Peace Prize of 1954. Guillén has also been elected to Cuba's National Assembly of People's Power, and he is a member of the Central Committee of the Communist Party of Cuba. In September 1981, he was given his country's highest honour, the José Martí National Order. Guillén's words of appreciation, a very recent public statement at the time of this writing, illuminate several of the points to be made in the following pages. He said:

Tonight I would have liked to give a speech here. A speech fired with emotion and with the friendship that gives us such strength and spirit. A speech, in short, to thank compañero Armando Hart for his generous words about me and my work, and compañero Fidel Castro for the distinction with which he has honoured me. Nevertheless,

I am going to say it in a poem. We have great poems in Cuba, some of which have transcended our national boundaries, poems which are permanent works and bear inexorable testimony to human progress. The Agrarian Reform, for instance, is one of the greatest poems in our history. The Literacy Campaign, the universalization of education, and the nationalization of property which was in the wrong hands, are also of limitless value. And all constitute the great poem which is the Cuban Revolution, the Revolution brought to victory by Fidel Castro. My poem goes as follows:

I HAVE

When I see and touch myself
I, only yesterday John with Nothing,
and today John with Everything,
I turn my eyes, I look,
I see and touch myself
and I ask myself how could it have happened.

I have, let's see,
I have the pleasure of walking about my country,
master of all there is in it,
looking very closely at what before
I didn't and couldn't have.
Sugar crop I can say,
countryside I can say,
city I can say,
army I can say,
now mine forever and yours, ours,
and a broad resplendence
of sun rays, stars, flowers.

I have, let's see,
I have the pleasure of going
I, a peasant, a worker, a simple person,
have the pleasure of going
    (here's an example)
to a bank to talk with the manager,
not in English,
not in Sir,
but to say compañero to him as it's done in Spanish.

I have, let's see,
that being black

nobody can stop me
at the door of a dance hall or a bar.
Or at a hotel desk
shout at me there is no room,
a small room and not a great big room,
a small room where I can rest.

I have, let's see,
that there is no rural police
to catch me and lock me up in jail,
nor grab me and throw me from my land
to the middle of the highway.

I have, well, like I have the land I have the sea,
no country club estate,
no high life,
no tennis and yacht clubs,
but from beach to beach and wave to wave,
immense blue, open, democratic:
in short, the sea.

I have, let's see,
I have already learned to read,
to count,
I have that I have already learned to write
and to think
and to laugh.

I have that I now have
a place to work
and earn
what I need to eat.
I have, let's see,
I have what I had to have.

GUILLÉN AND MARTÍ

It has seemed to Mirta Aguirre and to many other Cubans that their country has had two other 'national' poets, José María Heredia (1808–1839) and José Martí (1853–1895), who, with Guillén, were all born almost exactly fifty years apart. The nature of many references to Martí in this study suggests a brief summary here of the similarities between the two more recent national poets. Martí's poetry from its very early beginnings, his verse drama *Abdala*, and his sonnet '10 de octubre' (1869) showed his ardent desire for national liberation and an end to slavery. The underlying spirit of *Ismaelillo* (1882) is Promethean in the assertive, developmental, humanist sense in which Aeschylus understood the archetype (in contrast to the earlier Hesiod with his emphasis on Prometheus's deserved punishment for disruption of order and disloyalty to his class). Thus the book exudes the kind of confidence in a better future, in the capacity of man to improve his condition that abounds also in Guillén's work. The manifestations of patriotism and love of liberty continue in the *Versos libres* (*Free Verses*) (1882) and in *Flores del destierro* (*Flowers of Exile*), written in 1887 and published posthumously. A projection of a future Cuba in which justice would prevail is conveyed in the 'Carta rimada' ('Rhymed Letter') addressed to Néstor Ponce de León, and a variety of socio-political interests are demonstrated in the *Versos sencillos* (*Simple Verses*) (1882). Further, the special interest Martí showed in children as an audience, particularly in the work *La edad de oro* (*The Golden Age*) (1889), has its parallel in those poems addressed to children in several of Guillén's books. In fact, in the recent anthology of representative Guillén poems, *Poemas manuables* (*Handy Poems*) (1975), the section entitled 'Poemas para niños' contains the largest number of new poems. And the recent book, *Por el mar de las Antillas anda un barco de papel* (*Across the Caribbean Sea Sails a Paper Boat*) (2nd ed. 1978), a collection of 'poems for older children' published as part of the 'Colección Ismaelillo' reaffirms this link between Martí and Guillén. The final poem of the book, 'Fábula,' a fable about courage, typifies the Martí-like character-building attitude found in the book. But Martí did not foresee the possibility, realized by Guillén, of producing with consummate art a poetry whose social base and political message was constantly inescapable. In the hierarchy he established among the literary genres, he put primary emphasis on the essay as the medium for transmitting his ideology. His prose, however, is so artfully manipulated that the basis of comparison with poetry remains substantial. Martí wrote powerful prose attacking imperialism, racial discrimination, selfishness, economic exploitation, and in favour of the independence of Puerto Rico and of a liberated democratic Cuba that was just to the poor. He thus addressed, with thinking that was in the vanguard of his times, many of the topics addressed by Guillén.

Martí insisted that each Latin American country study, appreciate, and build on its indigenous, natural, living reality. He thereby rejected implicitly the concept of nation building proposed earlier in the nineteenth century by the Argentinian Domingo Faustino Sarmiento who, influentially in his country, equated civilization with European immigration and institutions. Guillén again reveals his close kinship with Martí by linking the idea of progress in Cuba and other Caribbean and Latin American countries with the concept of full participation by all their inhabitants in the national life.

In illustrating the character of imperialism there is in one case a coincidence of procedure in the metaphorical pattern employed by the two writers. In the poem 'Sensemayá,' as has been shown earlier, Guillén employed the parable of the killing of a snake. Martí, in his well-known essay 'Nuestra América' ('Our America'), depicts imperialism in the metaphor presented here in an abbreviated form:

El tigre, espantado del fogonazo, vuelve de noche al lugar de la presa ... No se le oye venir, sino que viene con zarpas de terciopelo. Cuando la presa despierta, tiene el tigre encima ... El tigre espera, detrás de cada árbol acurrucado en cada esquina. Morirá, con las zarpas al aire, echando llamas por los ojos.[2]

The tiger, scared away by the powder flash, returns at night to the site of the prey ... He isn't heard approaching for he comes with velvet paws. When the prey awakens, the tiger is upon him ... The tiger waits, behind each tree, crouching in each corner. He will die with his paws in the air, flames flying from his eyes.

Martí's 'tigre' and Guillén's 'culebra' are represented as clever, hostile, and surreptitious animals that threaten ingenuous people who are not fully alert to their wiles. Anaphora, used by Martí to strengthen the idea of persistence and danger, is used by Guillén to the same effect. Martí's sentence 'No se le oye venir, sino que viene con zarpas de terciopelo' is matched by Guillén's 'La culebra camina sin patas' ('The snake walks without feet'); and 'el tigre espera detrás de cada árbol acurrucado en cada esquina' corresponds to Guillén's 'la culebra se esconde en la yerba; / caminando se esconde en la yerba, / caminando sin patas' ('the snake hides in the grass; / walking it hides in the grass, / walking without feet'). According to both writers, the danger ends with the death of the animal when it is attacked decisively. The account by Augier (referred to in chapter 2, note 30) of the circumstances of the writing of 'Sensemayá' does not suggest that Guillén wrote it while taking any special cognizance of Martí's essay. Indeed, the correspondences between the two writers are not cited here as evidence of the literary influence of Martí on Guillén. They are treated rather as similarities and coincidences determined by the writers' responses to historical circumstances, some aspects of which had changed little in fifty years. The abiding identification made by Guillén in the 1930s of the necessity for a revolutionary approach based on class remains the ideological feature that distinguishes him most clearly from Martí.

GUILLÉN AND THE QUESTION OF BLACK POETRY

The conception that arises from the representation of blacks in Guillén's poetry, is a matter of much curiosity; Guillén is frequently categorized as a *negrista* poet.[3] In *Motivos de son* he allowed the dispossessed black sector of the Cuban population to show the impact of material deprivation on all aspects of life, particularly on its love relations. Thenceforth throughout his work, in a variety of settings and historical stages, conditions of oppression are condemned and rebellion is often urged in the period ending in the revolution. At the same time Guillén urged recognition of Cuba's Afro-Spanish identity as a unifying force.

The stage of oppression that evokes the greatest horror is, of course, slavery. The variety of ways in which Guillén deals with slavery suggests that it is searingly painful to his imagination. It is treated in a parable of horror in 'Balada del güije' ('Ballad of the River Spirit'), as blank past in 'Llegada' ('Arrival'). The victims are portrayed as white in *El diario que a diario*, and lethal violence affecting slave and slave master is shown in the poem 'Ancestros' ('Ancestors'). The slave driver's whip makes many appearances following its initial one in the 'Balada de los dos abuelos' ('Ballad of the Two Grandfathers'); the 'Sangre en las espaldas del negro inicial' ('Blood on the back of the first black man') is present in the 'Elegía a Jacques Roumain' ('Elegy to Jacques Roumain'); and the open sores caused by the whip are vividly displayed in 'Noche de negros junto a la catedral' ('Night of Blacks next to the Cathedral'). In 'El apellido' ('The Family Name') there is rage at the loss of an original identity:

> ¿Sabéis mi otro apellido, el que me viene
> de aquella tierra enorme, el apellido
> sangriento y capturado, que pasó sobre el mar
> entre cadenas, que pasó entre cadenas sobre el mar?

> *Do you know my other surname, the one I got*
> *from that enormous country, the bloody and captured surname,*
> *that crossed the sea in chains,*
> *that went in chains across the sea?*

There is rage too at the heritage and the continuing humiliations, at 'los fragmentos de cadenas / adheridos todavía a la piel' ('the fragments of chains / still sticking to the skin').

It has occurred to many to inquire about the relation of this kind of concern about the black experience to the much talked about concept of *négritude*. The concept emerged in France out of perceptions of colonial cultural tendencies made by a group of West Indian university students in Paris. In 1932, the group published one number of a periodical called *Légitime défense* in which they accused their compatriots of literary imitation and social conformity. The greater authenticity they required meant an emphasis on an African cultural heritage. This effort was followed by *L'Etudiant noir* with which the young poets Aimé Césaire of Martinique (who is credited with coining the term *négritude* to denote the required new spirit of rejection of cultural assimilation and the pursuit of authentic black cultural expression), Léopold Sedar Senghor of Senegal, and Léon Damas of French Guyana were prominently associated. A host of politicians and writers, Joseph Mobutu and Jean Paul Sartre among them, came later to express in their peculiar ways their allegiance to the vague concept. The vagueness is an inescapable consequence of the kind of all-encompassing definition that Senghor, for instance, has given of it, by calling it the 'sum of the cultural values of the black world as expressed in the life, the institutions and the works of black men; the sum of the values of the civilization of the black world.'[4] Always implied, and sometimes stated, is a conception of *négritude* as a metaphysical construct, as a distillation of the universal black soul. The concept has been insistently attacked from the early 1950s by the exiled Haitian poet, René Dépestre,[5] and more recently by other critics such as the Dahomeyan Stanislas Adotevi[6] and the Trinidadian Michael Dash.[7] All three converge on the excessive or irrational nature of the broad claims made for *négritude*, with Dépestre and Adotevi seeing its glorification of static values as a distraction from developmental tasks and an ideological base for neocolonialist penetration. And indeed it is clear, for instance, that the stereotype, sometimes pridefully accepted by Senghor and others, that blacks have a special closeness to nature, carries with it dissuasive impact from demanding a share in high levels of technology. Those levels of technology involved in the peaceful uses of nuclear energy, to take a contentious example, have tended to be publicized by certain industrialized countries in Third World countries with the emphasis placed not on their positive, productive uses in helping to provide for the needs of growing populations but on their possible dangers to man and nature. The insinuation is customary that such dangers are controllable only by the skills and temperament native to northern countries. Also, *négritude* is especially exploitable as an antidote to the development of political ideology in multiracial dependent societies where, as Guillén put it in his essay on Bola de Nieve, 'convivencia y connivencia' ('living together and connivance') of the different social currents are essential. While acknowledging the assistance it can give to morale among colonized blacks, Guillén has rejected the idea of a global neo-African culture as a focus of ideological orientation.[8] Given his historical and dialectical bent, it is not surprising that he should base his views on the course of concrete develop-ments in specific environments with their particular geographical and his-torical features. His intellectual formation took place in an environment in which the principal social factor was the presence of a population descended from Africans, from Spaniards, and from both in various mixtures. The African sector is comprised of the descendants of slaves, but a sociological analysis of this sector faces such complexities as the fact that (as Guillén has reminded me in conversation) there were some blacks in Cuba who were slave-owners. The intelligent appraisal of this kind of social experience is devastating to any system of racial belief that presupposes homogeneity. It points rather, as it did in Guillén's case, to a political ideology that facilitates harmonious interrelations among the whole population and an end to racial discrimination. This would result in the proper recognition and confluence in one national stream of the cultural contribution of blacks – a contribution that was separate and devalued during most of Guillén's years of writing. The point of synthesis reached by his dialectical process is constantly the national identity. If the Spanish cultural contribution is essential to Cuba, so is the African. It is to Cuba's disadvantage to deny equal opportunity to blacks, and it is incumbent on blacks as it is on the descendants of Spaniards to be constructively integrative and not to be divisive. Further, the efficacious way of forging national unity and incapacitating racism lies in striving for a nationhood free from class divisions.

Concomitant with this position is the minimal role played by folklore in Guillén's poetry. Poems that have usually been cited as representing folklore in his poetry, such as 'Sensemayá,' 'Balada del güije' ('Ballad of the River Spirit') 'Canción de cuna para despertar a un negrito' ('Cradle Song for Awakening a Little Black Child') decisively transcend that tradition. The collective unconscious as it reveals itself in Guillén's poetry is attuned to historical reality, and poems that appear in folkloric guise, such as those named above, speak of matters like imperialism, slavery, and combative opposition to racial discrimination.

MAGICAL REALISM

Absent from Guillén's poetry is that magical or marvellous realism that is elsewhere touted in Spanish-American and Caribbean literatures by such writers as Miguel Angel Asturias (Guatemala), Alejo Carpentier (Cuba), Wilson Harris (Guyana), and V.S. Naipaul (Trinidad), particularly in Nai-paul's recent collections of essays. The term 'Magischer Realismus' ('Mag-ical Realism') was employed by Franz Roh in 1925 to refer to a new objectiv-ity in painting following the impressionism / expressionism dichotomy and was soon applied to a European literary trend in which the boundaries between the real and the fantastic were obscured.[9] After observing the idea in France, Asturias and Carpentier came, with different nuances, to regard magical realism as characteristic of the Spanish-American world view.[10]

Asturias illustrates 'el realismo mágico' ('magical realism') by stressing preconscious, mysterious communication between people, between people and nature through the medium of spirits, or between people and spirits. There is often no distinction between the experienced and the imagined. All this is a reflection of the non-European – mainly Indian and African – mentality in Latin America. Carpentier's 'lo real maravilloso' ('marvellous reality') is manifested in focusing on acts that are preposterous, usually in the exercise of abusive power or in religious observances. A belief prevalent in Carpentier's characters that what is magical is real, is regarded by the novelist, along with other extraordinary phenomena, as marvellous. In a recent article that takes a penetrating look at *négritude* and magical realism, Horst Rogmann points to Asturias' expressed endorsement of Senghor's views and the coincidence of several of their positions. He suggests that these concepts arise from the writers' too distanced views of their societies:

The obvious lack of primary *identity* between the writer and the world that serves as the source of his inspiration yields to an *a posteriori identification*, and this is the origin of an illusory identity, the ideological base of 'el realismo mágico,' of 'lo real maravilloso' and of *négritude*. Thus the motifs of recovered infancy, lost steps, the return to the native country and to pre-colonial times characterized not by practicability, but by nostalgia and a strong reactionary accent.[11]

It might be added that the idea of working to effect change is powerfully opposed by the idea of magic – for the fundamental premise underlying magical conceptions is that human behaviour is controlled by forces that lie beyond human activity. Magic implants the delusion that people can get what they want automatically, and it induces a numbing fatalism. Thus, in situations of deprivation it is a pacifier or, worse than that, a policing force militating against organized socio-political action.[12]

The steadfast historical basis of Guillén's poetry leaves no room for the intrusion of magical conceptions. The idea of spiritual communion with mysterious nature that was broached in 'La canción de los sauces' ('Song of the Weeping Willows') (1921) of *Cerebro y corazón* is eschewed in his books published from 1930 onwards. It is replaced in such poems as 'Acana' ('Acana Tree'), 'Ebano real' ('Royal Ebony'), and 'Palma sola' ('Lonely Palm Tree') by the pragmatic and political emphases referred to in my earlier discussions of these poems. The moon in its many appearances in his poetry is a deaf mute, oblivious to man's difficulties; while hurricanes blindly wreak material damage, posing challenges for man. At the same time Guillén shows nature trembling before man's progressive resolve and extols, in poems such as 'El cosmonauta' ('The Cosmonaut'), achievements that demonstrate man's expanding scientific understanding of natural laws. All this is consistent with his basic view that the real, definable, demonstrable social, economic, and political problems are the ones that are to be faced unflinchingly. This outlook is consonant with a Spanish-American tradition that is obscured by the ontological claims of the promoters of 'magical realism' and is exemplified in literature by the considerable body of writings representing man in his struggle against and sometimes in his triumph over nature. In real life, it is exemplified by figures like Simón Bolívar and Augusto César Sandino. A simple coincidence in both liberators is that at important stages in their careers earthquakes occurred, devastating Caracas in 1812 and Managua in 1931. Bolívar reacted by saying, 'If nature opposes us we will fight against it and we will compel it to obey us.'[13] Sandino, referring to the sacredness of the national cause, told his guerrillas not to 'tremble before these things of divine origin precisely for the reason that our army itself has sprung from the same invisible impulse.'[14] This tradition of resolute struggle has been brought abreast of the times by Guillén.

FORMAL ACHIEVEMENTS

The scrupulousness about forms that Guillén has shown in conveying this historically based poetry is arrived at by a consciousness of the responsibility for producing elevated, though not hermetic, expression. The theoretical framework that has informed this approach was formulated early in Guillén's career and was expressed in his article, 'Emma Pérez: poesía y revolución' ('Emma Pérez: Poetry and Revolution'), of 1937, where he writes:

Social poetry has had a similar fate [to that of the so-called vanguardist poetry]: offering verses, and at times hardly verses at all, full of party sectarianisms, of invocations to Lenin and Marx, of apostrophes to the capitalists, of bad oratory, high sounding and hollow. The *cliché* then flourished and the *cliché* brought the standard poem, mass production, super production: soon we were drowned, sepulchered in a thick wave of 'revolutionary' songs, made up simply of words, shouts, wild gestures. What is the result of this? Very simply, the only survivors are those who in addition to being revolutionaries are poets and bring to their art, cleansing it, making it the substance of beauty, the conflict between a world that is disappearing and another that is being born. In this way revolutionary poetry stops being basically party slogans and transforms itself into a human concern without contradicting the slogans; and as for form, the already known – and often forgotten! – Horatian difficulty of simplicity must finally be faced. It is necessary to talk to the man in the street in a direct language, with clean energetic words that he himself knows how to use, and that becomes evident when we have a human, imperative message to transmit to him. We have been constructing a rhetorical poetry that is unintelligible to the worn-down being to whom it is addressed. Why don't we get closer to him and, abandoning the apocalyptic tone that frightens and confounds him, speak to him in his own simple way?[15]

In 1961, in his report to the First Congress of Writers and Artists, Guillén demonstrated the consistency of his views by suggesting that no writer would be able to win many readers among the people by catering to the lowest levels of intelligence or by supplying political slogans and books that rely solely on revolutionary themes, and he added: 'No, it is not true that it is necessary to talk down to the people in order to please them. We must give to the people the best of our spirit, of our technique, of our intelligence, of our work, in the certainty that they understand and know what we are giving them, acknowledging it with gratitude.'[16] Both statements consider form by presupposing that the transmitted content has potential and engaging importance for the reader, but with the awareness that even such content may be debased by inadequate attention to form. These views are similar to (and predate by two decades) those of García Márquez, examined in the first part of this study. The great emphasis placed on artistic quality is the distinguishing feature between them and views expressed by Mario Benedetti and others who believe the sacrifice of artistic finery in times of urgency to be worthwhile.[17]

The breadth of formal means exhibited by Guillén is unusual among twentieth-century poets. At the service of the comprehensiveness of his poetic world is a variety of techniques relating to point of view that are so wide in their embrace as to incorporate aspects of other genres. Not only is the whole range of personal points of view employed in his poetry, but within each one the possibilities are fully exploited. This is exemplified in his widespread use of the first person. A lyrical 'I' in monologue functions in a work such as 'Un poema de amor' ('A Love Poem'). An 'I' that speaks explicitly and authoritatively as poet to an assumed public appears in others such as 'Unión Soviética' ('Soviet Union'). An 'I' representative of the oppressed is used in 'No sé por qué piensas tú' ('I Don't Know Why You Think'). 'Tengo' ('I Have') illustrates one that functions with eclectic collectivity to represent the formerly oppressed. One representing the implied poet in dramatic monologue is exemplified by 'Frente al Oxford' ('Facing the Oxford'), and 'Búcate plata' ('Go Get Money') provides a case of an 'I' representing a character in dramatic monologue. The first-person plural, normally used to represent the oppressed in various attitudes as in 'West Indies, Ltd.,' 'Canción de los hombres perdidos' ('Song of the Lost Men') and 'España ...' is also used with irony to represent positions antithetical to the norm in Guillén's work, as in 'Llanto de las habaneras' ('Lament of the

Women of Havana'). All this makes obvious the error of necessarily identifying the first-person pronouns with Guillén himself and dictates the procedure of referring to the speaker of individual poems, a procedure that permits an enhanced view of the workings of the poems. The numerous poems written in the second-person singular, such as 'Negro bembón' ('Thick-lipped Negro'), and 'Responde tú' ('Answer!') and in the plural, 'La sangre numerosa' ('The Numerous Blood'), enjoy a dramatic intensity, which is achieved elsewhere in Guillén's poetry by dialogue, both within poems and in full-fledged dramatic pieces such as 'Poema con niños' ('Poem with Children') and 'Floripondito.' Also, in addition to the third-person poems that do not depend on irony (such as the 'Retratos' ['Portraits']) are those in which irony reigns, as in many of *El Gran Zoo* and *El diario que a diario*. The variety of points of view is one of the means by which the range of objective correlatives is made impressive in Guillén's poetry. It is a fundamental device for making the presented experiences, their emotional charge, and the ideology underlying them arise from the poems themselves.

Because the *son* is Guillén's strikingly original contribution, the reader is apt to imagine it to occupy a more dominant place in his poetry than it actually does. He employs, with balance, the gamut of verse forms, including *redondillas*, *quintillas*, quartets, tercets, *romances*, *coplas*, sonnets, *silvas*, and *décimas*,[18] often using them in innovative ways.[19] The sonnet 'Sic transit ...' ('Thus passes ...'), for example, possesses not only an *estrambote* or tail but also, inserted in the middle of the second quartet, a playful indication of time lapse – 'Pausa de 15 / segundos a / un año' ('A pause of 15 / seconds to / one year'). In addition, the rhythmic variety in his poems is unsurpassed.[20]

Verse form and rhythm in turn facilitate the creation of various moods in Guillén's poetry. The moods are distinct from each other, like those evoked in the poems 'Hay que tené boluntá' ('One Must Have Willpower'), 'Sensemayá,' 'La sangre numerosa' ('The Numerous Blood'), the poems of the section 'Salón independiente' ('Independent Salon') of *La rueda dentada*, in those of *El Gran Zoo*, and the moods evoked within the 'Elegía a Jesús Menéndez' ('Elegy to Jesús Menéndez'). Besides, the laughter / crying polarity encompasses a wide spectrum of emotions – joy, hope, faith, love, pathos, curiosity, incredulity, dismay, indignation, loss, grief. These emerge from the poems, affirming the authentic humanity they project. The polarity, while present in many of his poems, is thus compelling as an overall effect throughout his poetry.

Just as it would be possible to make separate collections of Guillén's poems on the basis of verse forms, so it would be possible to make or divide anthologies of his work on the basis of categories such as political, folkloric, black, love, satirical, elegiac, epic, lyrical, nature, or children's poetry. But while such a procedure carries the advantage of emphasizing Guillén's versatility, it is ultimately unsatisfactory because his poems are not contained by these categories. A crucial part of the meaning of the individual poems, the part that contributes most to the central character of his poetry, would be obscured. It was shown in the course of analyses that poems, at first glance belonging to any one of these groups, on closer examination exceeded those bounds to embrace aspects of the other categories. Beyond that, in their broad representation of life, particularly Cuban life, the poems have contributed to shaping the ideology of the Cuban revolution from its earliest stages. The breadth of relevance that makes Guillén's poetry specific and general, concrete and comprehensive, and (as the symbolic 'guitarra' of *El son entero* was described) 'universal y cubana' is in great part due to the poetry's simultaneous involvement with different generic categories while dealing with well-defined subjects. Thus when Guillén is properly spoken of as a social poet, 'social' is not to be understood as a sub-category of poetry but as a strategy in which an unusually wide range of poetic modes are made to merge, with consummate skill, in the conveyance of worthy and uncompromising human sentiments and aspirations.

This appealing distinctiveness within Guillén's work rests largely on its semantic features. Here his characteristic comprehensiveness is also in evidence. His expression ranges from the popular to the standard to the classical and the archaic. He creates words and draws from several languages and from all sectors of human activity over a vast historical expanse. One conspicuous feature of his use of figurative language is his preference for creating meaning by means of metonymy, which functions through contiguity, rather than metaphor which functions through contrast. This preference is a part of his broad inclination to avoid hermeticism, to regard poetry as communicative rather than cryptic, to keep it close to historical reality, and to enhance its didactic possibilities. A lesson often presented in Guillén's poetry – that man is the controller of his destiny and of his environment – has its repercussions in the function of language in his poetry. Thus, because man is capable of change and of altering his social systems, no pattern of linguistic signs will constantly represent his activity. Consequently, a semiological approach to the criticism of his poetry will be ineffective, as was shown in my analysis of the 'Elegía a Jesús Menéndez.' A structural analysis of the language of Guillén's poems is beset by paradoxes that can be resolved, as they were in that poem, only by taking into account the values attached to the participants in the struggle between progress and reaction. 'Metal' associated with Casillas is antithetical to 'metal' associated with Menéndez, and in this and other poems 'serpiente' may be an image of imperialism or of the fascination held by the locks of the loved one's hair. This kind of usage is a further indication of the fact that the generative principle at work in Guillén's poetry is dialectical rather than metaphysical. A reading of the 'Elegía a Jesús Menéndez' and of poems subsequent to it reveals that out of the conflict of 'metal' versus 'metal' comes a different form of reality, in which the 'metal' representative of Menéndez gains the ascendancy and evolves continuously in response to new challenges. The natural appeal that the struggle between progress and reaction holds for readers who are sympathetic to the idea of social progress is in itself one of the factors that prevents whatever difficulties may arise in Guillén's poetry from reaching the level of the hermetic. Even though potential hurdles to ready understanding such as archaisms and hyperbaton are functioning in his poetry at the semantic and syntactical levels respectively, these usages are fitted to engaging social contexts that elicit commitment, creating the impetus for and facilitating their resolution.

Guillén has found fitting forms in the macro sense at all stages of his poetry. For example, the *son* and popular speech provide appropriate forms for the newly emerged content of the *Motivos de son*; the newspaper, the keeper of the social record, itself satirized, conveys artistically the chaos of pre-revolutionary times in *El diario que a diario*; and post-revolutionary works tend to be characterized by a greater degree of difficulty reflecting the broader experience presented and the growing sophistication of his readers. He has also varied his forms considerably from one poem to the next. Thus in 'Guitarra en duelo mayor' ('Guitar in Grief Major') and 'Lectura de domingo' ('Sunday Reading'), which are two perspectives on the same event, different forms are fully operative in the different meanings, including the suggestions of the different levels of audience for which the poems are immediately destined. From the *Motivos de son* to *El diario que a diario* Guillén's unfailing sense of how to say what he has to say has led to the special appeal of his comprehensive achievement.[21] It has caused many of his poems to attain a degree of popularity that has made them part of the national oral tradition. At the same time, recondite features of his work – the unobtrusive artistic elements, his place within literary history, his creation of new expressive possibilities for use by his fellow practitioners – give him outstanding stature.

GUILLÉN AND THE THEORISTS

The achievement on which Guillén's stature is based makes him merit special consideration in light of the theories of poetry examined in the first part of this book. The two theoretical statements by Guillén quoted in the preceding section approximate those made by Marx and Engels concerning the need for attention to artistic demands. Guillén has abided by this concept while attaining comprehensiveness, a quality also admired by Marx and Engels, as well as by later theorists in the Marxist current such as Lenin and Lukács.

Marx and Engels used the example of Balzac, admiring the breadth of his world, but were outspoken about what they saw as his limitations, the chief of which was the conservative outlook that guided his work. Lenin, with similar reservations, made Tolstoy his main interest in the field of imaginative literature. Writing in our times, Lukács continued to dwell on these nineteenth-century novelists, adding to them other European novelists among whom he viewed Thomas Mann with particular favour. Guillén's work is to be recognized as an example *par excellence* of the kind of writing fostered by those who have built the core of Marxist literary theory because of its comprehensive reflection of society, the resultant validity of the vision with which it looks at successive historical stages, the staunchly revolutionary outlook that has constantly informed it, and the soundness of the artistic conception that governs its presentation. A strong tendency among the more recent European and North American contributors to Marxist theory is a failure to provide adequately studied examples, either positive or negative, to support their views. In any case, several of their pronouncements have been negated by Guillén's practice.

Just as Plekhanov's view that the writer who is seriously at odds with his society turns to art for art's sake is refuted by Guillén's whole pre-revolutionary work, so has the study of his poetry revealed shortcomings in certain theories of Gramsci, Sánchez Vázquez, and Demetz concerning the distinction they make between the poet and the politician and concerning the poet's incapacity to treat future time. By linking political to general cultural development, Guillén shows the ordinary man to be partial to the idea of progress, and by providing more challenging works for a post-revolutionary society he illustrates the views of Fischer to the extent that they are applicable to Cuban society at the historical stages at which Guillén has been writing. Thanks largely to the tension resulting from the entertainment/sobriety, laughter/crying duality that makes his poetry classifiable at once as art and as life, Guillén overcomes the problems (haunting to Brecht) caused by the distracting powers of art. His constantly demonstrated faith in a better future and the ideological initiative he has taken in plotting the path to that future distinguish him from Adorno and Macherey, respectively.

Given Guillén's alertness to aesthetic considerations, it cannot be said that the views of Ortega are wholly irrelevant to his work, for the positive aspect of Ortega's contribution lies in his having joined with other Formalists in directing attention to the internal demands of art, to how things are said. He thus helped to heighten sensitivities to artistic means. (Guillén has stated in the earlier mentioned interview by Ciro Bianchi Ross that Ortega was one of the writers he was reading in the early 1930s.) Yet Ortega's aggressive stance against human content in his campaign for art for art's sake exposes his incompleteness in the light of Guillén's achievement. One might well wonder about the feasibility of removing art from human life and while wondering ponder the case of the eminent scholar, A.C. Bradley. He produced, before Ortega, one of the most eloquent essays ever written on behalf of poetry for poetry's sake, arguing in it that the evaluation of art should not be tied up with social matters.[22] But Bradley shows improper psychical distance and reacts atavistically to the artistic treatment of a subject that is of crucial importance to Guillén's poetic and real worlds. In supporting Coleridge's view that Othello should be 'sunburnt' rather than black on the modern stage, Bradley writes in his *Shakespearean Tragedy*: 'Perhaps if we saw Othello coal-black with the bodily eye, the aversion of our blood, an aversion which comes as near to being merely physical as anything human can, would overpower our imagination and sink us below not Shakespeare only but the audiences of the seventeenth and eighteenth centuries.'[23] This statement precedes by five years his essay on poetry for poetry's sake. If one can conclude that his adoption of art for art's sake was a strategy to avert the kind of trauma he shows in his reaction to *Othello*, it might have served a useful purpose for him while demonstrating that poetry for poetry's sake tends to be for the sake of something else. However, in no case can Bradley's strategy be considered to be the best possible one, especially in view of the alternatives offered by Guillén in this regard.

The twentieth-century theorists with whom Guillén shows the strongest links are, not surprisingly, the Spanish-American ones. His practice is essentially in conformity with Mariátegui's views concerning the duty of the writer to possess a firm ideological base, to approach his task with ethical as well as aesthetic criteria, to put literature to the service of creating a society in which the interests of the vast majority would be directly served. This, in addition to the fact that Mariátegui generously praised the poetry of José María Eguren (whose work showed only faint nationalist sentiments and therefore did not reflect Mariátegui's theories) makes it possible for one to assume that he would have read Guillén's work with great satisfaction. Portuondo, whose views in important ways bring Mariátegui's theories up to the time of Guillén's production and also extend their historical roots, has used Guillén's work to illustrate his earlier expressed theories of literature. He does this evincing obvious pride in a body of work that, by occupying itself centrally with Cuban historical reality, represents a new stage in Spanish-American literary history.

The Spanish-American theorists are exceptional in another regard. It has been shown that the European theorists from Marx to Macherey tended to overlook the social possibilities of poetry and to concentrate their attention on the novel. Their underestimation of poetry may not be unrelated to the kind of Formalist classification that led Jakobson to marry metaphor to poetry and metonymy to prose. The Spanish-American quest to have poetry develop its social potential is, as was shown in the first part of this study, long standing, and the quest has obviated the genre-bound limitations of the Europeans.

GUILLÉN AND THE READER

The reader of twentieth-century 'Western' poetry is normally receptive to an approach to poetry that is quite different from Guillén's. In the English-speaking world, it is usual to encounter readers who consider such poets as T.S. Eliot, W.H. Auden, and Robert Lowell to have registered and defined the nature of modern consciousness. Modern consciousness so defined – and to such definers may be added such Third World poets as Octavio Paz, Jorge Luis Borges, and Derek Walcott – usually has to do with a sense of lost-ness, of the alienation of the individual in an abusive, confused, disintegrat-ing, absurd society. These contemporary versions of the *poète maudit* tend to make of poetry a means of self-affirmation. In the quest for identity and for nirvanas, society is sweepingly shown to be unsatisfactory, no gesture being made to rectify its specific defects. Thus Lowell as candid spokesman says: 'We are free to say what we want to, and somehow what we want to say is the confusion and sadness and incoherence of the human condition.'[24] Personal systems are constructed based on unique perceptions and reactions supplemented by borrowings from exotic, often nihilistic, religious and philosophical currents,[25] on claims to transcendence and a heavy reliance on irony – irony as a way of life, as characteristic of the 'human condition' rather than irony of the kind found in Guillén's work that is applied to specific social situations from a clear moral perspective. Conceits involving the abstruse reconciling of apparently dissimilar elements are common; and since the search for identity spurs a corresponding search for a supposed primor-dial purity of the word, hermeticism results and is usually accorded positive value. The contemporary reader, accustomed to the challenge of decipher-ing such obscure poetry, may well tend to regard as superficial, and react superciliously to, poetry that seems readily intelligible. But an illusion is at play here, for the difficulty present in poems that deal with idiosyncratic poetic visions and systems is in most cases one-dimensional because once the text has been deciphered, the game is over. The reader has had a viewing of a private world where factors such as maturity, cogency, and accountable knowledge are largely irrelevant. By contrast, the long literary tradition formed by the probingly humanist production of such writers as Aeschylus, Dante, Cervantes, and several Spanish-American writers – and to which Guillén has made his contribution in keeping with the scientific advances available to him – is multidimensional. Within this tradition the artistic means are remarkable in themselves, and they possess an altruistic function that is not limited to the promotion of art. They are used to evoke a critical view of a wide range of mankind's vital social experience. The reader is thus faced with the task of appraising artistic means that are bound up with aspects of the comprehensive viewing of society as these aspects are exposed. The reader is obliged to make reference to several areas of knowledge in the process of reading, and depth and maturity of vision become relevant considerations.

In Guillén's case, the reader is required to assess the effects of numerous artistic forms, for one of the attributes of Guillén's poetry is the functioning (with the result of clarity rather than obscurity) of semantic and musical devices that are not exceeded either in abundance or in range by the princes of darkness. Also, his integrative outlook is comprehensive, revealing itself in an attitude that is unfriendly to a disassociated cultural epistemology and in favour of linking the humanities with the sciences, of mobilizing 'sputniks y sonetos' in a unified struggle against backwardness. The reader must, therefore, have a capacity for absorbing material from the various fields with which he deals: from art, economics, history, literature, music, philosophy, politics, science, sociology, and sports. He must also be respectful of his fellow man. In fact, this last quality helps him to understand that the tendency to grasp the meaning of phenomena without the constraints of academic disciplines is widespread among readers and potential readers, and that works in this transdisciplinary vein are apt to be perceived or received naturally as being reflective of life as it is normally lived. Nor does such a reader necessarily defer to the specialist even in matters that in this context of comprehensiveness touch on the specialist's own field. It might be said, for instance, that because of his natural interest in growth, development, and the humanitarian ends of his labour, the ordinary worker is likely to have a better understanding of some essential aspects of economics than even a renowned economist of the monetarist school. Also, at a time when attempts are being made to lend reverence to the expression 'cado loco con su tema' ('to each madman his obsession') and irrationality and Dionysian attitudes are widespread (due to the efforts of such schools of psychiatry as that headed by R.D. Laing), the reader must resist the temptation to see any paradox in the fact that Guillén is a poet of accountable rationality. Where this poetry goes against the grain of the reader's ideological formation, which will usually be the case in the English-speaking world and indeed in most of the Spanish-speaking world as well,[26] he must show at least that 'willing suspension of disbelief' that Coleridge influentially prescribed for the appreciation of literature. But preferably he should read Guillén soberly; for the solid rationality that underlies his creations makes them apprehendable as truth and illustrations of how ever-broadening experience serves to determine consciousness. The steady expansion of consciousness, reflected in the content of successive books, forms an overall pattern that contrasts with the circularity, the trip from infancy toward maturity and back in old age, often found in the works of poets where the 'I' presumes to remove itself from its broad, evolving circumstances.

The opening up of paths to various fields is another aspect of the developmental attitude underlying Guillén's work. His wide span of interests has been channelled, by an ideological outlook that has grown in firmness with time, into a powerful current of poetry. Always a conscientious artist, he mastered early the conventional forms of Hispanic poetry and soon contributed innovations and variations, some of which derived from his discernment of the artistic possibilities of popular Cuban culture. This innovative virtuosity has constantly permitted him to find forms appropriate to expressing, first, advanced insights into the conditions of his country – for Cuba is the trunk of the tree of his poetry – and the universal ramifications of these insights. The lucidity and impeccable gracefulness with which his social perceptions emerge from his poems and the mature coherence of his total work make this Cuban, West Indian, and Spanish-American poet an outstanding international figure who occupies a high and secure place in the history of poetry.

Notes

INTRODUCTION

1 Nancy Morejón, ed., *Recopilación de textos sobre Nicolás Guillén* (La Habana: Case de las Américas 1974)
2 Angel Augier, *Nicolás Guillén: Notas para un estudio biográfico-crítico* I (La Habana: Universidad Central de la Villas 1965), and *Nicolás Guillén: Notas para un estudio biográfico-crítico* II (La Habana: Universidad Central de la Villas 1964)
3 Nicolás Guillén, *Obra poética 1920–1958* I (La Habana: Instituto Cubano del Libro 1972), and *Obra poética 1958–1972* II (La Habana: Instituto Cubano de Libro 1973)
4 Arturo Torres-Ríoseco, *The Epic of Latin American Literature* (Berkeley: University of California Press 1959), pp. 129–30, 132; and Enrique Anderson Imbert, *Historia de la literatura hispanoamericana* II (México: Fondo de Cultura Económica 1970), pp. 179–81, 182
5 Adriana Tous, *La poesía de Nicolás Guillén* (Madrid: Ediciones Cultura Hispánica 1971); and Jorge María Ruscalleda Bercedóniz, *La poesía de Nicolás Guillén* (Río Piedras: Editorial Universitaria 1975)
6 Ezequiel Martínez Estrada, *La poesía afrocubana de Nicolás Guillén* (Montevideo: Editorial Arca 1966)
7 Dennis Sardinha, *The Poetry of Nicolás Guillén* (London: New Beacon Books Ltd 1976); and Neville Dawes, *Prolegomena to Caribbean Literature* (Kingston: Institute of Jamaica 1977)
8 Wilfred Cartey, *Black Images* (New York: Teachers College Press 1970), pp. 111–48; and Frederick Stimson, *The New Schools of Spanish American Poetry* (Chapel Hill: University of North Carolina 1970), pp. 168–79
9 Martha Allen, 'Nicolás Guillén, poeta del pueblo,' *Revista Iberoamericana* 15 (1949): 29–43
10 Anthony George Dahl, 'La poética de Nicolás Guillén: Análisis estilístico integral de la "Elegía a Jesús Menéndez,"' MA thesis, Carleton University 1977
11 Cecil Maurice Bowra, *Poetry and Politics 1900–1960* (Cambridge: Cambridge University Press 1966), pp. 104–6

12 Lorna V. Williams, *Self and Society in the Poetry of Nicolás Guillén* (Baltimore: Johns Hopkins University Press 1982)
13 Nancy Morejón, *Nación y mestizaje en Nicolás Guillén* (La Habana: Ediciones Unión 1982)

CHAPTER I

1 For a detailed accounting of Marx's writings on literature and effective studies of the general topic, see Karl Marx and Friedrich Engels, *Sur la littérature et l'art*, selection of texts and introduction by Jean Fréville (Paris: Editions Sociales 1954); Adolfo Sánchez Vázquez, *Las ideas estéticas de Marx: Ensayos de estética marxista* (México: Era 1965); Raymond Williams, *Marxism and Literature* (London: Oxford University Press 1977); and Terry Eagleton, *Marxism and Literary Criticism* (London: Methuen 1976).
2 Karl Marx and Friedrich Engels, *L'Idéologie allemande*, trans. Henri Auger et al. (Paris: Editions Sociales 1968), p. 51. I have translated this and other subsequent quotations into English.
3 Frederic Jameson, *Marxism and Form* (Princeton: Princeton University Press 1971), p. 362
4 In *Sociology of Literature and Drama*, ed. Elizabeth and Tom Burns (Harmondsworth: Penguin Books 1973), pp. 159–60.
5 Ibid., p. 159.
6 Eagleton, *Marxism and Literary Criticism*, p. 41
7 V.I. Lenin, *Sur la littérature et l'art*, selection of texts and introducton by Jean Fréville (Paris: Editions Sociales 1957), p. 104
8 Georgi Plekhanov, *Art and Social Life*, trans. A. Fineberg (Moscow: Progress Publishers 1957), p. 16
9 Ibid., p. 17
10 György Lukács, *Problemas del realismo*, trans. Carlos Gerhard (México: Fondo de Cultura Económica 1960), p. 20
11 William Kurtz Wimsatt Jr, *The Verbal Icon* (Lexington: University of Kentucky Press 1954), pp. 69–83
12 See especially Roger Garaudy, *D'Un Réalisme sans rivages* (Paris: Libraire Plon 1963), pp. 153–4; and Lucien Goldmann, *Pour une sociologie du roman* (Paris: Editions Gallimard 1964), pp. 186–7
13 Sánchez Vázquez, *Las ideas estéticas de Marx*, pp. 263–71
14 Ibid., p. 264
15 Peter Demetz, *Marx, Engels, and the Poets* (Chicago: University of Chicago Press 1967), p. 211
16 José Ortega y Gasset, *La deshumanización del arte* (Madrid: Revista de Occidente 1956), p. 6
17 Ibid., p. 8
18 Ibid., p. 12
19 Ernst Fischer, *La necesidad de arte*, trans. Adelaida de Juan and José Rodríguez Feo (La Habana: Ed. Unión 1964), p. 259
20 Ibid., p. 270

21 Bertolt Brecht, *Sur le réalisme*, trans. André Gisselbrecht (Paris: L'Arche 1970), p. 126

22 Pierre Macherey, *Pour une théorie de la production littéraire* (Paris: Maspéro 1970)

23 Jean Franco, *Criticism and Literature within the Context of a Dependent Culture*, Occasional Papers, no. 16 (New York University: The American Language and Area Center 1975)

24 See the collection of his essays, *Understanding Brecht*, trans. Anna Bostock (London: NLB 1973).

25 Theodor W. Adorno, *Negative Dialectics*, trans. E.B. Ashton (New York: Seabury Press 1973)

26 In the course of doing so I will make reference to my article 'Literary American-ism and the Recent Poetry of Nicolás Guillén,' *University of Toronto Quarterly* 45 (1975): 1–18, which may be consulted for further details.

27 For an incisive study of these questions see Fernando Alegría, *Historia de la novela hispanoamericana* (México: Ediciones de Andrea 1966), pp. 5–9

28 Charles I's religious susceptibilities were also played on by the monetarist bankers, the Fuggers. They encouraged Charles and Philip II after him with loans to enmesh themselves in a series of religious wars in Europe. The desperate financial situation of Spain caused by the wars forced the monarchs into frantic dependency, of which the bankers knew how to take advantage. This situation prompted the voracious character of the looting (the word 'loot' came into the English language from the Hindi and originally described a British practice in India) of Spanish-American resources carried out by the Spaniards. When the flow of treasures from Spanish America ebbed, the debt to the Fuggers was paid by the transfer to them of some of Spain's mines and most fertile lands. In order to gain quick returns, the Fuggers introduced sheep on these lands, which ruined them for agriculture, turning them into dust bowls and leading to much poverty, two images that are recurrent in Spain's literature of the Golden Age. See Robyn Quijano, 'Erasmian Humanism and Ferdinand of Aragon,' *The Campaigner* 11, nos 3–4 (1975): 2, 78

29 José Enrique Rodó, *Obras completas*, ed. Emir Rodríguez Monegal (Madrid: Aguilar 1967), pp. 169, 191

30 See his prologue to his only novel, *Amistad funesta* (1885), in José Martí, *Obras completas*, (La Habana: Editorial Nacional de Cuba 1964), XVIII, 192

31 Jorge Luis Borges, *Discusión* (Buenos Aires: Emecé 1957), pp. 151–62

32 Two distinguished writers who represent the range are Mario Benedetti in its harsher aspects, particularly in his *Letras del continente mestizo* (Montevideo: Arca 1967), pp. 40–6; and Gabriel García Márquez, less harshly in conversa-tion with Mario Vargas Llosa, in *La novela en América Latina: Diálogo* (Lima: C. Milla Batres 1968). For what is perhaps the most developed argument against Borges's writing see Blas Matamoro, *Jorge Luis Borges o el juego trascendente* (Buenos Aires: A Peña Lillo 1971). Borges's work has enjoyed, of course, a great deal of favourable criticism, particularly from per-spectives other than sociological ones. The work that initiates this trend is Marcial Tamayo and Adolfo Ruiz-Díaz, *Borges enigma y clave* (Buenos Aires:

Nuestro Tiempo 1955). This trend has been well represented in English in such organs as the *New York Times Review of Books* and the *Times Literary Supplement*.

33 José Carlos Mariátegui, 'Arte, revolución y decadencia,' *Amauta*, no. 3 (1926): 1–2

34 Sánchez Vázquez, *Las ideas estéticas de Marx*, p. 260

35 For example, in Sánchez Vázquez's adopted country, Mexico, Diego Rivera, Clemente Orozco, and David Siqueiros contributed their various forms of painting, Nicolás Guillén first published his *Cantos para soldados y sones para turistas*, and Pablo Neruda first published his *Canto general*, all works that reached more than the privileged few.

36 Gabriel García Márquez and Mario Vargas Llosa, *La novela en América Latina: Diálogo*, p. 41

37 Ibid., p. 43

38 García Márquez also has founded a political party in his native Colombia and has faced the prospect of exile.

39 See the interview conducted by José Miguel Oviedo, 'Cortázar a cinco rounds,' *Marcha* 1634 (1973): 29–31

40 García Márquez and Vargas Llosa, *La novela en América Latina: Diálogo*, p. 36

41 See Jorge Ruffinelli, 'Cortázar: La novela ingresa en la historia,' *Marcha* 1644 (1973): 31

42 Cortázar replied to Ruffinelli praising his accurate perceptions ('de Julio Cortázar,' *Marcha* 1647 [1973]: 29)

43 *García Márquez: Historia de un deicidio* (Barcelona: Barral Editores 1971)

44 'Vade retro,' *Marcha* 1591 (1972): 31. The other articles by Rama in the series are 'Respuesta a Vargas Llosa: El fin de los demonios,' *Marcha* 1603 (1972): 30–1; 'Segunda respuesta a Vargas Llosa: Nuevo escritor para una nueva sociedad,' *Marcha* 1610 (1972): 30–1; and 'Un arma llamada novela,' *Marcha* 1612 (1972): 29–31. Those by Mario Vargas Llosa are 'Respuesta a Angel Rama: El regreso de Satán,' *Marcha* 1602 (1972): 30–1; and 'Segunda respuesta a Angel Rama: Resurrección de Belcebú, o la distancia creadora,' *Marcha* 1609 (1972): 29–31.

45 See his 'Segunda respuesta a Angel Rama ...' *Marcha* 1609 (1972): 29–31

46 Fernando Alegría, *Literatura y revolución* (México: Fondo de Cultura Económica 1971), p. 23

47 Two indigenous resisters whose names stand out are Hatuey who had fled to Cuba from the Spanish terror in Hispaniola and set up an area of combat in the mountains of eastern Cuba until he was killed in 1512, and Guamá who in 1530 led a damaging attack on Baracoa, the first Spanish settlement on the island. He was killed in action in 1533.

48 The essay by the venerable Cuban historian José Luciano Franco, 'Esquema de los movimientos populares de liberación nacional (1511–1868)' and others from his book *Ensayos históricos* (La Habana: Editorial de Ciencias Sociales 1974) are an indispensable source of information on these and other matters concerning Cuban history. See also the valuable book by Julio Le Riverend, *Economic History of Cuba* (La Habana: Instituto del Libro 1967).

49 Aponte is, of course, prominently alluded to in Guillén's poetry. The daring he

showed for his times has given rise to the saying that has survived in Cuba, 'Más malo que Aponte' ('Badder than Aponte').

50 Sergio Aguirre, 'Seis actitudes de la burguesía cubana en el siglo XIX,' *Dialéctica*, Año II, vol. 2, no. 6 (1943): 176

51 Quoted in José Antonio Portuondo's study of Cuban literary history, *Bosquejo histórico de la letras cubanas* (La Habana: Editora del Ministerio de Educación 1962), p. 20

52 There is an excellent brief portrayal of del Monte in Sergio Giral's masterpiece in film, *El otro Francisco* (La Habana: ICAIC 1975). The film undertakes an evaluation and re-creation of Suárez y Romero's *Francisco* in the light of the governing socio-economic conditions of mid nineteenth-century Cuba. With directors of the calibre of Giral and Gutiérrez Alea at its service, an ICAIC production of a film devoted to the career of the complex Domingo del Monte would be most interesting.

53 See Portuondo, *Bosquejo histórico de las letras cubanas*, p. 20

54 More than five million slaves were taken from Africa between 1807 and 1847, and in Cuba the trade continued until 1880 (see José Luciano Franco, *Ensayos históricos*, pp. 107, 123).

55 Quoted in Portuondo, *Bosquejo histórico de las letras cubanas*, p. 23

56 The word 'creole' which in Cuba meant originally descendants of Spaniards, born in Cuba, is at this stage in history taking on a meaning that includes making a definite choice of Cuba over Spain and thereby moving toward an identification with others whose patriotic ties are to Cuba.

57 Quoted in José Luciano Franco, *Ensayos históricos*, p. 230

58 Jorge Mañach, *Historia y estilo* (La Habana: Minerva 1944), p. 95

59 He wrote in a letter to Jorge Mañach: 'I destroy my verses, I despise them, I forget them: I am interested in them to the same extent that social justice interests the majority of our writers,' Rubén Martínez Villena, *Orbita de Rubén Martínez Villena*, ed. Raúl Roa (La Habana: UNEAC 1965), p. 211.

60 Juan Marinello, 'Arte y política,' *Revista de Avance*, Año II, no. 18 (1928): 6 and 'Plástica y poética,' *Revista de Avance*, Año III, no. 32 (1929): 100

61 *Jitanjáfora* is the term used by Alfonso Reyes to denote a 'word' created to serve only for its phonic value. The word *jitanjáfora* appeared first in a poem by Mariano Brull.

62 Mañach, *Historia y estilo*, p. 94

63 See Guillén's essay entitled 'Marinello' in *Prosa de prisa* I (Habana: Editorial Arte y Literatura, 1975), pp. 237–9 and his obituary in *Casa de las Américas*, Año XVIII, no. 103 (1977): 10–11

64 In one of her final contributions before her recent death, Mirta Aguirre includes comment on this period in her comprehensive and eloquent essay on Guillén in her book *Ayer y hoy* (La Habana: UNEAC 1980)

65 Raúl Roa, *Bufa subversiva* (La Habana: Cultural 1935)

66 Portuondo, *El concepto de la poesía* (México: Colegio de México 1944)

67 Portuondo, *El heroísmo intelectual* (México: Tezontle 1955). For an effective brief study of Portuondo and Mariátegui as literary theorists see Lynherst Peña, 'Trends of Literary Criticism in Spanish America, 1900–1950, PHD dissertation,

University of Toronto 1970. Among the essays in Roberto Fernández Retamar's valuable book, *Para una teoría de la literatura hispanoamericana* (México: Editorial Nuestro Tiempo 1977), is 'Lecciones de Portuondo,' pp. 30–8

68 Portuondo, *Estética y revolución* (La Habana: UNEAC 1963), and *Crítica de la época y otros ensayos* (La Habana: Universidad de las Villas 1965)

69 José Lezama Lima begins with these words his collection of essays, *La expresión americana* (Santiago de Chile: Editorial Universitaria 1969) p. 9

70 José Rodríguez Feo, 'Cultura y moral,' *Ciclón* I, no. 6 (1955), no pagination

71 Roberto Fernández Retamar, 'Teoría (y práctica) de la literatura,' *Universidad de la Habana*, no. 155 (1966): 9–10

72 Mirta Aguirre, 'Recuerdo Juan ...' *Casa de las Américas*, Año XVIII, no. 103 (1977): 13. Among Guillén's many poems dealing with the hardships of exile is 'Pero señor' (1958), dedicated to Mirta Aguirre. The above level of literal, unrhymed translation will be evident in my subsequent renderings of Guillén's poems. For accomplished translations of many of his poems see *Man-making Words; Selected Poems of Nicolás Guillén*, trans. Robert Márquez and David Arthur McMurray (Amherst: University of Massachusetts Press 1972); *¡Patria o Muerte! The Great Zoo and Other Poems*, trans. Robert Márquez (New York: Monthly Review Press 1972); and *Tengo*, trans. Richard J. Carr (Detroit: Broadside Press 1974).

73 See my article 'Cuban Literature and the Revolution,' *Fidel Castro's Personal Revolution in Cuba: 1959–1973*, ed. James Nelson Goodsell (New York: Alfred A. Knopf 1975), pp. 243–8

74 My translation of parts of the address quoted in Adolfo Sánchez Vázquez, *Estética y marxismo* (México: Era 1970), II, pp. 403–8.

75 The most important of these documents, 'La actividad cultural,' a section of the *Declaración del Primer Congreso Nacional de Educación y Cultura*' (1971); 'La cultura,' a selection from the *Report of the Central Committee of the Communist Party of Cuba* (1975); 'Sobre la cultura artística y literaria,' *Thesis and Resolution of the First Congress of the Communist Party of Cuba* (1976), in addition to the 'Palabras a los intelectuales,' appear in the book *Política cultural de la Revolución Cubana. Documentos* (La Habana: Editorial de Ciencias Sociales 1977).

76 For an attractively presented example of the tendency in some places to persist in interpreting Cuban cultural activity in a way that is unduly hostile to the revolution, see Tomás Gutiérrez Alea, 'Memorias de *Memorias (del subdesarrollo)*,' *Casa de las Américas* 122 (1980): 67–76.

77 For an extensive examination of this, see Charles Hollingsworth, 'The Development of Literary Theory in Cuba, 1959–1968,' PH D dissertation, University of California, Berkeley 1972). See also J.R. Pereira, 'Towards a Theory of Literature in Revolutionary Cuba,' *Jamaica Journal* 9, no. 1 (1975): 28–33.

78 The poem may be found in *Casa de las Américas* 108 (1978): 72–3.

79 For affirmations of this and for a clear discussion of related theoretical questions see Roberto Fernández Retamar, *El intelectual y la sociedad* (México: Siglo XXI 1969).

80 A useful chapter entitled 'La Rhétorique restreinte' on the recent emphasis on metaphor and its relation to metonymy is to be found in Gérard Genette's *Figures III* (Paris: Editions du Seuil 1972), pp. 21–41. He takes into account earlier reflections on the topic by Roman Jakobson in 'Two Aspects of Languages and Two Types of Aphasic Disturbance,' *Fundamentals of Language* (The Hague: Mouton and Co. 1956), pp. 55–82. Jakobson had tended to distinguish between the language of prose and the language of poetry and had linked metaphor to poetry and metonymy to prose. Genette rectifies this view by making no such distinction in his promotion of metonymy.

81 André Breton, *La Clé des champs* (Paris: Editions du Sagittaire 1953), p. 114

82 See my analysis of each of these three Darío works in my book *Critical Approaches to Rubén Darío* (Toronto: University of Toronto Press 1974), pp. 85–101.

83 This is a prominent preoccupation throughout his books: *Brecht on Theatre*, trans. John Willett (London: Methuen 1964), *Sur le réalisme*, trans. André Gisselbrecht (Paris: L'Arche 1970), and *Les Arts et la révolution*, trans. Bernard Lortholary (Paris: L'Arche 1970).

84 I.A. Richards, *Science and Poetry* (London: Kegan Paul 1926), pp. 56–9

CHAPTER 2

1 Angel Augier's *Nicolás Guillén: Notas para un estudio biográfico-crítico* I (La Habana: Universidad Central de las Villas 1965), and *Nicolás Guillén: Notas para un estudio biográfico-crítico* II (La Habana: Universidad Central de Las Villas 1964) are the main sources of the biographical information given here.

2 See Guillén's article 'Nací en una imprenta,' *Prosa de prisa* III (La Habana: Editorial Arte y Literatura 1976), pp. 386–7.

3 Augier, *Nicolás Guillén* ... I, p. 39

4 See n. 1 above, vol. I

5 In giving away the manuscript to Gustavo E. Urrutia in 1931, he called it in his inscription 'this little assassination, perpetrated in Camagüey,' ibid., p. 48.

6 In selecting poems for the collection, Guillén excluded a relatively large number (eight) of Alexandrine sonnets.

7 A later echo of *Cerebro y corazón* probably exists also in the name that was given in 1936 to the journal *Mediodía*, edited by Guillén. In the collection, the word 'Mediodía' appears in the poems 'Sol' and 'Agua fuerte,' and in the latter in the phrase 'el fuego eternal del Mediodía.' It is possible that the journal was named in the hope that its flame would be eternal.

8 For a document that sheds clear light on all of this period, see Guillén's 'Charla en el Lyceum,' *Prosa de prisa* I (La Habana: Editorial Arte y Literatura 1975), pp. 287–305.

9 It is perhaps for this reason that this poem has not been commented on, to my knowledge, by Guillén critics.

10 Ramón Guirao, *Orbita de la poesía afrocubana* (La Habana: Ucar García 1938), p. xxii

11 José Juan Arrom, *Estudios de literatura hispanoamericana* (La Habana: Ucar García 1950), p. 127
12 See Guillén's account in his *Prosa de prisa* I, p. 291.
13 Notice Guillén's consistent attitude and closeness to Urrutia as well as his early relations with Marinello in the following selection from the tribute to Marinello: 'Troubled early in his career about the destiny of Cuba, Marinello recognized in their time the labours of the ingenious nobleman Don Gustavo Urrutia, at war against the infamous racist discrimination which was unrelenting in a society freshly out of slavery. Marinello sent us at that time a letter (5 May 1929) placing himself beside us in the face of a problem that was basic for national unity. One year later our friendship was consolidated forever on the publication of *Motivos de son* which he received with pure joy, very different from the reticences of *ad usum* criticism in whose roots the reactionary tendency which would culminate in the most repugnant betrayal was evident' (*Casa de las Américas* 103 [1977]: 10). For Guillén's account of his first meeting with Rubén Martínez Villena, see 'Palabras de gratitud,' *Prosa de prisa* III, pp. 384–5.
14 *Prosa de prisa* I, p. 292. Through his persistent efforts, Urrutia had managed to get the *Diario de la Marina*, beginning in March 1928, to create the page entitled 'Ideales de una Raza,' dedicated to the cultural interests of the black community. It is clear from Guillén's statement in the preceding note that both he and Urrutia understood the task to be undertaken by the page to be a national rather than a merely ethnic one. Lino D'ou had been the channel through which these ideas had flowed from Martí and Maceo to Urrutia and Guillén; for Guillén's deep admiration of him, see Guillén's 'Estampa de Lino D'ou,' *Prosa de prisa* I, pp. 269–77. See also, regarding Lino D'ou and racial discrimination in Cuba, the first article published by Guillén in *Ideales de una Raza* (21 April 1929), 'El camino de Harlem,' *Prosa de prisa* I, pp. 3–6.
15 Augier, *Nicolás Guillén* I, p. 119
16 *Prosa de prisa* I, p. 294
17 Some blacks shared this attitude in an exaggerated form: see Gustavo E. Urrutia's article on Guillén's speech given at the Club Atenas in 1930 in Nancy Morejón, ed., *Recopilación de textos sobre Nicolás Guillén* (La Habana: Casa de las Américas 1974), pp. 321–2. Morejón's collection of articles, with her excellent prologue, is indispensible for Guillén studies.
18 The present director of the Septeto Típico Habanero, Manuel Furé, has been, in personal interviews, a helpful source of information on its history.
19 The statement was made in answer to a question by Ciro Bianchi Ross in his extensive and probing interview of Guillén entitled 'Conversación hacia los 70,' *Cuba Internacional*, Año IV, no. 34 (1972): 14–21. The question and Guillén's answer may be found on p. 19.
20 A.J. Greimas, for instance, in *Semantique structurale* (Paris: Larousse 1966), a study in which he deals almost exhaustively with his subject, fails to discuss *jitanjáfora*, whether so named or not.
21 These are, of course, all plural in the text. Apocope is at work here silencing the 's' sounds or the final syllables, a phenomenon widely observable in Cuban popular

speech and reflected in such traditional *sones* as the Septeto Habanero's 'Qué dirán la gente' (1926).

22 The tendency to elevate popular speech and musical forms to a level of true art shown here in Guillén is strong in poetry now being written in the English-speaking Caribbean, particularly by Edward Braithwaite and Bruce St John. For an astute assessment of some essential differences between Guillén and such leading contemporary English-speaking Caribbean poets as Braithwaite and Derek Walcott, see Neville Dawes, *Prolegomena to Caribbean Literature* (Kingston: Institute of Jamaica 1977).

23 Responding to a question posed by Nancy Morejón on this matter, Guillén stated: 'The blacks cried out to the heavens over what they considered to be a profanity. One of them, very distinguished, very European, very sensible, told me: "We suffered discrimination at work, in the hotels and restaurants, in the public parks, in the schools and now you are hitting us with literary discrimination." It was impossible for them to understand that I was not planning to create "one more discrimination," that it was not a matter of a "black" poetry as opposed to a "white" poetry, but the search for a *national* poetry through the artistic expression of the whole Cuban social process, from the arrival of the first African slaves to our own times, its slow process of fusion not only physical, but spiritual. Finally, I won the battle, and the letter Don Miguel de Unamuno sent me from Madrid in 1932 was very useful to me.' Nancy Morejón, *Recopilación de textos*, pp. 45–6. Obviously, such blacks as Gustavo E. Urrutia and Lino D'ou are not to be thought of as sharing the above attitudes.

24 *Obra poética 1920–1958*, p. 176

25 Ibid., p. 175

26 Cintio Vitier, *Lo cubano en la poesía* (La Habana: Universidad Central de Las Villas 1958), pp. 357–8

27 *Prosa de prisa* III, p. 381

28 The use of sugar production as a symbol of imperialist control of Cuba had surged in the late 1920s. The publication of Ramiro Guerra's *Azúcar y población en las Antillas* (1927) had been preceded by Felipe Pichardo Moya's 'Poema de los cañaverales' (1925) and Agustín Acosta's 'La zafra' (1926). A similar wave of anti-imperialist writing focusing on sugar in the English-speaking Caribbean was produced in the 1960s by the New World Movement.

29 Juan Marinello's essay, entitled 'Poesía negra,' is to be found in his book, *Poética: Ensayos en entusiasmo* (Madrid: Espasa Calpe 1933), pp. 99–143. Unamuno's letter dated 8 June 1932 and sent from Madrid, was published in *Sóngoro cosongo y otros poemas* (La Habana: La Verónica 1942). It may be found in Nancy Morejón, *Recopilación de textos*, pp. 324–5. In the former, the Spanish-American relevance of Guillén's book is stressed, while Unamuno writes of its universal projection.

30 See Augier, *Nicolás Guillén* I, pp. 226–7

31 I need to translate only: no se mueve = it doesn't move; se murió = it died. The idea of finality is skilfully supported by the versification in this final stanza

where the pattern of *verso agudo* (final stress) in the odd verses and *verso llano* (penultimate stress) in the even ones is broken in the final verse which, although it is an even verse, is a *verso agudo*. 'Murió' being the final word of the verse, the music contributes to the decisiveness of the concept.

32 The Cuban term *güije* is used to refer to an evil river spirit.

33 For some of these, see José Luciano Franco, *Ensayos históricos* (La Habana: Editorial de Ciencias Sociales 1974), pp. 112–24.

34 It is unfortunate that Cintio Vitier misunderstood all this so extremely as to have written, in his well-known book *Lo cubano en la poesía* (La Habana: Universidad Central de las Villas 1958), p. 358: 'The theme dealt with here [in 'Balada de los dos abuelos'] with open human sympathy, reappears in ironic dress in the sonnet "El abuelo." Here he deals with *only one*, the black grandfather. He confronts one racism with another. Guillén has not wanted to preserve the beautiful equilibrium in "Balada ..."'

35 In reply to a question from Jaime Sarusky about the events that had been most influential in his life, Guillén replied: 'I could mention five. The death of my father, in 1917. The fall of Machado, in 1933. My association with Spain, in 1937. My joining the Communist Party, in that same year. The Revolution, in 1959' (Nancy Morejón, *Recopilación de textos*, p. 51).

36 The interview, done by Rafael Heliodoro Valle, was published in the Mexican journal, *Universidad*, in February 1937. A sequel to it, from which the quotation is taken, appears in Angel Augier, *Nicolás Guillén* II, p. 51.

37 An indication of the significance of the collection for the revolution is the importance attached to it by Raúl Castro, the Cuban vice-president in charge of the Revolutionary Army Forces. He cited the book repeatedly in his essay commemorating Guillén's seventieth birthday. See *La Gaceta de Cuba*, no. 104 (1972): 2

38 Augier, *Nicolás Guillén* II, p. 91

39 For an important study of the elegiac mode in Guillén see José Antonio Portuondo, 'Sentido elegíaco de la poesía de Guillén,' *La Gaceta de Cuba*, nos 8–9 (1962): 2.

40 Note the intense representation of abuse achieved by the metaphor that is built on the simile.

41 For Guillén's account of this campaign effort in Las Villas see his article 'Viajando con Menéndez,' *Prosa de prisa* I, pp. 246–8. This article may be thought of as a prefiguration in essay form of the 'Elegía a Jesús Menéndez.'

42 The mere facts of the assassination of Jesús Menéndez are that while serving as general secretary of the National Federation of Sugar Workers and a member of the Cuban legislature, he was killed on January 22 1948 by army captain Joaquín Casillas as he got off a train in Manzanillo following his visits to troubled sugar estates. Casillas was executed eleven years later when the revolution came to power. Casillas, according to Guillén, responded to the poem with the threat to the poet: 'When I catch up with that mulatto no one can save him from my kicking the hell out of him.' For this and other Guillén statements concerning the circumstances of the composition of the poem, see Nancy Morejón, *Recopilación de textos*, pp. 51–2. Some important studies of the poem are

Mirta Aguirre, 'En torno a la "Elegía a Jesús Menéndez,"' *La Ultima Hora*, Año
II, no. 23 (1952): 3–4, 48; Anthony George Dahl, 'La poética de Nicolás
Guillén: Análisis estilístico integral de la "Elegía a Jesús Menéndez,"' MA thesis,
Carleton University 1977; and Mónica Mansour, *Análisis textual e intertextual
[de] 'Elegía a Jesús Menéndez' de Nicolás Guillén* (México: UNAM 1980).

43 Madrigal no doubt had in mind poems such as these when he wrote with
complimentary intention that most of Guillén's poetic compositions have nothing
to do with ethnic or social topics. He regards this majority of Guillén's poems
only as demonstrations of traditional motifs of Western poetry. See Luis Iñigo
Madrigal, ed. *Nicolás Guillén: Summa poética* (Madrid: Ediciones Cátedra 1976),
p. 34

44 Guillén was in Guatemala in 1954 when the United States intervened militarily
to overthrow the newly elected government of Jacobo Arbenz. Guillén found
refuge in the Ecuadorean embassy and left subsequently for Mexico.

45 See Augier's note to the poem in *Obra poética* II, p. 396.

46 The poems were published under the title 'Romances de guerra y vida' in
Granma, 17 April 1973, p. 2.

47 The title is a Cuban saying that has its origin in a simile applied to the arrival in
Cuba in 1799 of the Spanish administrator Salvador de Muro y Salazar despite
heavy patrols of the Cuban coasts by the English. He was said to have
arrived 'as if rained down from heaven.'

48 This poem and the 'Letrilla cubana' were written as Guillén's contribution to a
workshop on combative poetry that he organized during the 'Cuban Missile
Crisis' of October 1962.

49 These were published in *Lunes de Revolución*, 29 June 1959.

50 The translation into Greek was done by the distinguished Greek poet Yannis
Ritsos and published as *El Gran Zoo* (Athens: Zemelio 1966). The distinguished Haitian writer, René Dépestre did the translation into French,
published as *Le Gran Zoo* (Paris: Seghers 1967).

51 In one of the thirty-one trenchant epigrams comprising one section of *La rueda
dentada*, the tendency to burden blackness with a negative value is satirized.
The epigram is number XXIII: 'Pienso: / ¡Qué raro / que al tiro al blanco / no
le hayan puesto *tiro al negro*!' ('I think: How strange that instead of saying
target practice [literally "shooting at the white"] they didn't say *shooting at
the black!*').

52 The attitude shown here cannot be classified as deriving from the irreverent view
of a healthy man. The poem was written, as Augier states (*Obra poética* II, p.
457), in early 1971 while Guillén was hospitalized in Havana with a serious
heart ailment. It derives from Guillén's characteristic tranquil rationality.

53 The presence of pathos here and in other parts of Guillén's work leads one to
think of the writer whose work is characterized by pathos, Juan Rulfo (see
Donald K. Gordon's fine study, *Los cuentos de Juan Rulfo* [Madrid: Playor
1976]). The distinction must be borne in mind, however, that in Guillén's
work pathos is never removed from satire or from some other mood that
indicates an urging to defiance. This is not as clearly the case with Rulfo.

CHAPTER 3

1 See his comments in this regard in my 'Conversation with Nicolás Guillén,' *Jamaica Journal* 7, nos 1–2 (1973): 79.
2 José Martí, *Obras completas* VI (La Habana: Editorial Nacional de Cuba 1963), p. 19
3 For studies that include the treatment of diverse aspects of Guillén's poetry that emphasize racial matters and his defence of blacks, see Richard L. Jackson's valuable book, *Black Writers in Latin America* (Albuquerque: University of New Mexico Press 1979), pp. 80–92, passim; Mónica Mansour, *La poesía negrista* (México: Ediciones Era 1973), pp. 209–64; and J.A. George Irish, 'Nicolás Guillén's Position on Race: A Reappraisal,' *Revista Interamericana* 6 (1976): 335–47. A relevant anthology of poetry is Aurora de Albornoz and Julio Rodríguez Luis, *Sensemayá: La poesía negra en el mundo hispano hablante* (Madrid: Editorial Orígenes 1980).
4 Sylvia Washington Bâ, *The Concept of Négritude in the Poetry of Léopold Sédar Senghor* (Princeton: Princeton University Press 1973), p. 44
5 Dépestre's views, published regularly since the 1950s in *Optique* and other journals and presented in a series of lectures given at the University of the West Indies, Mona, in 1977, have been summarized in his essay 'Saludo y despedida a la negritud,' *Africa en América Latina*, ed. Manuel Moreno Fraginals (México: Siglo XXI 1977), pp. 337–62. His views differ substantially from those of G.R. Coulthard in his essay, 'Nicolás Guillén and West Indian Négritude,' *Caribbean Quarterly* 16, no. 1 (1970): 52–7
6 Stanislas Adotevi, *Négritude et négrologues* (Paris: Union Générale D'Editions 1972)
7 Michael Dash, *Jacques Stéphen Alexis* (Toronto: Black Images 1975)
8 I quote below from my 'Conversation with Nicolás Guillén,' p. 78, Guillén's answer to my question concerning his views on *négritude*: 'As your question implies, *négritude* is a very vague concept. And my answer to your question ["... do you consider yourself to be one of the poets who represents *négritude*?"] would have to be no. The problem with *négritude* is the same kind of problem that we encounter with other definitions, like that of socialist realism, for example. Almost everyone has a different definition of these terms; and perhaps these definitions are all correct. Sometimes this reminds me of the definition given by Voltaire of metaphysics: the search in a dark room for a black cat that is not in the room. I believe that *négritude* is a phenomenon which is produced in countries where there is a black population exploited by a white colonial sector. The blacks find it necessary to strive to expose their cultural values: their music, their sculpture, painting, and so on. In countries where a revolution has taken place, as in Cuba, the problem of *négritude* does not make sense, because it would be a kind of racism, a dispersing element rather than an agglutinating one. If I had continued after the Revolution with a black line of writing, I would be isolated. And more so when I personally believe that the aim of the struggle is not to separate whites from blacks but to unite them. And that struggle cannot be racist

but revolutionary in order to abolish the division of society into classes, since this very division is the source of racism.

'In Cuba itself, before the Revolution, an emphasis on blackness was explainable because the artistic, political, cultural, indeed the human, values of the black man had to be stressed in the face of discrimination or slavery; and one had to give emphasis to this element within the national culture. It was one of the manifestations of the class struggle. But when a revolution erases that struggle and gives power to the working class without any regard for skin colour, the concept of racial superiority does not exist any more.

'There are moments – historical moments – when *négritude* is linked to movements of national liberation; but it is impossible to maintain *négritude* as a primary attitude because then it would be converted into another form of racism. In 1929, for example, I wrote the "Oda a Kid Chocolate," exalting the black boxer, exalting his blackness. But today in Cuba this would not make sense.'

9 See Enrique Anderson Imbert, '"Magical Realism" in Spanish American Fiction,' trans. Roger Moore, *International Fiction Review* 2, no. 1 (1975): 1–9

10 Fernando Alegría, *Literatura y revolución* (México: Fondo de Cultura Económica 1971), pp. 104–5, perceives well the imposed nature of the concept on Spanish-American literature.

11 Horst Rogmann, '"Realismo mágico" y "*négritude*" como construcciones ideológicas,' *Actas del Sexto Congreso Internacional de Hispanistas*, ed. Alan M. Gordon and Evelyn Rugg (Toronto: Department of Spanish and Portuguese 1980), pp. 632–6

12 A reigning magical conception has been seen to apply not only to Latin America and the Caribbean but also to Europe: see Anna Varga's study 'The Miracles and Martyrdom of St. Antonio Gramsci,' *The Campaigner* 7, nos 4–5 (1974): 63–79.

13 This, ironically, is quoted in Germán Arciniegas, *América mágica* (Buenos Aires: Editorial Sudamericana 1959), p. 304. The quotation betrays the fallacy that underlies Arciniegas' title.

14 Quoted in Neill Macaulay, *The Sandino Affair* (Chicago: Quadrangle Books 1971), p. 171

15 Nicolás Guillén, 'Emma Pérez, poesía y revolución,' *Mediodía*, no. 16, 26 April 1937, p. 8

16 Nicolás Guillén, 'Informe al Congreso de Escritores y Artistas,' *Islas* 4, no. 2 (1962): 85

17 For a thorough study of these matters see Robert Pring-Mill, 'The Scope of Spanish American Committed Poetry' in *Homenaje a Rodolfo Grossman*, ed. Sabine Horl et al. (Frankfurt: Verlag Peter Lang 1977), pp. 259–333.

18 Guillén's recent *El libro de las décimas*, ed. Nancy Morejón (La Habana: Ediciones Unión 1980) consisting mostly of already published poems, reveals the enormous inventiveness and versatility with which he employs the *décima*, adapting this form to enhance the overall meanings of the different poems. Collections of his poetry on the basis of the different verse forms would be equally revealing of his unsurpassed dominance of verse forms.

19 For a statistical accounting of the different verse forms used in Guillén's poetry up to *El Gran Zoo*, see Jorge María Ruscalleda Bercedóniz, *La poesía de Nicolás Guillén* (Río Piedras: Editorial Universitaria 1975), pp. 197–8.

20 For a detailed study that has been done on this, see Adolfina Cossío, 'Los recursos rítmicos en la poesía de Nicolás Guillén,' *Santiago*, no. 5 (1971): 177–223.

21 See Roberto Fernández Retamar's chapter entitled '¿Quién es el autor de la poesía de Nicolás Guillén?' in his book *El son de vuelo popular* (La Habana: UNEAC 1972).

22 Andrew Cecil Bradley, 'Poetry for Poetry's Sake' in *A Modern Book of Aesthetics*, ed. Melvin Rader (New York: Holt, Rinehart and Winston 1966), pp. 309–23

23 Andrew Cecil Bradley, *Shakespearean Tragedy* (London: Macmillan 1904), p. 202

24 In Warner Berthoff, *A Literature without Qualities* (Berekeley: University of California Press 1979), p. 15

25 The horrible effects on humanity that lie potentially in the extremes of some of these exercises are sometimes realized. In his article, 'La diabolique douceur de Pol Pot,' *Le Monde Dimanche*, 18 May 1980, pp. 1 and 20, the Cambodian professor of literature and philosophy, Soth Polin, has shown how Pol Pot, the former Buddhist teacher of French literature, turned the combination of the music of language and a nihilistic world view into an effective instrument of extermination.

26 For a thoughtful study of this question see Nelson Osorio, 'Las ideologías y los estudios de literatura hispanoamericana,' *Hispamérica*, Año IV, Añejo 1 (1975), pp. 9–28. See also Terry Eagleton, *Criticism and Ideology* (London: NLB 1976)

Glossary of frequently used literary terms

alexandrine	see 'sonnet' and 'caesura'
anaphora	the repetition of words or phrases at the beginning of successive verses or clauses
annominatio	see *paronomasia*
anticlimax	the undermining of the impressive effect of a climax by a following inferior contribution
antithesis	occurs when contrasting ideas are expressed in contiguous sentences or phrases
aphaeresis	the suppression of an initial letter, syllable, or syllables of a word
apocope	the suppression of a final letter, syllable, or syllables of a word
apostrophe	a figure of speech in which an absent person or a personified object or abstraction is addressed as if present and capable of understanding
assimilation	a process by which two different adjacent or neighbouring phonemes (q.v.) become identical or similar ('acordarte'/'acoddadte')
assonance	or 'vocalic rhyme' occurs when identical vowels, and not identical consonants, recur in final stressed position in lines of a poem. Within a line of a poem, assonance is the repetition of the same vowel sounds with different consonantal sounds intervening
asyndetical	consisting of the omission of conjunctions and sometimes articles for the creation of special effects in a poem
caesura	the pause that marks the end of a phrase within a line of poetry. Caesura may occur, for example, after the seventh syllable of a fourteen-syllable (Alexandrine) line, marking the division of the line into two seven-syllable hemistichs
calligramme	a poem written so that the disposition of its lines on the page sketches an image related to the subject of the poem
catachresis	the improper use, in a literal sense, of an expression. Catachresis has rich expressive possibilities and is related to metaphor in usages such as 'eloquent tears,' 'metallic wind,' and so on
chiasmus	occurs when the terms in the second of two parallel phrases reverse the order of corresponding ones in the first
copla	a stanza or group of lines of verse that may be arranged according to a wide variety of schemes, usually in twelve-syllable quartets or *redondillas* (q.v.)

cultismo	a learned word
dactylic	refers to verse with a basic metrical unit of a long syllable followed by two short ones
décima	also known as the *espinela*, the *décima* is a ten-line poem each line of which usually is composed of eight syllables. The usual rhyme scheme is *abba ac cddc*; but, as Guillén demonstrates, there are many possible variations
ellipsis	the omission of one or more words that are normally needed to express completely the sense of a statement
enjambment	the continuation without pause of one line of poetry into the next
envoi	the final, usually shortened, stanza affixed to some poems that summarizes the poem or commends it to the reader or the person to whom it is dedicated
epigraph	a short quotation placed at the beginning of a book, a chapter, a poem, a section of a poem, etc.
estrambote	an addition of one or more lines to the normal fixed length of a poem
glosa	consists of a *redondilla* (q.v.) in which a subject is stated and four *décimas* (q.v.), which each end by repeating the successive lines of the *redondilla*
hemistich	see 'caesura'
hyperbaton	the transposition of words out of their normal syntactical order
hyperbole	the use of bold exaggeration to effect emphasis
irony	a form of speech in which one meaning is stated and a different, usually antithetical, one is to be understood
langue	following the French terminology introduced by Ferdinand de Saussure, *langue* designates the complete language system used by a group or community, while *parole* designates individual speech usage in a given case
leitmotiv	a central motif repeated within a work or in all the works of a poet
letrilla	a poem generally written in short lines, often having a refrain, and dealing usually with a light or satiric topic
lexical	relating to the words of a language
madrigal	a lyrical poem, dealing with matters of love, of between three and twenty lines in length and without a fixed rhyme scheme or length or lines
metaphor	is the tacit comparison or contrast between an idea, image, or symbol and another idea, image, or symbol. The process of metaphor involves a tenor, the basic idea, image, or symbol and a vehicle, the illustrative idea, image, or symbol
metathesis	the transposition of the order of sounds within a word
metonymy	which may well be considered to embrace synecdoche, is the substitution of one element for another to which it is closely related: the part for the whole or the whole for the part, the material for the product, the trait for the individual, the individual for the group, the cause or means for the effect, the date for the event, and so on
onomatopeia	the formation of words from sounds that seem to suggest or reinforce the meaning

oxymoron	contiguous words that unite contradictory or mutually exclusive ideas. Oxymoron is condensed paradox or antithesis (q.v.)
paradigm	a cluster of word associations that form a model, pattern, or example
parallelism	the repetition of the same construction in consecutive phrases or sentences
Parnassian	reflecting the devotion to descriptive precision and craftsmanship of a group of French poets known as the Parnassians, who became prominent after 1860
parole	see *langue*
paronomasia	or *annominatio*, is a play on words that are similar or identical in sound, but which have related or diverse meanings
personification	a manner of speech in which human attributes are given to things or abstractions
phoneme	a minimum unit of speech sound
quartet	a four-line stanza in which various rhyme schemes and lengths of lines are permitted
quintilla	a stanza or poem comprised of five usually eight-syllable lines with rhyme and / or assonance in various combinations
realism	the literary representation of life as it appears to the normal human consciousness. Since such consciousness is sympathetic to human advancement, a comprehensive representation of life contains, depending on the society portrayed, varying degrees of critical realism, which implicitly urges change. A broadly based developmental impulse, presented as being reflective of the interests of the working classes especially in post-revolutionary socialist societies, is characteristic of socialist realism
redondilla	the typical manifestation of the *redondilla* is four eight-syllable lines, rhyming *abab* or *abba*
romance	a traditional Spanish verse form usually consisting of eight-syllable lines with assonance (q.v.) in alternate lines
semiological	a semiological or semiotic study of a poem is concerned with an examination of its phonic, lexical, syntactical, and semantic aspects as parts of an autonomous system of signs
silva	irregular combinations of seven- and eleven-syllable lines
simile	an explicit comparison of tenor with vehicle (cf. 'metaphor')
Son	one of the basic forms of Cuban music, containing African and Spanish elements. It is played usually by a septet or octet consisting of guitar, *tres* (an instrument of the guitar family with three pairs of strings), bass, bongo drums, maracas, *claves* (two small rounded sticks of hard wood), and trumpet. The *son* is structured as an interplay between the refrain or *montuno*, sung by several members of the orchestra, and the *motivo* sung by the lead singer. The *son* with its refrains, firm percussion, pulsating cords, and rhythmic variations has been adapted by Guillén to his poetry and is now, both as a musical and a poetic form, an important part of Cuba's national cultural identity
sonnet	a fourteen-line poem of Italian origin, consisting of two quartets and two

	tercets. The rhyme scheme is normally *abba abba cde cde*; but there are variations, particularly in the tercets (q.v.). Sonnets in Spanish are usually composed of eleven- or fourteen-syllable lines. The latter are known as alexandrines (q.v.)
syllepsis	a figure in which a single word although seeming to be equally related to a pair of others has to be understood in different ways to be appropriate to each
synaesthesia	the merging of an image perceived by one of the senses with an image perceived by another; for example, colour may be attributed to sounds, taste to colours, and so on
tenor	see 'metaphor'
tercet	a stanza of three lines, usually containing rhyme
tertulia	a salon or café gathering for literary, social, or other conversation
topos	a conventional rhetorical theme
trochaic	refers to verse with a basic metrical unit of a long syllable followed by a short one
vehicle	see 'metaphor'
zeugma	a figure in which a single word is applied to two other terms, though being strictly appropriate to only one of them

Bibliography

BOOKS OF POETRY BY NICOLAS GUILLÉN

Motivos de son. La Habana: Rambla, Bouza 1930
Sóngoro cosongo. Poemas mulatos. La Habana: Ucar García 1931
West Indies, Ltd. La Habana: Ucar García 1934
Cantos para soldados y sones para turistas. México: Masas 1937
España. Poema en cuatro angustias y una esperanza. México: México Nuevo 1937
El son entero. Suma poética. 1929–1946. Con una carta de Miguel de Unamuno.
  Textos musicales de Eliseo y Emilio Grenet, Alejandro García Caturla, y Silves-
  tre Revueltas. Ilustraciones de Carlos Enríquez. Buenos Aires: Editorial Pleamar
  1947
Elegía a Jesús Menéndez. La Habana: Páginas 1951
La paloma de vuelo popular. Elegías. Buenos Aires: Editorial Losada 1958
Buenos días, Fidel. México: Gráfica Horizonte 1959
¿Puedes? La Habana: Ucar García 1960
Balada. La Habana: Movimiento por la Paz y Soberaniía de los Pueblos 1962
Tengo. La Habana: Universidad Central de Las Villas 1964
Poemas de amor. La Habana: La Tertulia 1964
Antología Mayor. La Habana: Ediciones Unión 1964
El Gran Zoo. La Habana: Ediciones Unión 1967
Che Comandante. La Habana: Instituto Cubano del Libro 1967
Cuatro canciones para el Che. La Habana: Consejo Nacional de Cultura 1969
La rueda dentada. La Habana: UNEAC 1972
El diario que a diario. La Habana: UNEAC 1972
Obra poética. 2 vols. (I: 1920–1958; II: 1958–1972.) Compilación pró-
  logo y notas de Angel Augier. La Habana: Instituto Cubano del Libro 1972
El corazón con que vivo. La Habana: UNEAC 1975
Poemas manuables. La Habana: UNEAC 1975
Por el mar de las Antillas anda un barco de papel. La Habana: UNEAC 1977
Música de cámara. La Habana: Ediciones Unión 1979
El libro de las décimas. Ed. Nancy Morejón. La Habana: Ediciones Unión
  1980

ENGLISH TRANSLATIONS

Carr, Richard J., trans. *Tengo*. Detroit: Broadside Press 1974

Hughes, Langston and Ben F. Carruthers, trans. *Cuba libre*. Los Angeles: The Ward Ritchie Press 1948

Márquez, Robert, trans. *Patria o muerte. The Great Zoo and Other Poems*. New York: Monthly Review Press 1972

Márquez, Robert and David Arthur McMurray, trans. *Man-making Words; Selected Poems of Nicolás Guillén*. Amherst: University of Massachusetts Press 1972

Prentice, Roger, trans. *In the Turmoil of the People: Three Cuban Poets*. (Roberto Fernández Retamar, Manuel Navarro Luna, Nicolás Guillén). Vancouver: Cuban Friendship Committee 1967

SELECTED STUDIES OF NICOLAS GUILLÉN'S POETRY

Aguirre, Mirta. 'En torno a la "Elegía a Jesús Menéndez."' *La Ultima Hora*, Año II, no. 23 (1952): 3–4, 48

Albornoz, Aurora de and Julio Rodríguez Luis. *Sensemayá: La poesía negra en el mundo hispano hablante*. Madrid: Editorial Orígenes 1980

Allen, Martha E. 'Nicolás Guillén, poeta del pueblo.' *Revista Iberoamericana* 15 (1949): 29–43

Antuña, María Luisa and Josefina García Carranza. *Bibliografía de Nicolás Guillén*. La Habana: Biblioteca Nacional 'José Martí' 1975

Arrom, José Juan. *Estudios de literatura hispanoamericana*. La Habana: Ucar García 1950

Augier, Angel. *Nicolás Guillén: Notas para un estudio biográfico-crítico*. Vol. I. La Habana: Universidad Central de Las Villas 1965

– *Nicolás Guillén: Notas para un estudio biográfico-crítico*. Vol. II. La Habana: Universidad Central de Las Villas 1964

Boulware-Miller, Patricia. 'Nature in Three "Negrista" Poets: Nicolás Guillén, Emilio Ballagas, and Luis Palés Matos.' PH D dissertation, University of California, Berkeley 1978

Bowra, Cecil Maurice. *Poetry and Politics 1900–1960*. Cambridge: Cambridge University Press 1966

Cartey, Wilfred. *Black Images*. New York: Teachers College Press 1970, pp. 111–48

Cossío, Adolfina. 'Los recursos rítmicos en la poesía de Nicolás Guillén.' *Snatiago*, no. 5 (1971): 177–223

Coulthard, Gabriel R. 'Nicolás Guillén and West Indian Négritude,' *Caribbean Quarterly* 16, no. 1 (1970): 52–7

– *Race and Colour in Caribbean Literature*. London: Oxford University Press 1962

Dahl, Anthony George. 'La poética de Nicolás Guillén: Análisis estilístico integral de la "Elegía a Jesús Menéndez."' MA thesis, Carleton University 1977

Davis, Stephanie Jo. 'Development of Poetic Techniques in the Works of Nicolás
Guillén (1927–1972).' PH D dissertation, Princeton University 1976
Dawes, Neville. *Prolegomena to Caribbean Literature*. Kingston: Institute of Jam-
aica 1977
Dill, Hans-Otto. 'Methodenumbruch und Kubanische Revolution in Werk Guilléns.'
Weimarer Beiträge 24, no. 12 (1977): 171–6
Ellis, Keith. 'Cambio y continuidad en la poesía de Nicolás Guillén.' In *Actas del
simposio internacional de estudios hispánicos, Budapest, 18–19 de agosto de 1976*.
Ed. Mátyás Horányi. Budapest: Akad. Kiadó 1978, pp. 229–33
– 'Conversation with Nicolás Guillén.' *Jamaica Journal* 7, nos 1–2 (1973): 77–9
– 'Literary Americanism and the Recent Poetry of Nicolás Guillén.' *University of
Toronto Quarterly* 45 (1975): 1–18
Fernández Retamar, Roberto. *El son de vuelo popular*. La Habana: UNEAC 1972
Guirao, Ramón. *Orbita de la poesía afrocubana*. La Habana: Ucar García 1938
Irish, J.A. George. 'Nicolás Guillén's Position on Race: A Reappraisal.' *Revista
Interamericana* 6 (1976): 335–47
Jackson, Richard L. *Black Writers in Latin America*. Albuquerque: University of
New Mexico Press 1979
King, Lloyd. 'Nicolás Guillén and Afrocubanism' *Tapia*, 2 June 1974, pp. 6–7,
and 9 June 1974, pp. 5, 8
Liddell, Janice Lu. 'The Whip's Corolla: Myth and Politics in the Literature of the
Black Diaspora: Aimé Césaire, Nicolás Guillén, Langston Hughes.' PH D disserta-
tion, University of Michigan 1978
Madrigal, Luis Iñigo, ed. *Nicolás Guillén: Summa poética*. Madrid: Ediciones
Cátedra 1976
Mansour, Mónica. *Análisis textual e intertextual [de] 'Elegía a Jesús Menéndez.'*
Mexico: UNAM 1980
– *La poesía negrista*. México: Ediciones Era 1973
Marinello, Juan. *Poética: Ensayos en entusiasmo*. Madrid: Espasa Calpe 1933
Martínez Estrada, Ezequiel. *La poesía afrocubana de Nicolás Guillén*. Montevideo:
Editorial Arca 1966
Melon, Alfred. 'Guillén: poeta de la síntesis.' *Unión* 9, no. 4 (1970): 96–132
Morejón, Nancy. *Nación y mestizaje en Nicolás Guillén*. La Habana: Ediciones Unión
1982
– ed. *Recopilación de textos sobre Nicolás Guillén*. La Habana: Casa de las Américas
1974. (This important item contains an extensive bibliography, which I do not
attempt to reproduce.)
Ross, Ciro Bianchi. 'Conversación hacia los 70.' *Cuba Internacional* 34 (1972):
14–21
Ruscalleda Bercedóniz, Jorge María. *La poesía de Nicolás Guillén*. Río Piedras:
Editorial Universitaria 1975
Salvioni, Giovanna. *L' "Africa nera" a Cuba: Tradizione popolare e poesia di
libertà di Nicolás Guillén*. Milano: Vita e Pensiero 1974
Sardinha, Dennis. *The Poetry of Nicolás Guillén*. London: New Beacon Books Ltd
1976

Stimson, Frederick S. *The New Schools of Spanish American Poetry*. Chapel Hill: University of North Carolina 1970, pp. 168–79
Tous, Adriana. *La poesía de Nicolás Guillén*. Madrid: Ediciones Cultura Hispánica 1971
Vitier, Cintio. *Lo cubano en la poesía*. La Habana: Universidad Central de Las Villas 1958, pp. 340–68
Williams, Lorna V. *Self and Society in the Poetry of Nicolás Guillén*. Baltimore: Johns Hopkins University Press 1982

OTHER RELEVANT WORKS

Adorno, Theodor W. *Negative Dialectics*. Trans. E.B. Ashton. New York: Seabury Press 1973
Adotevi, Stanislas. *Négritude et négrologues*. Paris: Union Générale D'Editions 1972
Aguirre, Sergio. 'Seis actitudes de la burguesía cubana en el siglo XIX.' *Dialéctica* 6 (1943): 153–77
Alegría, Fernando. *Historia de la novela hispanoamericana*. México: Ediciones de Andrea 1966
– *Literatura y revolución*. México: Fondo de Cultura Económica 1971
Anderson Imbert, Enrique. '"Magical Realism" in Spanish American Fiction.' Trans. Roger Moore. *International Fiction Review* 2, no. 1 (1975): 1–9
Arciniegas, Germán. *América mágica*. Buenos Aires: Editorial Sudamericana 1959
Bâ, Sylvia Washington. *The Concept of Négritude in the Poetry of Léopold Sédar Senghor*. Princeton: Princeton University Press 1973
Benedetti, Mario. *Letras del continente mestizo*. Montevideo: Arca 1967
Benjamin, Walter. *Understanding Brecht*. Trans. Anna Bostock. London: NLB 1973
Berthoff, Warner. *A Literature without Qualities*. Berkeley: University of California Press 1979
Borges, Jorge Luis. *Discusión*. Buenos Aires: Emecé 1957
Bradley, Andrew Cecil. 'Poetry for Poetry's Sake.' In *A Modern Book of Aesthetics*. Ed. Melvin Rader. New York: Holt, Rinehart and Winston 1966, pp. 309–23
– *Shakespearean Tragedy*. London: Macmillan 1904
Brecht, Bertolt. *Les Arts et la révolution*. Trans. Bernard Lortholary. Paris: L'Arche 1970
– *Brecht on Theatre*. Trans. John Willet. London: Methuen 1964
– *Sur le réalisme*. Trans. André Gisselbrecht. Paris: L'Arche 1970
Breton, André. *La Clé des champs*. Paris: Editions du Sagittaire 1953
Dash, Michael. *Jacques Stéphen Alexis*. Toronto: Black Images 1975
Demetz, Peter. *Marx, Engels, and the Poets*. Chicago: University of Chicago Press 1967
Dépestre, René. 'Saludo y despedida a la negritud.' In *Africa en América Latina*. Ed. Manuel Moreno Fraginals. México: Siglo XXI 1977, pp. 337–62
Eagleton, Terry. *Criticism and Ideology*. London: NLB 1976
– *Marxism and Literary Criticism*. London: Methuen 1976
Ellis, Keith. *Critical Approaches to Rubén Darío*. Toronto: University of Toronto Press 1974

- 'Cuban Literature and the Revolution.' In *Fidel Castro's Personal Revolution in Cuba: 1959–1973*. Ed. James Nelson Goodsell. New York: Alfred A. Knopf 1975, pp. 243–8

Fernández Retamar, Roberto. *El intelectual y la sociedad*. México: Siglo XXI 1969
- *Para una teoría de la literatura hispanoamericana*. México: Editorial Nuestro Tiempo 1977
- 'Teoría (y práctica) de la literatura.' *Universidad de la Habana* 155 (1966): 9–10

Fischer, Ernst. *La necesidad de arte*. Trans. Adelaida de Juan and José Rodríguez Feo. La Habana: Ediciones Unión 1964

Franco, Jean. *Criticism and Literature within the Context of a Dependent Culture*. New York University Occasional Papers, no. 16. New York: The American Language and Area Center 1975

Franco, José Luciano. *Ensayos históricos*. La Habana: Editorial de Ciencias Sociales 1974

Garaudy, Roger. *D'un réalisme sans rivages*. Paris: Libraire Plon 1963

García Márquez, Gabriel and Mario Vargas Llosa. *La novela en América Latina: Diálogo*. Lima: C. Milla Batres 1968

Genette, Gérard. *Figures III*. Paris: Editions du Seuil 1972

Giral, Sergio, dir. *El otro Francisco*. La Habana: ICAIC 1975.

Goldmann, Lucien. *Pour une sociologie du roman*. Paris: Editions Gallimard 1964

Gordon, Donald Keith. *Los cuentos de Juan Rulfo*. Madrid: Playor 1976

Greimas, A.J. *Sémantique structurale*. Paris: Larousse 1966

Guillén, Nicolás. 'Emma Pérez; poesía y revolución.' *Mediodía*, 26 April 1937, p. 8
- 'Informe al Congreso de Escritores y Artistas.' *Islas* 4: no. 2 (1962): 85
- 'Juan Marinello.' *Casa de las Américas* 103 (1977): 10–11
- *Prosa de prisa*. 3 vols. La Habana: Editorial Arte y Literatura 1975–76

Gutiérrez Alea, Tomás. 'Memorias de *Memorias* (*del subdesarrollo*).' *Casa de las Américas* 122 (1980): 67–76

Hollingsworth, Charles. 'The Development of Literary Theory in Cuba, 1959–1968.' PHD dissertation, University of California, Berkeley 1972

Jakobson, Roman. *Fundamentals of Language*. The Hague: Mouton and Co. 1956

Jameson, Frederic. *Marxism and Form*. Princeton: Princeton University Press 1971

Knight, Franklin W. *Slave Society in Cuba during the Nineteenth Century*. Madison: University of Wisconsin Press 1970

Le Riverend, Julio. *Economic History of Cuba*. Trans. María Juana Cazabón and Homero León. La Habana: Instituto del Libro 1967

Lenin, Vladimir Ilyich. *Sur la littérature et l'art*. Ed. Jean Fréville. Paris: Editions Sociales 1957

Lezama Lima, José. *La expresión americana*. Santiago de Chile: Editorial Universitaria 1969

Lukács, György. *Problemas del realismo*. Trans. Carlos Gerhard. México: Fondo de Cultura Económica 1960

Macherey, Pierre. *Pour une théorie de la production littéraire*. Paris: Maspéro 1970

Macaulay, Neill. *The Sandino Affair*. Chicago: Quadrangle Books 1971

Mañach, Jorge. *Historia y estilo*. La Habana: Minerva 1944

Mariátegui, José Carlos. 'Arte, revolución y decadencia.' *Amauta*, no. 3 (1926): 1–2

Martí, José. *Obras completas*. La Habana: Editorial Nacional de Cuba 1964

Marx, Karl and Friedrich Engels. *L'Idéologie allemande*. Trans. Henri Auger et al. Paris: Editions Sociales 1968

– *Sur la littérature et l'art*. Ed. Jean Fréville. Paris: Editions Sociales 1954

Ortega y Gasset, José. *La deshumanización del arte*. Madrid: Revista de Occidente 1956

Osorio, Nelson. 'Las ideologías y los estudios de literatura hispanoamericana.' *Hispamérica*, Año IV, Añejo I (1975): 9–28

Pereira, Joseph R. 'Towards a Theory of Literature in Revolutionary Cuba.' *Jamaica Journal* 9, no. I (1975): 28–33

Peña, Lynherst. 'Trends of Literary Criticism in Spanish America, 1900–1950.' PH D dissertation, University of Toronto 1970

Plekhanov, Georgi. *Art and Social Life*. Trans. A. Fineberg. Moscow: Progress Publishers 1957

Portuondo, José Antonio. *Bosquejo histórico de las letras cubanas*. La Habana: Editora del Ministerio de Educación 1962

– *El concepto de la poesía*. México: Colegio de México 1944

– *Crítica de la época y otros ensayos*. La Habana: Universidad de Las Villas 1965

– *Estética y revolución*. La Habana: UNEAC 1963

– *El heroísmo intelectual*. México: Tezontle 1955

Pring-Mill, Robert. 'The Scope of Spanish American Committed Poetry.' In *Homenaje a Rodolfo Grossman*. Ed. Sabine Horl et al. Frankfurt: Verlag Peter Lang 1977, pp. 259–333

Quijano, Robyn. 'Erasmian Humanism and Ferdinand of Aragon.' *The Campaigner* 11, nos. 3–4 (1978): 2, 78

Rama, Angel. 'Vade retro.' *Marcha* 1591 (1972): 31

– 'Respuesta a Vargas Llosa: El fin de los demonios.' *Marcha* 1603 (1972): 30–1

– 'Segunda respuesta a Vargas Llosa: Nuevo escritor para una nueva sociedad.' *Marcha* 1610 (1972): 30–1

Richards, Ivor Armstrong. *Science and Poetry*. London: Kegan Paul 1926

Roa, Raúl. *Bufa subversiva*. La Habana: Cultural 1935

Rodó, José Enrique. *Obras completas*. Ed. Emir Rodríguez Monegal. Madrid: Aguilar 1967

Rodríguez Feo, José. 'Cultura y moral.' *Ciclón* 6 (1955): n.p.

Rogmann, Horst. '"Realismo mágico" y "négritude" como construcciones ideológicas.' *Actas del Sexto Congreso Internacional de Hispanistas*. Ed. Alan M. Gordon and Evelyn Rugg. Toronto: Department of Spanish and Portuguese 1980, pp. 632–6

Roucek, Joseph S. 'A History of the Concept of Ideology.' *Journal of the History of Ideas*, 5 (1944), 479–88.

Sánchez Vázquez, Adolfo. *Estética y marxismo*. 2 vols. México: Ediciones Era 1970

- *Las ideas estéticas de Marx*: *Ensayos de estética marxista*. México: Ediciones Era 1965
Steiner, George. 'Marxism and the Literary Critic.' In *Sociology of Literature and Drama*. Ed. Elizabeth and Tom Burns. Harmondsworth: Penguin Books 1973, pp. 159–60
Varga, Anna. 'The Miracles and Martyrdom of St. Antonio Gramsci.' *The Campaigner* 7, nos. 4–5 (1974): 63–79
Vargas Llosa, Mario. *García Márquez*: *Historia de un deicidio*. Barcelona: Barral Editores 1971
- 'Respuesta a Angel Rama: El regreso de Satán.' *Marcha* 1602 (1972): 30–1
- 'Segunda respuesta a Angel Rama: Resurrección de Belcebú, o la distancia creadora.' *Marcha* 1609 (1972): 29–31
- 'Un arma llamada novela.' *Marcha*, 1612 (1972), 30–1.
Williams, Raymond. *Marxism and Literature*. London: Oxford University Press 1977
Wimsatt Jr, William Kurtz. *The Verbal Icon*. Lexington: University of Kentucky Press 1954

Index

Index of Poems and Collections Cited

UNIVERSITY OF TORONTO ROMANCE SERIES